CRIMES
OF THE
CROSS

CRIMES
OF THE
CROSS

The Anglican Paedophile
Network of Newcastle,
Its Protectors and the
Man Who Fought for Justice

ANNE MANNE

Published by Black Inc., an imprint of Schwartz Books Pty Ltd
Wurundjeri Country
22–24 Northumberland Street
Collingwood VIC 3066, Australia
enquiries@blackincbooks.com
www.blackincbooks.com

9781863959681 (paperback)
9781743823460 (ebook)

 A catalogue record for this
book is available from the
National Library of Australia

Cover design by Akiko Chan
Text design and typesetting by Beau Lowenstern
Cover image: Shutterstock/New Africa

CONTENTS

INTRODUCTION

I BEGAN WRITING about child sexual abuse in 2013, in an essay for the online human rights journal *Right Now*, about the cover-ups of the abuse of children by clergy in the Catholic dioceses of Melbourne and Ballarat. I then decided to research and write a book on the Royal Commission into Institutional Responses to Child Sexual Abuse, which ran over five years, from 2013 to 2017. The underlying pattern – of denialism, cover-up and corruption, with the devastation of the lives of survivors – was depressingly similar, no matter the religious denomination or institution, whether it was the scouts, dance schools, exclusive private schools, the Catholics, the Anglicans, a Jewish school or, worst of all, the "care homes", which dealt out to orphans a special form of cruelty: physical as well as sexual abuse. Of the Catholic cases, the concealment of Gerald Ridsdale's rampant paedophilia by the Catholic hierarchy over decades, continually moving him on to another parish and new victims, stood out. But the inner workings of the secret, mysterious Catholic committees such as the Ballarat diocese's College of Consultors, responsible for the cover-ups, were opaque and hard to get at.

Then, in July 2016, my project suddenly changed. From a report on ABC TV's 7.30 program, screened just before the royal commission's public hearing into the Anglican diocese of Newcastle commenced, I learned of a sinister paedophile ring of priests demonic in their cruelty. A bishop and a few church officials turned whistle-blowers were openly talking. Michael Elliott, an ex-policeman hired by the diocese to deal with sexual abuse complaints, told of files tampered with and documents gone missing. He told 7.30 that former bishops undoubtedly knew of the paedophile priests, and that one of the priests answering a child-abuse hotline was an abuser himself. "There were groups of child sexual abusers that were working together," he said. As Elliott went about his work, he was targeted; there were death threats, his car and home were repeatedly vandalised, and his beloved family dog disappeared. John Cleary, the diocesan business manager who had hired Elliott to investigate, was also targeted. He told 7.30 of a death threat received just before he gave evidence in the Supreme Court about Graeme Lawrence, the former dean of the cathedral, who was facing defrocking for child sexual abuse. The bishop of Newcastle in 2016, Greg Thompson, spoke of having been sexually abused by a former bishop, Ian Shevill, in 1975, when he was a teenager. Thompson spoke of "mates protecting mates" and a *Sopranos*-style protection racket.

Two other survivors, Paul Gray and Nick Brown, spoke to 7.30 of the abuse they had suffered. In Newcastle, one of the lynchpins of the paedophile ring was Father Peter Rushton, a powerful senior priest and archdeacon. Rushton took Gray to Yondaio youth camp. The camp had been sold to parents as being all about boys hunting for wildlife with torches, all jolly and innocent fun. In reality, the predators were the priests and the boys were their prey.

Gray described being taken out at night at the camp with another boy and at least five men. "I recall the men saying, 'We are going to get you.' From my previous experience, I knew this meant that they were going to sexually abuse me." The two boys started running, hearts beating fast. It was dark as they ran through the thick scrub, and brambles tore at their clothing. Then they could run no more, for they had reached a cliff with a steep drop down to the sea. They hid in the bushes and listened while the men came closer, flashing their torches. Then the men found them. Paul Gray said, "After I was dragged from the bushes, I was raped by the two men. While I was being raped, I could hear another boy screaming." He was haunted ever after, wondering whether he should have jumped off the cliff.

Nick Brown was also a member of the Church of England Boys' Society and was brutally raped at the same camp. Brown told 7.30, "One of the worst things that happened … was I had my backside split open. My clothes were taken from me, they were burnt. I can't remember the names of the people that done this to me."

At an orphanage, St Alban's Home for Boys, multiple men sexually abused children, often at the same time, watching each other. Paul Gray was taken to St Alban's by Father Rushton, who was his godfather. Rushton left him there to be raped. Paul called out to Rushton, begging him not to leave him, but he did, many times. Rushton was on the board that ran the boys' home. His lover Jim Brown, another paedophile, abused a former St Alban's boy, Phil D'Ammond, who was also interviewed by 7.30.

John Cleary, the diocesan business manager, told 7.30, "It's not uncommon for survivors to have attended group parties where there may have been multiple perpetrators." Michael Elliott, the ex-policeman, said that Rushton had been on all the committees investigating child sexual abuse. He was influential in choosing who would train as a priest at St John's College, Morpeth, the college from which one-quarter of convicted Anglican paedophiles had graduated. Elliott said, "There's evidence there was an awareness of Rushton's offending. It had been brought to the attention of various bishops on a number of occasions."

From the moment I heard this story, in 2016, I was riveted by the Newcastle case. So much attention has been paid to the Catholic Church, for understandable reasons. It is the most sexually repressive church, while being responsible for so many crimes against children. Yet that focus, unfortunately, has enabled child sexual abuse in other institutions to slip under the radar – almost as if it didn't happen. But it did happen. And the Newcastle Anglican Church was clearly responsible for some of the worst of the worst. Few in the Catholic hierarchy had spoken openly or truthfully about their church's cover-ups. But here was the Newcastle bishop, Greg Thompson, who had been abused himself, talking frankly about a "sense of self-entitlement" among clergy, as if sexual abuse of children came with the role.

This was like drilling down into the earth and finding the history of what had finally caused a volcanic eruption. Here, it seemed, was a chance to understand the multilayered history of denial, and to investigate a protection racket that enabled a network of abusers to flourish unchecked for decades.

I am a planner, the opposite of impulsive. I don't travel much except to see family. But I had to go to the Newcastle hearing of the royal commission. I immediately booked my flights and accommodation. I spoke to Nick Feik, editor of *The Monthly* magazine at the time, about writing an article; he agreed straightaway. My husband was startled but agreed with my instinct that this was an extraordinary story: "You must do it."

In May 2017, six months after the royal commission hearing ended, I published an essay, "Rape Among the Lamingtons", about the Newcastle case – Case Study 42, in the royal commission's parlance – in *The Monthly*.

By 2019, I had decided to give a fuller account. Before Covid struck in early 2020, I made many trips to Newcastle, reconstructing the paedophile network, how it worked, who knew about it and when they knew. One of the stories that most affected me at the royal commission hearing was that of Steve Smith. Steve was abused by Father George Parker between the ages of ten and fourteen, from 1971 to 1975. His extraordinary, brave struggle to get the church to acknowledge what happened, and to bring Parker to justice, took more than forty years.

In early 2020, Steve took me around Newcastle and its surrounds to where the abuse happened. We came to Yondaio, where Gray and Brown were raped at the church camp, on a steamy summer day. We parked my little hire car on the main road and walked down to the former campsite through dense forest on an ochre-coloured track. The sound of traffic from the highway receded and became a distant rumble. The bellbirds sounded like piping flutes. Otherwise, it was silent. The bush was lush, thick, even oppressive. In Victoria, where I live, summers bring hot north winds from central Australia, drying out the bush and grass until it crackles. Here, our footsteps could hardly be heard in the soft, damp leaf litter beneath our feet. The gums were tall, with a lower canopy of thick scrub. There was a beauty to it that made me shiver – a jarring discordance between this pretty patch of bushland and the evil done here. Paul Gray's words, "'We are going to get you,' the men said," kept ringing in my ears.

"Where did they run to? Where are the cliffs?" I asked.

Steve answered, "Over there, just before it drops to the ocean."

We walked through the bracken and blackberry until we confronted large rocks, where the land dropped steeply down the rocky cliff face.

"It's so thick," I said. "Imagine trying to run away through this. When you know what's coming."

Steve agreed. There was no doubt; the boys could not have escaped. He told me he couldn't escape his abuser, either. "I'd run away and hide, but sooner or later he was going to get me." He paused and looked around in silence before continuing. "You think – if these trees could talk. The horror. I know it's not as extreme, but it's like walking through Belanglo Forest, where the Ivan Milat murders took place. That eerie sort of feeling ... you think of a little kid running through the bush at night with a pack of bastards chasing them, knowing what's going to happen. Even if they went over the cliffs they'd have to come back. And they'll get you when you come back ... The church, if they had any decency, would put a memorial down here. Because there have been kids who lost their lives because of it."

Steve was talking about all the suicides.

Steve's comment that it is a place like Belanglo Forest is not so far from the mark. Because what took place, here and all over the Newcastle Anglican diocese, may not have been murder, but it was soul murder of little children who struggled ever after with what was done to them.

Children like Steve Smith.

PART ONE
CHILDHOOD

CHAPTER ONE
SMILEY

STEVEN SMITH WAS born in 1961. He was the third of four boys and was a happy little kid, so much so that his nickname was "Smiley". There is a photo from when he was nine years old, his face smiling widely, bursting with life and joy. Steve describes his parents, Robert and Margery, as "normal, suburban" people. They lived in Edgeworth, a working-class outer suburb of Newcastle.[1]

They were members of the local Anglican church, and Margery was especially devout. She had poor health, suffering from kidney disease. Perhaps that was one reason for her strong religious faith. Margery was a nurse and worked night shifts, so that she could be there for her children during the day. She went to work after they went to bed and was back before they got up. Steve's father, Robert, was a sheet-metal worker at BHP for forty years until he retired. He was also a justice of the peace. Most people in Newcastle at that time worked for BHP or down the mines. The Smiths were working class and money was scarce. Newcastle was divided into workers and managers, and everyone was aware which side of the tracks they lived on.

Steve took me to see his childhood home, a modest bungalow in a quiet street, Laurel Avenue, lined with 1950s and '60s worker's cottages. His dad built most of these houses, Steve told me proudly: "Dad could turn his hand to anything." Pointing to a front bedroom, he explained that this was where he and his three brothers slept, all bunked in together. The house sits opposite Brush Creek, which was brown and muddy from recent rain. Mangroves twisted into crooked shapes lined its banks. The only sounds to be heard were birds and cicadas. On the other side of the wide stream were scrub and bushland. Further along the creek was a dense tract of camphor laurels. That's how the street got its name.

Life for the Smith family revolved around the church and its community: "it was the centre of our universe ... we were part of something". Steve's mother was musical and was the church organist. She was not only devout but her life was full of good works and attentiveness to others. She ran the local Girls' Friendly Society and Mothers' Union, and each week she cleaned the church and festooned it with fresh flowers. Steve and his brothers would help, polishing the brass and vacuuming.

Steve still has a photo of Margery at a Mothers' Union celebration at Christ Church Cathedral in Newcastle around 1956. She looks radiant, wearing a white peaked hat, a little like a nun's steeple. He remembers his mother "always helping someone". When the Smiths eventually got a car, elderly women often needed transport, so Margery would drive them, lurching along in her rickety little white Hillman. "She was a terrible driver ... There was always some wayward soul at our door, God knows what hour of the night, needing help ... And they never turned anyone away." Father Peter Rushton from the neighbouring parish of Wallsend would bring orphans from St Alban's Boys' Home to stay, for Margery to "patch up". The Smith boys would grow jealous of the fuss their mother made of these boys.

Steve's father, Robert, was a church warden, responsible for the church finances and for the maintenance of the grounds and building. Steve describes his father as a gentle, fair man, who was always looking out for other people. Before the family had a car, on Saturdays, Robert would lift one kid onto his shoulders, pile most of the other boys into a wheelbarrow along with his tools and walk the mile or so to church "to do some work there, on the toilet block or something". One kid would push the lawn mower. On the way they would stop at a pub, the Traveller's Rest, and Robert would nip in to pick up the flagon of communion wine and, Steve suspected, have a schooner or two. Steve's mum would come up later with a picnic hamper and drinks, and the whole family would work together to make their place of worship immaculate.

On the way back from church, the kids would be allowed to roam through the bush, "and five hundred adventures later, you'd turn up home. They never knew where we were half the time. But we were safe. It was adventure central."

Sundays were a day of ritual, worship and community. Margery would play the organ and Robert, wearing his Sunday best, would pass the collection plate around for donations. After church, the priest would come back to the Smiths' house for Sunday lunch, a roast chicken with all the trimmings. "So that made me feel important, like we must be important people."

Steve describes his early life as very happy. He thinks he was his mother's favourite. He was intelligent, dux of every year and then, in year six, second to dux of the school at Edgeworth Primary. "You'll be a priest one day," Margery told him. She thought he had the right qualities.

Steve's maternal grandfather, Pop McGregor, was "very left". He hated banks and priests. He had eloped as a young man, and his hatred of the church remained. His wife – Margery's mother – had died young, and he had been on his own all those years. He was a "cantankerous old Scotsman. A good bloke. I loved him." Although Pop McGregor "would never step inside a church", he quite liked the local priest during Steve's early life, old Reverend Neville Spohr, who was a former tradie and, like the Smith family, a staunch Labor man. "My family was Labor Party to the core."

After Sunday lunch, Father Spohr, Pop McGregor and Steve's father would sit in the backyard, drinking bottles of beer. "I have this memory of stinking hot days, sitting out under the peach tree out the back. We'd sit on the grass, and I'd just sit there and listen. Or I'd sit up in one of the branches up the peach tree and listen to the men talk." The men's voices drifted upwards to where Steve sat in the leafy canopy. Steve loved it. The conversations were about justice and what was right and wrong, especially for the workers. "Everything they talked about was a sense of fairness … People need to be treated properly … the conversation was always that. And I had great respect for the priest because he subscribed to the same credo."

Steve's outlook on life and political views were formed by listening to them. This was the bedrock of his character, along with the example of his mother and father being so good to people. Steve couldn't remember a single sermon he'd ever listened to that wasn't "bloody gibberish", and "nothing's changed my view of that". "But sitting on the branch of the peach tree, listening to the three men talking, and talking about what I thought were really important things, were really the best days of my life."

Steve puts his academic success at primary school down to hearing "sensible people talking about sensible things. You learned how to think, and I got to the point where I'd ask questions. I'd jump out of the peach tree every now and then and say 'But why …?' A lot of the talk was about the unions, what they should be doing, and the rights of workers. They also hated Menzies and his successors, so the talk was often about toppling the Liberal government. 'We'll get them [the Liberals] this time.'"

Steve's sense of justice meant he also sometimes played devil's advocate. He'd climb down from his perch in the peach tree and ask, "But what if the men aren't working hard enough?" "They would answer that they only had to work as hard as they've got to work. Silly stuff, probably childish stuff … every now and again it was ideas that I'd get into my head, and I'd ask, and they'd answer me. It was great."

Ken Booth, a member of the NSW parliament and state treasurer, was a family friend and used to visit the Smiths. "That made you feel important." Every election day, Steve's mother would dress her boys in their white sports uniforms to hand out Labor how-to-vote cards. It might have been the 1960s, but she spoke up too. "Mum wasn't averse to getting into the conversation either, like, she wasn't scared of the blokes' world … It was a really great way to grow up … I'd do it again tomorrow, I enjoyed it that much. I was really proud to be a part of that family. I really loved it."

Lack of money did not mean any shortage of amusement. They made their own fun. Summers were oppressively hot and humid. In Brush Creek, out the front of their house, they would cool off by fishing and swimming. Steve's father used his metal-working skills to build canoes for many kids in the neighbourhood, "so long as they could swim".

> There'd be these fleets of these tin canoes, which were really well made [with] air compartments in them, so they couldn't sink. So, on any summer's day there'd be twenty or thirty of these things floating around in the front of our house, kids fishing out of them, sitting with their dog in the front of it or swimming behind. It was just perfect. Paradise.

Money might have been tight, but the Smith children were enterprising. They would swim across the creek to the golf course, find lost golf balls and sell them back to golfers. "Rastus, our old dog, who used to swim across the creek with us, helped pinch golf balls for me. We'd swim across the creek, pinch a few golf balls and swim back."

The children's lives centred on the creek. Brush Creek joins Cockle Creek, which runs all the way to Lake Macquarie, a beautiful saltwater lake, the largest in the southern hemisphere. The Indigenous people of the area called it Awaba, or "a plain surface", referring to its glassy stillness. It is huge, twice as large as Sydney Harbour. These waterways were the Smith boys' playground. They would put Rastus, and then their next dog, a Labrador called Baz, in the canoe, or let him paddle behind.

Steve tells me, "It was a Tom Sawyer or Huckleberry Finn existence." We are standing on the green grass next to Brush Creek, and Steve looks around with affection. "It used to be farms all down there, and where I used to hide as a kid. But this was sanctuary, this was heaven … it's a really hidden part of the world. A lot of people didn't even know it's here." Steve loved it so much he moved back there when he was first married, wanting his kids to have the same kind of childhood.

The one cloud on his childhood horizon was that his parents were unhappy in their marriage. There was constant, simmering conflict. "Mum and Dad didn't get on … you sort of knew that but didn't really see it. Often the bedroom door would be shut, and you'd hear them having a go at each other." Steve was especially close to his mother. "She was so caring, a great mum."

Margery's devotion to the church meant three of the Smith boys were altar boys. However, it was Steve who his mum felt should become a priest, perhaps because of his interest in justice. "She was determined I was going to be a priest … She just decided that was what I was going to be." His brothers didn't have that interest, so Steve was more often at the church with her. "I think she saw that I had a similar nature to her. So that's what I remember her telling me: 'You'll be a priest one day, Stevo.'"

Steve respected and trusted Reverend Spohr completely. Sadly, however, Spohr, "the good priest", who, along with Steve's father and Pop McGregor, had taught him so much about justice, fairness and how to live, eventually left. "It broke the parish's heart to see him go."

It was 1971, just before Steve's tenth birthday. It was at this point in Steve's young life that Father George Parker arrived.[2]

CHAPTER TWO

THE KIDNAPPING

WHEN GEORGE PARKER arrived at Edgeworth in 1971, he had been an assistant priest under Father Peter Rushton at nearby Wallsend, where Steve's parents had been married. Parker was thirty years old, single, wore his hair long and drove a "cool" Volkswagen beetle. He had a good singing voice and strummed a guitar. In every way he was very different from the old priest. Parker was a part of a strong Anglo-Catholic faction in the Newcastle diocese, which included Peter Rushton, Michael Cooper and James Brown. This faction wanted a return to many aspects of Catholicism, including being called "Father" rather than "Reverend". They espoused the value of celibacy, even though marriage for priests had been permitted in the Anglican Church for centuries. According to Steve, "Parker was more Catholic than Anglo." Liturgy at Edgeworth now became "very High Church".

The women of the parish, in particular, "fell in love" with Parker. Reverend Rod Bower remembered Parker as a great "kisser" of women after church services. Ian, Steve's older brother, remembered "Parker prancing around the church with a guitar. He was a talented musician ... popular among the church ladies, including my mum." Steve agreed.

> He was charismatic ... Merely by his position as the local parish priest, my
> mother held Parker in the highest regard. She really put him on a pedestal.
> It was like he was as close to being God as she'd get. He would regularly
> attend our home, where Mum would provide him meals pretty well every
> Sunday and randomly on weekdays.

However, gone were the halcyon days when Steve, sitting up in the peach tree in the backyard, would listen to the priest, his dad and his grandfather talking about justice. "The whole dynamic of Sunday changed." Now the other men vanished, and Parker would stay inside with Margery, Steve and his younger brother. Robert, Pop McGregor and Steve's older brothers Graeme and Ian all took an instant dislike to Parker. When Robert arrived home after work, Parker's Volkswagen would often be parked outside. There would be no beer left in the fridge; Parker had drunk it all during the day. "Dad just couldn't cop a bloke who drank another man's beer." But it was more than that. "Dad didn't like him, really didn't like him. Pop couldn't stand him."

Ian recalled getting a creepy feeling when Parker looked at him. "I immediately picked up a bad vibe from him." Parker was a close friend of Peter Rushton, and they'd often turn up with a little orphan boy called Michael, about Steve's age, from St Alban's Boys' Home. Michael would be left with the Smiths for weeks at a time for Margery to care for. Steve described him as a "very sad, very hurt boy" who would "attach himself to Mum like a leech". Then he'd be picked up and taken back to the orphanage.

Despite the dislike of Father Parker by the male members of the Smith family, "it was rare not to see him almost daily ... There has been some scuttlebutt that he was having an affair with my mum. Was he? I don't know. He could have been. It wouldn't surprise me ... Mum and Dad weren't particularly happy, and he's a young man coming around, paying her attention."

However, Father Parker likely had a very different motive for getting close. He was grooming the whole family. Winning Margery's trust and acting as her intimate confidant, Parker gained free access to Steve and his brothers. The Smiths were a good family, but they were vulnerable because of his parents' marital problems. "He would have known there was disharmony. Mum would have talked to him. The priest is the most trusted person."

When Parker arrived in the parish, Steve told me, "the me being a priest stuff ramped up extraordinarily." Parker took Steve under his wing. Margery could not have been more pleased. "His interest in me was extraordinary. Above the other kids, I think. He just really seemed to want to be around me all the time. Even sitting at dinner, I had to sit next to him, all the time. He would say, 'Come and sit with Father George.'"

Parker would also pay Steve to wash his car, and "we never had any money", so Steve did so frequently. Steve felt proud of the attention, of being Father Parker's favourite. His mother was proud, too, that this "up and coming" priest had taken a shine to one of her boys. For a working-class family, to have a priest take an interest in Steve's future vocation seemed a golden opportunity. Such opportunities didn't come along every day. Steve said it felt as though "this bloke's [interested], and my son is destined for the priesthood; here's a free kick."

For his tenth birthday, Steve was given a bright red Repco Mustang bicycle. "It was the most wonderful thing I had ever seen. I wasn't game to ride it at first in case I scratched it. I have no idea how my parents afforded the thing, but I had never felt so happy in my life." Pop and Robert patiently watched him ride proudly up and down their street. They solemnly told Steve that now he was a young man.

Parker turned up for Steve's birthday too, hugging him and giving him a dollar. Steve felt a "peculiar unease". He pushed the priest away "because I felt something pressing against me. I thought he had something in his pocket." The men in Steve's household shook hands; they never hugged.

Now ten, Steve was old enough to begin training as an altar boy. Although kids at school teased him, he knew he was making his mother proud. At Sunday lunches, Parker would put his hand on Steve's leg under the table. "Not long now," he would say. On Wednesday afternoons, Steve eagerly ran the 500 metres from school to the church for training. A couple of other boys were training too, but "Parker paid special attention to me." Parker would offer to drive Steve home. "If he dropped a few [boys] home, I was always last."

Then it started.

"He just sort of touched me on the leg ... he'd want to give you a hug."

No one, Steve said, "would have thought anything of it. It was a different era." For Steve, "at first there was no particular threat to it."

Once Steve was an altar boy, everything changed.

Parker had to give Sunday services in four churches in his parish. First up was the main church, St James in West Wallsend, then St Anne's in Edgeworth. Afterwards, Margery went home to organise Sunday lunch, while Parker would drive Steve in his VW beetle either to nearby Killingworth or, through rolling hills, to the pretty little stone church at Minmi, an old coal-mining settlement.

The church at Minmi sits in a quiet, bushy street, surrounded by a leafy garden. Ivy curls up its walls. To one side of the steeply gabled roof is a small annex, containing a quaint vestry. It was there that Parker would get changed into his priestly robes, and Steve into his white altar-boy garments. And it was there, in that pretty little church, that Parker first sexually assaulted Steve.

After the service, Parker told Steve to go and get changed in the old vestry. The timber floor was rotten, so Steve had to step carefully when he walked in. As he was getting changed, he suddenly felt Parker behind him. The priest started feeling Steve's buttocks over his underpants. Then the priest reached around and fondled Steve's penis. Parker was a big man, about six feet tall. Steve was a little boy of ten. Parker pinned him against the vestry table, trapping him by wrapping his powerful arms around Steve's middle and by positioning his bulky form behind Steve, preventing escape. Steve was frozen with fear. There were still people moving around outside. Steve felt the pressure of Parker's erect penis rubbing firmly against him. Parker kept pressing Steve hard against the chest-high vestry table. After about five minutes, he finished.

"My knowledge of sexuality then was nil. The first time, I had no idea of what's going on. I was shocked, confused, scared." After the assault, Parker behaved as if nothing had happened. Then, while driving Steve home, he said for the first time, "This is our secret. You can't tell anyone." That was his mantra: "This is our special secret. Remember how good a friend Father George is." And "God sent you to me."

This command not to tell left Steve:

> really confused, because it heightened my sense that this was all wrong. I remember thinking, if I couldn't tell anyone, maybe it shouldn't have happened … However, a priest was someone of extremely high standing back then. I was a ten-year-old kid whose family held Parker in reverence. There was no way in my child mind that I could divulge Parker's secret, because no one would've believed me.

Parker told Steve repeatedly that "no one would believe him". The priest drew Steve into a circle of secrecy, placing responsibility on Steve not to tell, or else his "special friend", Parker, would get into trouble. He also straightforwardly threatened Steve with physical harm, telling him that he'd bash up Steve or his family if Steve told. On one occasion, Parker told the mute, terrified child, mid-assault, that Steve mustn't tell because his mother would be upset if she knew what Steve was doing. Steve was flabbergasted. What *he* was doing?

The type of sexual assault Parker committed on that first occasion happened at least a dozen more times at Minmi. There were also multiple assaults when they were driving to the next church. Parker would fondle Steve nonchalantly, and Steve, trapped in a moving vehicle with his seatbelt on, could do nothing about it. "It was always like that with him. I was amazed. It just seemed like nothing to him. He just kept driving straight ahead, with an indifferent but smug look." Once, on a long drive west to Cessnock to meet with Father Rushton, the abuse lasted for the entire forty-five minutes in each direction. On another occasion, Parker drove to The Entrance parish church, in a long trip down the coast, and molested Steve the whole way, there and back. When they went inside the church, there was another priest. Steve didn't know who he was, but recalled him laughing and saying to Parker, "It's not like you to share, George." "He thought it was hilarious." That laughter stayed in Steve's mind. He never forgot it. He could hardly look at the other priest because he was utterly terrified that *both* priests would assault him. They didn't, however.

The abuse escalated over time. What started as sexual assault through clothing became fondling naked genitals under clothing, then anal digital penetration, which "hurt like crazy". Steve estimated Parker raped him digitally forty to fifty times at St Anne's in Edgeworth.

Steve's mother trustingly sent Steve on numerous occasions to help Parker at the rectory, to mow the lawns or wash the car. These visits provided opportunities for Parker to be alone with Steve and to sexually assault him. The *modus operandi* was always the same. When Parker digitally penetrated Steve, "I immediately felt trapped, because I was being pressed up against the sink." He couldn't escape. Frozen, Steve focused on the house next door, through the window, before closing his eyes in horror as he was assaulted. Afterwards, Parker said nothing; he just walked away as if nothing had occurred. "There was no exchange of words." Steve would pull his pants up, go outside and finish the mowing, then put the mower away and be driven home, sitting silent and shocked in the car. Sometimes Parker would talk about the weather.

There were even times when, despite other people being present at church or a social occasion, Parker would furtively grab or touch Steve's penis or buttocks as he brushed past. It was like he owned Steve. Steve always tried to keep other people between him and Parker.

By the time Steve was in year five at Edgeworth Primary, he had been sexually assaulted many times. On the day of scripture class, to avoid Parker, Steve bunked off from school. He ran home. He wanted to tell his mum but was too fearful of not being believed, so she took him back to school. The principal, Mr Hammond, was angry about Steve playing truant.

> [He] talked to the class about leaving school without permission and said I needed to be made an example of. Mr Hammond then made me put my hands out and gave me four strokes of the cane. I had never been caned before. I cried a fair bit. I was then made to sit in the front of the room with my back to the class. It became clear to me that no matter what I did, Parker would be able to get me.

Over time, the abuse escalated to include oral and anal rape. The abuse happened "at least fortnightly".[1] At St Anne's in Edgeworth, when Steve came for altar service, Parker would lock the door to the church, walk down the aisle and bend Steve over the altar, before assaulting him.

The first time he was anally raped by Parker, Steve had been mowing the lawn at the rectory at West Wallsend. Parker told Steve to go inside to get a drink of cordial. Then Parker came in and moved behind him in the kitchen, pinning him against the sink, trapping him. "I closed my eyes out of fear for what was about to happen." This time Parker forced anal penetration with his penis. It was agonisingly painful.

> It hurt a lot more than the finger. Parker ejaculated inside my anus. When he was finished, Parker simply pulled up his trousers and walked away from me towards the front portion of the house, but I don't know where he went. I went to the toilet and just sat there. I wiped [the mess away]. I felt sick. The whole thing just felt really violent – like you're being punched. Like, what was that all about?

I was always trapped when Parker got me. I had nowhere to go. I didn't scream and didn't say anything because I was frozen with fear, I literally felt like I could not physically move or speak – again, I was petrified.[2]

After that time, anal penetration happened on many occasions. Steve came to learn Parker's bodily movements and "pig grunting" noises, which meant the ordeal would soon be over. Steve always felt he was just an object to be used. Parker would drive Steve home afterwards, either silent or chatting about inanities. Steve would "go bush" to the Three Creeks area, where Brush Creek, Cockle Creek and Cocked Hat Creek meet, about a kilometre from his home. In the privacy of the creekbank, shaken and miserable, he "cried and cried". Then he had to clean himself up. "My undies were a mess with blood, shit and semen on them. I rinsed them in the water and used them to wipe myself down." Then he would bury them in the dirt next to the creek, put his shorts back on and walk home, hoping Parker had left. Once home, Steve would sneak a new pair of underpants out of the drawer, so his mother never knew.

Steve was abused by Parker at the local church at Edgeworth, in the kitchen at the rectory in West Wallsend, in the garage at the rectory, and in a parked Jaguar car owned by a friend of Parker's. He was molested in Parker's own car and at other churches in the parish. The very culture of doing good works, of volunteering, his family's impressive contribution to church and community life, meant Steve was frequently delivered to Parker's door by his unwitting mother, to help "the man of God". "I used to wash his car, mow his lawn, get raped." After the rapes, Steve would feel devastated, disgusted, angry, frightened, ashamed, humiliated and panic-stricken.

Steve was just a kid. He had no idea what to do. He couldn't escape. He felt utterly trapped and powerless.

A little church with few parishioners, like the one at Minmi, was a perfect opportunity for abuse. "You'd go out there and there would be no one … And so, he had free access to me. After an hour or so he would go home to my place in Edgeworth, and he'd sit and have lunch with my family." Parker's effrontery is one of the things that especially angers Steve. After sexually assaulting their child, he would turn up at the family table, to be treated to a special roast dinner prepared by Steve's devout mother.

He'd sit at the table opposite ... and put his leg over my leg. Like, this guy has just raped me, and he's sitting there eating our fucking food, and he'd do that. And I'd sit there and say nothing ... That was him saying to me, "I can do whatever I want, when I want" ... It was the power he got off on.

Steve was in no doubt that the sexual acts were about power over him, and that this was what Parker was aroused by.

From the age of ten, Steve's world was split in two. The boys' world of brothers, mates and school, of canoes and adventures at the creek, of Mum, Dad and the church had been suddenly shattered. Steve was catapulted from that safe world into a bewildering new and secret one – a subterranean world of adult male sexual perversity. Suddenly he had the shock of new and unwelcome knowledge of adult penises, erections, the strange smells of semen and of Parker's tobacco and alcohol, the ugly noises Parker made, and the ghastly aftermath on his own body. Father Parker, the trusted family priest, had split Steve's world into these two irreconcilable pieces. There was the surface world that most people, including his mother, inhabited, where priests were respected men of God who could do no wrong. That world of faith and trust now seemed unreal. What was real was the sordid world of the paedophile that Steve was being forced to inhabit.

Not only was Steve trapped in a frightening world utterly beyond his understanding, but he was also isolated there. Steve had sexual knowledge that had to be kept secret from other children as well as adults. His feelings of terror, disgust and shame he had to deal with entirely alone. He couldn't escape. He had to live, day after day, with this enormous, explosive, shame-ridden secret and the fear of its discovery.

During one of my visits to interview Steve, there was a terrible crime in Newcastle: a young girl was kidnapped and raped several times by a paedophile. Steve, like everyone in Newcastle, was upset, outraged and horrified by what had happened to the little girl. He quietly said to me that what had happened to him, and to other child sexual abuse victims, was another kind of kidnapping. He couldn't escape. He endured rape after rape, never knowing when the next ambush would take place, over five years. The only thing certain was that Parker would get him again, no matter how much Steve tried to stay out of his clutches.

*

Everything in Steve's universe changed. A clever kid with bright prospects, his schoolwork now deteriorated. Living in fear of the next assault, "Smiley" was no more; "I stopped smiling."

"I was terrified all the time," he remembered. "I couldn't focus on anything, I got to a point where I got up early on a Sunday morning and [would] shoot through. I'd go bush. I knew what was going to happen … I always had vantage points where I could make sure his car was gone before I came home. Mum would be sitting in a big old-fashioned armchair and say, 'Come here.' And I'd get a backhander … And Mum, she'd give good backhanders. I made a decision early I was prepared to wear that."

Steve's mother did not understand it as anything more than her boy playing truant. Her conscientious son, her "good boy", the future priest, was changing, and she couldn't understand why. Angry and disappointed, wise to his early morning escapes, she would call out as he went, stopping him.

When Steve started disappearing on Sundays, Parker responded by coming to Steve's school. That meant even school, which Steve had always loved, was no longer a place of safety. Parker would randomly turn up and, hiding behind his priest's collar, take Steve out of class. Steve couldn't concentrate, worrying and waiting for Parker to get him. He remembers vividly being in a high-school French lesson with Miss Bickley, when he was twelve or thirteen. Parker casually walked in and said, "I'm here to get Steven." The teacher, instinctively obeying the priest, said, "Steven, put your books away" – "no questions asked".

Parker never had to sign Steve out or get permission from the school office. He did not have to inform Steve's parents. He just took him. This was humiliating: among Steve's mates, to be a priest's boy had meaning. "The kids gave me a hard time about that, calling me a 'priest's boy', a 'church boy'." But worse, far worse, was that Parker "would have me for the rest of the day to do whatever he wanted".

Sometimes they drove to the Woodlands Boys' Home or St Alban's Boys' Home. There would be other kids in priests' cars parked outside. Like Steve, they waited outside the boys' home while the priests went inside. "We knew what they were doing." Peter Rushton's car was often among them. The partner of a Woodlands Boys' Home victim described how "These men came, got the boys, used them, and put them back … It was like buying a bottle of milk to them … If you don't like it, put it back. Get another one."[3] By this time, Steve had formed the opinion that Rushton was also sexually abusing kids. Jokes circulated among the altar boys: "arses against the wall, Rushton's on the crawl." And that sad little boy, Michael? Steve now thought both Parker and Rushton were abusing him.

Going to YMCA camps was the only way Steve could escape. "After Parker started abusing me, it was one place he couldn't get me, because they wouldn't let anyone come in to get a kid." The safety of the YMCA camps, however, cost ten or eleven dollars for the week. That sum was not easy for the Smiths, so "it didn't happen often". By the time Steve was fourteen, he had worked his way up to be a junior leader at the camp. The sexual abuse was still going on, and he would "volunteer for everything. I'd just stay and stay and stay, as long as I could." At the camps there was relief, "enjoyment and security. He couldn't get me."

Of his inability to disclose the abuse, Steve said, "I don't expect lay-people to understand the power of the church and the fear this instilled in me about speaking out against its clergy."

Steve's intelligence, his perceptiveness about people, his innate kind-ness and capacity to see things from another person's perspective actually made it harder for him to tell anyone. It wasn't just that he knew that he would likely not be believed, but that the inevitable, catastrophic fallout would harm the people he loved. Steve felt he had to protect his family, and especially his mother, by not telling anyone what Parker was doing to him. Steve was close to his mother and understood her. He felt disclosing the abuse would be like taking an axe to his mum; her whole world, her faith, her trust, would be utterly destroyed. He also worried that his grandfather, Pop, an old bushie, "if he ever knew, would get his rifle and shoot Parker."

Steve had absolutely no idea how to get out of the situation.

One incident deeply impressed upon Steve that he must not tell. He went to church one day and there was whispering behind people's hands, a scandal about another family. These were "lovely people". The older brother of one of Steve's fellow altar boys had told his parents that Parker had been abusing him.

It turned out Parker was getting it on with [him]. And he was underage … he was a kid. The family apparently raised it with Parker. Parker carved these people up. That family went from front row, front pew. [The mother] was a glamourpuss with gloves and the big hat, she always had the best frock … They disappeared. The congregation ran them out of the church.

The social ostracism, the informal excommunication, was a strong discouragement to Steve speaking to anyone. "I watched what the community did when the priest was challenged."

Later, a friend from those times saw a newspaper article about what had happened to Steve. He said, "Smithy, why didn't you tell me?"

I said, "What the fuck was I going to tell you? You know, 'What did you do on the weekend?' 'Oh, you know, I went for a surf, went kayaking, oh and I got raped by a priest …' I'll give you the heads up, mate. I know what would have happened if anyone had known what was happening. Your families would have run my family out of town. Your mother would not have let you play with me. No question of it. I understood that at the time. That was the consequence of raising that."

Early in 1975, George Parker was transferred to another parish, Gateshead. The Edgeworth parishioners – especially the women – were heartbroken over losing the wonderful Father George. Steve was relieved and elated.

Parker's place was taken by Reverend John Sherlock. Steve was by now very wary of a popular, charismatic priest. He described the new vicar as "like an old English village priest, a lovely bloke. Dry as a bone … The personality of a house brick. But he was a nice old bloke … I thought, 'It's over.' I thought the nightmare was over."

But it wasn't.

A few weeks later, at the end of April or the beginning of May 1975, on a Saturday, Steve and his brother came home from playing at the creek. His mother told them to pack their bags. Father George had called. He had no altar boys at the new church and wanted the boys to serve tomorrow.

Steve immediately knew what was coming if they stayed over, so he asked if they could go in the morning. His mother replied that Father George thought it would be a treat for them to sleep over.

"I thought, 'Yeah, righto. What do I do here?' If I don't go, my little brother is going to go, and I know what will happen to him. My *younger* brother." Steve was now fourteen, and his younger brother was eleven. I will call his brother B, after the last letter of the pseudonym he was allocated by the royal commission, CKB. So, to try to protect his little brother, Steve went.

Parker picked up the boys in his car, a white Galant station wagon. Steve told me, "I can even tell you the rego number – GKD999." The car stank; Parker was a heavy smoker of Kent cigarettes, and the ashtray was stuffed full of stubs. "And off we all went, chucked our bags in the back. My brother was sitting in the back. Parker kept reaching through the seats the whole time, trying to get him [to touch his genitals], and I'm trying to distract him. I was thinking about how we were going to get through the night."

At Charlestown, they stopped and bought chicken and chips for a treat. Parker then insisted B have a shower before dinner. "Next thing I know ... apparently Parker went into the shower and molested him." Parker took off B's pants and underpants and rubbed his hands on B's buttocks. B managed to get away and get into the shower, pulling the curtain around him. He tried to shut the bathroom door, but Parker said the door had to be left open. When B emerged from the shower, they had the chicken and chips. Parker put large wine glasses on the table, "like brandy glasses", and filled them with red wine. He told the boys, "Don't tell your mother I'm letting you drink. She'll be really cranky at me."

"And I'm thinking, fuck, if she only knew. The least of your worries, mate. Like, he loaded us up."

Parker insisted B go to bed and took him into the second bedroom, shutting the door behind them. Steve was worried about what might happen behind the closed door, so intervened and told Parker that at home, they always kept the bedroom door open. Parker ignored him. He had other plans – for Steve.

Parker made up a bed out of couch cushions on the lounge-room floor. He told Steve to get undressed and observed admiringly how muscly he was now. Parker then took Steve's underpants off. Steve was heavily affected by the alcohol. Parker leant him over a lounge chair and pushed him into it face first. Steve still remembers the scratchy material. Parker fondled Steve's anal area, undid his own trousers, and rubbed his erect penis over Steve's buttocks. He attempted to penetrate but was unsuccessful. Steve cried out in distress. But for the first time, now aged fourteen, he was old enough and strong enough to rebuff him.

I was fourteen and I was bigger … I could have knocked him down. I should have. But then he tried again, and I fought back. It was like "No, fuck you. Enough." He got pretty uppity with me … I was still pissed, I think. There was all sorts [of], "Remember what a good friend Father George is to you. You can't be telling your mother what has happened."

Parker finally gave up and went to bed, saying, "Now, you know where my room is if you want me through the night."

Steve was so frightened he hardly slept, keeping one eye open all night. He expected Parker to come back, but he didn't. "The next morning, we got up and it was all very quiet in the house. I could see something had happened to my brother. I saw that he was terrified." In turn, his brother thought Steve looked frightened; he knew that something had happened.

The two boys dressed in their white lace robes and performed as altar boys. They listened while Parker preached about virtue. The women of the church had set up trestle tables with cups, saucers and cakes they had baked for morning tea afterwards. An urn was bubbling away. After the service, Parker was "eyeballing both of us". Luckily, "some old lady came walking along with a cup of tea for him and a plate with a cake on it". When Parker turned to talk to her, Steve said to his brother, "C'mon, we're out of here." They bolted fifty metres across a small grass paddock to the rectory.

Steve was worried that if they didn't get out then, they would be there all day with Parker. From the rectory, full of fear, Steve rang home. "My brother Graeme answered the phone and I said, 'Where's Mum?' He said, 'Oh, she's still at church.'"

"As soon as she gets home, tell her to come and get us," Steve said.

Steve told his little brother, "Get out of your robes, get your street clothes back on, bag all your shit up." They had to be quick before Parker came back. "Mum turned up in pretty record time. For me to ring her, she knew something was up."

His mother drove over in the old white Hillman with the green stripe. She asked them, "Aren't you going to say goodbye to Father George?"

"NO! Just go!" Steve told her.

His mum raised an eyebrow at this, but sensed something was very wrong and started driving.

Steve remembers exactly where he first told his mother that he had been sexually abused by George Parker. There was a little bridge in

Edgeworth, not far from their home. There's a McDonald's there now.

After he'd told her, she didn't say anything at first.

"Because we were only 500 metres from home, she waited. When she pulled into the driveway, she told B to get out. We sat together, in the car, in the shed.

"[She said] 'Tell me what's happened?'"

"So, I told her."

Steve's mum believed him straightaway. It was not at all what he was expecting. Steve had feared for so long that if he told, he would not be believed. It would be his word, a child's word, against the word of a revered priest. And how could he cope with what he had endured only to be told *it did not happen*? How could he go on having a relationship with anyone who didn't believe him once he spoke?

Later, Steve wondered if Margery's quickness to accept his account showed that "there'd really been something else going on" between her and Parker. "There was never any hesitation. And that really caught me off-guard, because I had thought, 'I'm going to be sitting in front of the grand inquisition here.' The tendency then was to blame kids for everything." There has been debate in Steve's family about that: "Some of the brothers in years gone by have said, 'Why did she even let you go there?'" Steve says, "I try not to get into it, because I can't change what happened. And I'm not going to bag Mum. For her to think, 'This bloke is doing that to my boy ...'"

Telling his mother was momentous for Steve. He had got over the first hurdle. He had told his mother and she believed him. She told Steve: "I'm going to talk with your father, and we'll deal with this."

However, that was the end of the conversation. The family didn't ever discuss it with Steve or tell him what they had done about it. "She never ever spoke to me about it again." But Parker was no longer welcome in their house.

A psychologist's report years later stated that Steve had gone through one of the most extreme cases of sexual abuse that she had ever encountered. The silence that descended was not ill-intentioned. But it meant Steve was left to deal with the trauma, the meaning of it, the emotional repercussions and psychological aftermath of those horrific five years, all by himself. He had been raped hundreds of times from the age of ten to fourteen. And he was utterly alone with it.

CHAPTER THREE

THE BODY REMEMBERS

STEVE WAS TRAPPED for five years at a formative time in his development. He could not escape. All the spaces that should have been safe for him – church, school, the bus stop, even his own home – were now places of opportunity where Parker could attack without warning and with impunity. No one suspected the priest was a paedophile. The clerical collar provided the perfect cover.

Steve could not avoid him, no matter how hard he tried. Steve was as resourceful as any child. He hid up a tree for hours, heart beating fast, only climbing down when he saw Parker's car depart. Or he went bush on a church morning and hid where the priest's greedy eyes could not see him. But it was no use. During the week, Parker could walk into the school and pluck Steve out with the teacher's permission. On weekends, Steve was delivered by his mother straight to the predator's lair.

Steve was a bright spark of a kid who saw with sharp clarity the social world around him. He knew the consequences for his mother and family should the situation be made public – shame, expulsion from the church, ostracism from the community. He knew that homophobia was rife and that he would be branded a "poofter" and rejected and bullied by his peer group if it became known he was sexually abused by a priest.

There was no escape. He never knew when the next attack would happen. Only that it *would* happen.

When a person has no escape from a traumatic situation, something terrible happens. They freeze. Freezing is a mechanism that evolved to give the organism a chance of surviving, like a mouse in a cat's mouth playing dead. In a human being, when in a situation of extreme danger, like sexual assault, the brain can be flooded with chemicals which prevent movement. Recent neuroscience on trauma has revealed that it is not something the person being attacked has control over. It is an involuntary reaction; the person literally cannot move. It is likely an evolutionary adaptation, because by remaining motionless in life-threatening situations, a person might survive.

Another evolutionary mechanism for the human being in the hands of a predator is to float out of their body, as if looking down, remotely observing, as if the abuse is happening to someone else. This is dissociation. It is a way of psychologically surviving the attack. Floating high above the body, or focusing on a blind, a wall, a speck of light, during a rape, they can experience the attack in a detached or disembodied way. Steve remembers focusing on the window above the rectory sink while Parker assaulted him.

When a human being is subject to this kind of trauma, such frequent triggering of the freezing and dissociation responses is bad news. Fight or flight responses at least give a person the sense that they can do something.

The very worst form of trauma, as understood by specialists from the 1990s onwards, is when the person cannot use any agency or take any action to escape. This is when the gravest possible harm is done to the human psyche. The consequences are long-lasting. The victim can't just "move on" after the assaults have stopped. The experiences and their effects are often not accessible to simple talk therapy. They can be stored at a bodily level. For example, a child victim of oral rape might find themselves panicked at a dentist because of the forced opening of their mouth, without knowing why. Trauma memories may be stored in a different region of the brain from language. If you have to flee from a predator, you need cortisol and adrenalin coursing through your body, enabling you to take the necessary action to escape. For someone trapped in a traumatic situation long-term, however, these very survival mechanisms work against the victim. Their body is constantly being flooded with cortisol, and the effects go way beyond the emotional and psychological; trauma actually *changes the brain*.

If the red-alert button in a person is permanently switched on, extraordinary damage is done. A cascade of neurological and physical changes occurs. After prolonged inescapable trauma, the brain becomes hypervigilant. That hypervigilance continually triggers states of fear and panic, which then become a source of fear themselves. The person has a racing heart and intense startle reactions. Normally cortisol in a person's body follows a daily rhythm. It is a stimulant hormone that rises in the morning and falls during the latter part of the day. At night-time, the hormone melatonin surges and provides for sleep and restoration. In trauma, this mechanism is disrupted. Cortisol surges and remains high, circulating constantly and setting off chain reactions. Small, seemingly unrelated events, words, phrases and images act as triggers. The person can't "downward regulate" their emotions – in simple terms, they can't calm down. It is as if they are taking stimulants constantly. That means racing thoughts, anxiety, disrupted sleep and nightmares. Lack of sleep further damages the capacity to cope. Sometimes trauma memories are fragmentary, of sounds, smells and sensations. Or, as in Steve's case, the traumatic memories may be so vivid that flashbacks and intrusive thoughts dominate, even when he was supposed to be relaxing or enjoying a family occasion.

The worse it gets, the worse it gets. The reason is that when neurons fire together, they wire together. Self-blame and the spiral into depression and panic occur faster and faster. The more the person's life – entirely explicably, entirely understandably, entirely predictably – goes off the rails, the worse the panic and depression become.

The person becomes hardwired to react as if they are in a battle zone, leaping or erupting in anger when a loud noise occurs, even if it is only a car backfiring. They begin to live in the past, constantly preoccupied by racing thoughts that dominate their conscious and unconscious moments, when they are trying to do schoolwork, study or watch TV. They might explode into rage seemingly inexplicably – except it is entirely explicable because of the movie reel running in their heads. They may find it hard to relate to people they love or work with who have no idea what is going on inside them, the wildfire in their brain. They may suffer mood swings, alternating between inappropriate anger for their present situation and weeping fits. They often turn to alcohol or drugs to try to numb themselves. They may self-harm. Physiologically, self-harming can work to temporarily distract from, or override, the overwhelming psychic pain. All this may seem inexplicable to families who don't know what their loved one has been through.

The feeling of being out of control, of being unable to cope, may make it impossible to hold down a job. That plunges the person into poverty and welfare dependency, a source of further self-blame when our society does everything it can to shame welfare recipients. Why can't I make a go of things? What is wrong with me? Blame is not directed where it belongs, at the perpetrator, but at themselves.

And so often the survivor is not believed. There are few things worse for the survivor than being told, "It did not happen." As the horrifying cascade of psychic pain and neurophysiological change continues, a downward spiral may end in the person not wanting to live anymore. All those single-car "accidents". The slow suicides by alcohol and drug abuse. And the suicides by hanging, jumping off buildings, overdosing and slitting of wrists. It is a miracle that Steve is still here. Many others are not. Michael, a fellow altar boy, told Steve when they were both in their early twenties and working at BHP that he had also been abused by Parker as a child. A couple of years later, Michael jumped off the roof of a multi-storey motel near the Sydney Cricket Ground. Paul Gray, another survivor, told me he thought there were up to fifty suicides connected to Anglican child sexual abuse in Newcastle.

Steve froze during the attacks and at the priest's house at West Wallsend because he was trapped. Parker's well-choreographed moves showed he knew how to render a child powerless. Steve could not fight off someone three times his size. He could not flee. He felt he could not tell anyone. Every response involving agency had been blocked. In many court cases, victims of sexual assault are asked, "Why didn't you say no or do something to fight back?" when the person was literally paralysed with fear, flooded with neurochemicals preventing movement. It is one of the cruellest responses to sexual assault, and entirely misunderstands the effects of fear on the body. These responses are not from lack of will – they are involuntary neurological and physiological processes.

According to trauma expert Bessel van der Kolk, being trapped and unable to do anything has a huge effect on whether or not the person develops Post-traumatic Stress Disorder (PTSD). He writes:

> Being able to move and do something to protect oneself is a critical factor in determining whether or not a horrible experience will leave long-lasting scars ... Dissociation is the essence of trauma. The overwhelming experience is split off and fragmented, so that the emotions, sounds, images, thoughts, and physical sensations related to the trauma take on a life of

their own. The sensory fragments of memory intrude into the present, where they are literally relived.[1]

That was what happened to Steve. Triggers happened all the time. If he saw a priest out walking, he'd have to cross to the other side of the road, heart racing, panic setting in. He hated going near a church. Like most trauma victims, Steve startled easily. Van der Kolk explains that "many people may not be aware of the connection between their 'crazy' feelings … and traumatic events … They have no idea why they respond to some minor irritation as if they were about to be annihilated." Steve was angry a lot, and misdirected anger is a typical response. Another is to drink heavily to anaesthetise the pain and to try not to feel so much. Steve did that too. Van der Kolk writes:

> the bottom line is that the threat-perception system of the brain has changed, and people's physical reactions are dictated by the imprint of the past. The trauma that started "out there" is now played out on the battlefield of their own bodies, usually without a conscious connection between what happened back then and what is going on right now inside.[2]

After trauma, people often feel numb and disconnected in social situations, even ones meant to be joyful. They can be physically present but emotionally absent. Van der Kolk makes a crucial point:

> Social support is not the same as merely being in the presence of others. The critical issue is *reciprocity*: being truly heard and seen by the people around us, feeling that we are held in someone else's mind and heart. For our physiology to calm down, heal, and grow, we need a visceral feeling of safety … trauma can turn the whole world into a gathering of aliens.

Steve's brother, Ian, said to me, "After Parker, Steve seemed a different person."

Actually, after the abuse, Steve *was* a different person. Van der Kolk tells us the scientific reason:

> After trauma the world is experienced with a different nervous system. The survivor's energy now becomes focused on suppressing inner chaos,

at the expense of spontaneous involvement in their life ... In PTSD the body continues to defend against a threat that belongs to the past.[3]

A Western Australian survivor of child sexual abuse, Andrew, put this very well:

In many ways, adult survivors are still children, who have been jettisoned from the normal life experience into a parallel existence. We continuously struggle to reconcile our inner world with the world and people around us, we are no longer living a truly shared experience with our fellows, and we struggle to understand why.[4]

He might well have been talking of Steve.

CHAPTER FOUR

SMOKING VOLCANOES EVERYWHERE

PARKER MIGHT HAVE been out of his life, but he had not been evicted from Steve's mind.[1] In fact, as is the case for most child sexual abuse survivors, Steve's perpetrator was permanently lodged there. Steve now had a new set of problems. Like fear of discovery.

> In the panic about what might happen, your life is where you are walking down this path with all these smoking volcanoes everywhere, and you never knew when one of them was going to erupt … I couldn't focus on anything besides self-protection … That's just what your life turns into. I have to protect myself, I have to protect my family, but I didn't know how to do it. Like, I don't know what to do.

Steve told me this in 2021, yet in his last sentence he moved into the present tense. With PTSD, that's what happens: the trauma is not "just" memories. There are times when that past is still fully alive, as if the person is still living through it. When he was a teenager, and for many years after, Steve was still:

> really trapped in those feelings and trapped in the fear of what might happen with my family. I didn't know what my mum or dad had done about it. I never knew when I was gonna walk back into this … you wouldn't know if anyone knew about it … You just never knew when it was going to re-emerge.

After the last assault at Gateshead, Steve no longer had to cope with the continual, unpredictable sexual assaults, but he now lived with the shame of what had happened and the terror of people discovering it. He also knew the cruelties of the schoolyard and the contempt with which homosexuals were often regarded in the 1970s.

Steve never shared that view. He never confused same-sex preference among adults with predation on children. He knew Parker was not a homosexual. He was a paedophile, aroused by sex with a child because it gave him complete power over his victim. "It was so impersonal. It was entirely about him, what he wanted or needed or however you want to describe it ... It didn't matter what I felt or how upset I was, how painful, like I was an object."

Steve lived in a state of constant anxiety and panic. It drenched every activity. Was he partly to blame, he wondered? He liked girls, but did Parker's abuse mean he was queer? What did it mean that Parker picked on *him*? Was there something wrong with him? Even though he'd been a ten-year-old kid, he felt bad that he had not fought off the six-foot-tall burly man who'd threatened him. He beat himself up over his freeze response and the state of helplessness he had been reduced to. He felt scorching shame over having been penetrated. He could not speak of it to anyone. If anyone found out, he felt, the shame would land on him, not Parker.

The abuse might have stopped, but the aftermath had just begun.

Apart from telling Steve it was "our special secret" and that "no one will believe you", Parker had never once discussed what he had done to Steve. Afterwards Parker would be casual, chatting about anything but what had just occurred. It was a tactic of disconfirming Steve's reality, as if the sexual assault hadn't happened. The attacks were violent but silent.

Despite the extreme trauma of his late childhood and early adolescence, Steve received no help. "There was a void," he told me. Steve is by character a stoic. He belongs to the "boys don't cry", working-class school of hard knocks. It's how he was raised. A man had to be in charge of himself, had to be strong. To admit vulnerability was seen as a weakness. His perceptions about the likely reactions of people around him at that time were – sadly – correct. "I always thought it was a matter of great shame for the family." He is also courageous, a fighter. So he struggled to cope by himself. He tried, and he tried, and he tried to "move on". That was how it was in the 1970s.

As the abuse went on, Steve's alarm system had been on red alert for over five years. "I was just terrified ... I was fearful of copping it from the kids. I think that's where I got my hypervigilance. I was watching *all the time*." He befriended a boy whom he thought was also being abused. The boy was called "Poofy P" and bullied mercilessly. "I would stick up for him, and other people who were being bullied." Steve was likeable and popular at school. But he knew that would be his fate too if anyone knew about Parker. This meant he had to conceal his inner turmoil and present a tough image. Given how macho the world was, he learned what he calls "front".

Steve reminded me of a phrase I had once used: "impression management". "I loved that phrase ... you become a master of it. You'd just have to present this image – of show no weakness. I went to a school where weakness was punished. If you showed any sign of weakness, they gotcha!"

Casual drug use was widespread among Newcastle youth in the 1970s, especially alcohol, marijuana and acid. One of the things that scared Steve, when a joint was passed around, was that he might lose control and reveal something of his terrible secret. At a deeper level, he had experienced the complete loss of control with Parker, so the novelty of losing control by taking drugs held zero appeal.

Steve struggled to trust anyone. It wasn't just about not showing any weakness. He also felt he had to manage every situation he got into, lest it turn into a volcano that would blow up him, his family and his life. The road ahead was strewn with potential volcanoes, ready to erupt if he let his guard down even for a millisecond. "You are forward planning all the time," he told me. He lived his young life, every moment of every day, every week, every year, in fear of what might happen, trying to avoid exposing his secret. That affected his performance at school. As his grades plummeted, where once he felt pride, now he felt shame.

The silence that descended over the Smith household about Parker didn't help. Did his dad know? What if his dad decided to confront the church? What if his mother told people? What would happen to her?

What if, what if, what if ...

Steve was finding school very difficult. He couldn't concentrate on anything. However, he battled on. He was involved as a voluntary leader in YMCA youth camps – not Church of England boys' camps – held around Lake Macquarie. Mowing was one of his duties. One Sunday in March 1976, at about 10.30 in the morning, Steve was mowing when he stopped to clear a big cobweb from the path in front of the mower. He didn't realise, but the mower had no guard fitted. As he bent down, a spider suddenly jumped at him, and he leapt backwards. The toes on his right foot caught in the blade of the mower. The blade struck his foot twice, causing extensive damage.

Max Lean, the camp director, found Steve lying on the ground in agony, bleeding profusely. At Newcastle Hospital, Steve was rushed into surgery, and three bones were removed. He had another operation the next morning to stop the bleeding. Steve lost all upward movement in his first two toes – he had severed the tendons in his foot. He required a third operation to fuse the stub of tendon on his big toe, so that he didn't trip over all the time. The camp director's written report grimly predicted that "Steve will walk with a limp for the rest of his life."[2] Even worse, he contracted chronic osteomyelitis, a dangerous bone infection. This would flare up from time to time and almost cost him his life at one point.

For Steve, something else happened that was as bad as the accident. Parker turned up at the hospital to visit him as if nothing had occurred, as if his presence was welcome. Utterly vulnerable, shocked after the accident, in pain and immobile, Steve remembers being terrified by Parker's presence.

Steve was now at the pointy end of school, where study became a serious matter of setting oneself up for opportunities for the rest of your life. He was already struggling with increasingly intrusive memories and flashbacks of Parker's abuse, and the accident only made it worse. He was preoccupied all the time and had trouble concentrating. Although he went back to school after the accident, he was on crutches. His headmaster told him he shouldn't be there with all those stairs and sent him home. Steve missed most of the year but still managed to pass year 10. He did reasonably in English, history and commerce and had a spelling score of 90 out of 100. It is striking, despite his inner struggle, how often teachers reported him being co-operative, consistent, reliable and friendly. But it is clear from Steve's reports that there was a disparity between his ability and his results. Steve was not fulfilling the high potential he had shown before Parker's abuse.

In 1977 he tried to start school again, to do year 11 and finish his Higher School Certificate, when there came another terrible blow.

*

Steve and his brothers lived with constant rowing between their parents. One day in 1977, after one of these arguments, his mother "just got in her car and went". Steve chased her car up the street, pleading with her to stop. She kept driving. And then she didn't come home. For days.

That was completely out of character. No one else in the family pursued her or seemed worried. Steve's dad thought she had left him and was angry – he refused to try to find her. "Perhaps he was relieved that the unhappy marriage was over."

Steve was beside himself with worry. The hospital said she hadn't turned up to work. That was extremely unusual. Steve was too young to drive, so on foot he searched for days and nights in the pouring rain. He hitchhiked all over Newcastle. He looked for her at the house of her father, Pop McGregor. Pop was in hospital with prostate cancer. Steve couldn't see her car there, so kept on looking. After she'd been missing a few days, Steve went to the police station at Wallsend and tried to file a missing person's report. He was told by Sergeant Shanahan that at sixteen he was too young to file such a report. It had to be his father. His father refused. He just thought his wife had left him.

Pop hadn't been told that Margery was missing while he was in hospital, because they didn't want to worry him. But when he came home, he found Margery there. Her car was hidden behind the house, which was why Steve hadn't seen it. Pop rang the family and told them, "She's here and she's been beat up. She's black and blue."

But she hadn't been beaten up. She was black and blue because she had been dead for four days.

Steve and his brothers drove straight around to Pop's, where there were police cars. Steve ran up the steps to the front door and managed to get to the bedroom door, where he caught a glimpse of his mother. At that point, Steve believed she was still alive. But he was "grabbed by a big copper", who "shuffled me back out and said, 'You can't go in there, she's dead.' That was the gentle way of telling us."

To the grief-stricken boy, the police then said, "She's drunk weedkiller." They had found an empty weed-killer bottle on the kitchen table and assumed she had committed suicide. Steve later thought, "Why would a trained nurse with all the access in the world to lethal drugs drink weedkiller?"

But in that moment, Steve believed the police. The thought that Margery had committed suicide pierced his soul, not only with grief for the loss of his beloved mother, but also with guilt and terror that he was to blame. That his disclosure had cracked her world into little pieces and destroyed it, destroyed her. That she could no longer believe in anything and had taken her own life. He felt utterly responsible for her death. "It just broke my heart, I just stood there and crumbled. I just ... was convinced she killed herself because of what I told her."

Another shock came at his mother's funeral, on 20 July 1977. The church arranged that Father Parker should deliver the eulogy.[3] It was full of breathtaking hypocrisy and sentimental flourishes. Steve had to listen to Parker "rejoicing" in the life of Margery, in order to give "strength, comfort and our love" to her family.

"When the history of this Parish comes to be written," Parker said, "... the name of the Smith family will loom large ... But most of all will be written about this complex and wonderful lady in whose honour we have gathered in the place she loved."

Describing "the lady" – whose heart he had broken by abusing her son – Parker spoke of her "force of personality" and many "amazing acts of kindness, so often unexpected but so infinitely precious". How, for "Marge", the church organist, music was at the heart of her religious experience. She was a "doer of the word and not just a hearer" who had touched people's lives in a way that was "incredible". She brought food for unexpected guests, she hired taxis to help parishioners without transport get to church, and as a nurse "she wiped away our tears, comforted us in our mourning ... and took away our pain." He noted that no less than four former Edgeworth priests had come to pay their respects to Margery, because of "the love the Smith family has given us".

At one point in the eulogy, Parker expressed regret about not having said sorry to her: "How are we to live with that sense of dread, of guilt, because we have not been able to say the things we ought to have said to Marge and did not say them ... So often we leave it too late to say 'I love you, I'm sorry, thank you, can you help someone else, help me.' These five things are the foundation upon which all human relationships are built."

Steve had to listen, knowing the truth about Parker and what he had done to him and his mother. As a pallbearer, he had to walk behind his abuser, holding the coffin containing his mother's body. "The coffin was incredibly heavy. I was so upset about Parker being at the funeral that I was terrified about dropping Mum's coffin." When Parker and Rushton turned up at the house for the wake, Steve fled.

After Margery died, Steve decided to disclose the abuse to one of the policemen who had attended his mother's death. In 1977, Steve walked into Wallsend police station and told Sergeant Shanahan that he wanted to talk about a priest who had sexually assaulted him. "I thought that I'd get help from him because he had been pretty good when Mum died. I'd picked him out, but just nothing." Shanahan told him to go "talk to a priest". "Mate, why would I want to talk to one of them?" Another rebuff.

The inquest into Margery's death was finally held two years later, in mid-1979. The coroner was "very gentle". His conclusion was that Margery had had a heart attack. She had been ill with kidney disease for a long time. There was no foul play. And she had not committed suicide. But even with the coronial judgement, by now Steve's conviction that he had caused her to kill herself was so entrenched that he couldn't shake the idea that the coroner might be wrong, or that he *was* to blame … for her heart attack. He was in a spiral of self-blame.

I asked Steve if he thought that the Christian teachings about good and evil – the belief that God was always peering into your soul, judging you, deciding whether you would go to heaven or to everlasting damnation – affected his response.

He answered without hesitation. "Yeah. Because I still hadn't processed whether or not *I'd* done anything wrong. You've got all this stuff just piled on top of what Parker was doing to me. And by the time I was eighteen, I was thinking I should have stopped him, I should have stopped him—"

I interjected, protesting: "Steve, you were a little boy, you were only ten when it started."

Steve went on: "So then it's my fault and then I told Mum, and she dies and that's my fault, she didn't kill herself, but she had a heart attack, is that my fault? That it affected her so badly – so that's caused that. You are sitting there questioning your whole being."

Such thoughts raced around his mind, over and over. *What have I done?*

*

"I'd got to the point where I wasn't even surviving. You just exist. You just stumble from one thing to another."

Margery's death ended any further thoughts Steve had of continuing his schooling. He did not complete year eleven or the Higher School Certificate. After he left school, he kept working at the YMCA youth camps and took over much of his mother's role around the house, cooking, washing and cleaning. "Dad couldn't make a sandwich." Robert didn't drive, so once Steve got a licence, he drove his father wherever he wanted to go. Robert had also met, and eventually married, Jean, Steve's stepmother. Jean moved into Steve's childhood home.

Steve took his father's remarriage hard. He felt "chucked aside" and acknowledges that he was difficult. "I gave Jean a hard time. I would go out of my way to make her life unpleasant. I don't want to step back from that."

After one altercation, Steve was thrown out of home. He had no car, so Jean and Robert drove him to the suburb of Toronto, on Lake Macquarie, where Steve had friends and worked at the YMCA camps. "I was just cast out." They stopped the car by the side of the road, popped the boot so Steve could retrieve his bag and left him there. It was pouring rain. Steve was now homeless. Typically, Steve defends his father: "I don't want to pick on him." They had a good relationship later in Robert's life and Steve always thought his dad "was a good man". But at the time, standing on the side of the road with nowhere to go, Steve felt "just despair". He thought, "What do I do now?" "I had to stay in a caravan my brother Graeme had. He let me stay for a while. It was unsuitable but better than being out in the rain."

From that point, "everything went downhill from drinking too much". Soon there was another blow. Despite his inner torment, from his mid-teenage years Steve had a long-time girlfriend, Kate, whom he admired and respected. Kate was also involved in the YMCA camps. Kate's mum, who'd been a close childhood friend of Margery, mothered him. Their home was a safe haven and Steve felt like he had a family there, as well as a girlfriend.

By this time, Steve was running the youth centre and it was going well. He was popular and the camp and school programs were thriving. He was very protective of children, very strict about the behaviour of adults around them – something others noticed. He seemed to have found a niche and, despite his own struggles, was swept along by Kate's positive energy and upward trajectory in life.

But it was all precarious. As so often happens with child sexual abuse victims, the abuse severed a whole series of possibilities that would otherwise have come from staying on at school and undertaking training or further study. Steve blamed himself for leaving school early. He felt he hadn't lived up to his potential and that "I'd let my family down. I felt, 'I've failed here.'" He suffered mood swings that seemed to flash out of nowhere and depression, particularly after drinking. He was often overcome with unquenchable sadness, weeping. He couldn't fully disclose the abuse to Kate. "It wasn't something you could discuss with your girlfriend ... I did talk to her about what had happened, but in no great detail."

After high school, Kate began studying nursing and was "setting the world on fire". Steve felt he was just "wallowing". She was facing forward, full of optimism; Steve was always looking back. When the relationship ended, it was entirely amicable, but his final remaining mooring was gone. He lost not only their closeness but also the important safety net he had felt in her family, and in particular with her mum. "That's not anybody's fault but my own. I own that. The relationship failure was entirely on me." ("I own that. That was entirely on me" was Steve's most common phrase in describing many things that went wrong.)

After being thrown out of home and losing the steady relationship with Kate, things degenerated. Life "revolved around the pub. Heavy drinking was just a normal thing ... And I drifted in and out of that." Although he drank to obliterate the past, the opposite occurred. At first, alcohol had a pleasantly numbing effect. But then all of a sudden, like "a flood", memories of the rapes would wash over him, as if they were happening right then and there. "It wouldn't come as a niggle ... All of a sudden, this wave would come over me." It was like an ambush. He would "fall apart really quickly".

He'd be in what should have been an enjoyable social situation, but instead of being happy he'd get anxious and teary. It was confusing and frightening, and it was getting worse. He couldn't sleep. He had recurrent nightmares. He couldn't walk or drive past a church. Seeing a priest in the street would trigger a panic attack. He began to feel estranged from almost everyone, even from his family.

Steve didn't understand why he wasn't coping. At first, he compartmentalised the sexual abuse and saw individual decisions that he made, such as leaving school, as failures caused by his own mistakes. "I blew that." It took a long time for him to realise that everything was linked, and that it was Parker who had messed him up. But by the time he had put two and two together, the intrusive memories and flashbacks were running out of control. He could hardly think about anything else. When Steve could no longer control his PTSD symptoms, he finally came to a devastating understanding of the impact of Parker's abuse. This insight did not erase the ongoing pain. Engulfed in sadness, Steve realised he could not get back the life he could have had.

As Steve spiralled down, Parker "was rolling up" the clerical ladder; "there'd been no repercussions for him". On 28 May 1980, there was a puff-piece about "Father George" in the *Lake Macquarie Post*, praising his work with jobless youth and congratulating him on his important new post in an Anglican parish at North Lake Macquarie. Father George, the article gushed, "had become well known to young people" at the Jobless at Gateshead centre, "as a committee chairman who was prepared to participate in activities as well as organise them". Parker told the newspaper that he would miss the centre, because of "the opportunity it had offered to work with young people … close up".

Meanwhile Steve's belief that the church was all-powerful was confirmed by something his older brother Ian now told him. A few months after Steve had disclosed the abuse, Ian had taken their mother to see Bishop Shevill to make a complaint. She came out sobbing, completely hysterical. Steve realised that his mother had been savagely blown off and humiliated by the bishop when she tried to get justice for her son. "They knew, but nothing had happened." This deepened his feelings of powerlessness, anger and despair.

Steve turned twenty in 1981. "By this stage, I thought, 'This is never going to get any better.'" Steve was reconciled to not making it to twenty-one. He lived with a death wish. "I was seriously suicidal because I wanted to end my suffering. I drove stupid, I drank stupid, like reckless behaviour, just, like, what does it matter? I was crashing cars, I cut my wrists a few times. I made that conscious decision that I just don't want to be alive anymore. I just don't want to be here."

CHAPTER FIVE

BREAKDOWN

ONE NIGHT IN the early hours of the morning in 1981, Steve was walking along a road, bleeding heavily. He had cut himself up and didn't care whether he lived or died. A man pulled up in a panel van. He was a government contractor who picked up dead bodies in the middle of the night. "I was bleeding like a stuck pig. He worked out pretty quickly what was going on, so he gave me a towel to wrap up my arms."

The man took Steve to Newcastle Hospital, stopping to pick up a body on the way. "He actually started lecturing me," Steve recalled. "He said, 'I see lots of dead people, mate. I've picked one up now. If you don't wake up, you'll end up dead in the back of my van. Wake up to yourself, you are only a young bloke, you've got it all in front of you.' He walked me into the casualty ward at the old Newcastle Hospital."

A doctor or nurse sewed Steve up without anaesthetic, as if to teach him a lesson. He was not sent for counselling or referred to a psychiatrist. He wandered out of the hospital at three or four in the morning, "feeling like shit", into "dark streets of rain".

Steve was by now both overdosing and cutting himself regularly. His family did nothing. "I was cast out and no one did anything ... no one was interested, and I found that very confusing and confronting and I couldn't understand that." Finally, friends of his said, "We can't help you, but you need help." They took him to the James Fletcher Psychiatric Hospital (called Watt Street at the time). "I just remember walking in and saying, 'I need help.' A huge thing at that time for anyone ... I was there for six weeks."

The psychiatrists decided that Steve was drinking way too much and that this was the main issue. They didn't probe deeply into the causes of his drinking. At the time, "encounter groups" were popular in psychiatry, and there were group therapy sessions. The head counsellor was a tough, no-nonsense bloke. Steve got on well with him. He took Steve under his wing, and they had long talks. Steve enjoyed the assertiveness-training sessions, where he learned that he could speak up without blowing up. For the first time in a long time, he ate properly and was becoming healthier. The nurses and psychiatrists cared, and Steve had not felt that anyone cared in a long time. "It saved my life. There is no question of that."

He also met his present wife, Rachael, at the hospital. She was visiting her mum, who was suffering from alcoholism. Steve was immediately smitten. Rachael's mum invited him to stay at her place when he was discharged. However, her stepfather, Tom, didn't like the developing relationship, perhaps because Rachael's mother was still fragile, or perhaps because Steve had been in a psychiatric hospital. Tom kicked Steve out by driving him to a caravan park in Salamander Bay, north of Newcastle. Steve told me, with his usual bending-over-backwards fairness, that "Tom was a good guy; he was just looking out for Rach."

But Steve felt abandoned again. He ended up in the pub, full of grog, and then went back to the caravan and swallowed all the Valium the psychiatrist had given him. One of his drinking buddies realised Steve was missing and came looking for him at the caravan park. He found Steve unconscious. Steve went back into hospital.

Despite this setback, Steve began to inch forward in life. The hospital became his safety net. He enjoyed going to the outpatient clinic fairly regularly. He became friends with some of the nurses, and they'd come outside and have a smoke and a chat with him. He went back to work at the YMCA. He had a new job and a flat with cheap rent in a beautiful spot near Newcastle beach, looking over the ocean baths and the sea.

Steve's life was back on track, but it took only a little to derail it. He was still extremely fragile. His brother Graeme moved into "the little nest I'd built", and then moved in another friend of his as well. Now, the flat no longer worked for Steve. It was 1982, and things were falling apart again. He descended into a deep despair. "I can remember sitting down at a little shelter seat, down in the ocean baths in Newcastle ... I found a Coke-can lid, an old ring-pull lid, and I remember carving into the seat, 'Steven, you're a fuckwit.'"

Steve hitched to Queensland, thinking he'd leave all his troubles behind. *If I just lived somewhere else* was a frequent refrain in his life at this time. He got a job up north, driving a truck. After a couple of months, he came back and went to work at the YMCA again. There he met Lisa, whom he hired as a ballet teacher for the youth group. They gradually became close and eventually married in 1984.

Before they married, there was another moment when Steve tried to tell the church what had happened with Parker. He had left the YMCA and started working with Father Arthur Bridge, who was opening an Anglican youth centre in Edgeworth. Steve thinks that agreeing to work with Bridge was an act of self-sabotage, given the Edgeworth church was where a lot of the abuse had happened. "It was like a series of explosions going off in your brain. Blowing up."

Steve visited Bridge to tell him the news that they had won a government grant, worth many thousands of dollars, to set up the youth centre. Bridge invited Steve inside to celebrate, poured two little whiskies and then put his hand on Steve's knee. That was the trigger; Steve refused to continue working for him.

Steve went to Assistant Bishop Appleby to express his concern about how effectively Bridge was administering the grant money. Appleby's residence was a smart modern house, and Appleby met Steve in a beautiful book-lined study with large windows and sunlight streaming in. Appleby was very welcoming and the model of affability. He seemed receptive and caring. At the end of their conversation about Steve's concerns about Father Bridge, Appleby said words to the effect of "I'll deal with this." Steve replied sceptically that he knew "what you blokes do", and that he knew how the church "sorted things out". Appleby asked him what he meant.

Steve hadn't planned it, but now he told Appleby that Parker had abused him as a child and that it was widely accepted among the altar boys that Peter Rushton was also a child molester. Steve also named Father James Brown.

Appleby seemed genuinely concerned. "How terrible," was the tenor of his response, and he seemed resolved to do something about it: "Leave it with me." Steve was heartened and immensely relieved. He trusted Appleby. It was an extraordinary load off his shoulders. At last, someone was going to do something.

Steve waited for the "something" to happen. And waited. However, he heard not a word from Appleby. Steve imagined that his accusation would at least quietly stall Parker's career. But some time afterwards, he realised that Parker had been promoted to archdeacon of the South Lakes district. His career was flourishing.[1] "It was only a month ago I was talking to this bloke – Appleby – and all of a sudden Parker gets a promotion. The anger then was red-hot."

Meanwhile, Steve's family had taken another hit. Not long after the meeting with Appleby, Steve's father, Robert, who had returned to involvement in the Anglican Church alongside his second wife, Jean, was summarily dismissed from all church roles. Robert wrote an eloquent letter to the then bishop, Alfred Holland, quoting from Shakespeare's *Othello*:

> Who steals my purse steals trash; 'tis something, nothing
> … But he that filches from me my good name
> Robs me of that which not enriches him,
> And makes me poor indeed.[2]

Steve was left with the distinct impression that this was how the Anglican Church of Newcastle would deal with anyone disclosing child sexual abuse. Do nothing about the priest, destroy the victim's credibility, destroy the credibility of their family. His father had been, he thought, collateral damage.[3]

Steve married his first wife, Lisa, shortly after this, and tried to get on with his life. Soon they had children. Taking on the church was not something he wanted his young wife or children to have to cope with.

Steve was working for a printing supply company, ACP, and then moved to Pasminco, the sulphide works. He stayed at Pasminco for ten years and worked hard to provide for his growing family. Steve always had a good work ethic. It wasn't long, however, before the marriage was under pressure from the dark shadows cast by his past. He was often withdrawn. He had flashbacks which billowed out of nowhere without warning. He was still struggling with depression, anxiety and panic attacks. Alcohol numbed the pain, so he drank too much and had mood swings. He was overprotective, he says, with his children, and definitely didn't want them being altar boys or girls (girls could now be servers). His wife was a Catholic, and this became an issue.

Buried unresolved trauma is like an internal abscess that has never been lanced. It can threaten the whole person with systemic sepsis. Steve's trauma sat in his psyche, cordoned off but unresolved, leaking into everything. He tried to get through each day, providing for his family while compartmentalising his history as best he could. But then came an event which made it no longer possible to suppress it.

In 1995, Vince Ryan, a Newcastle Catholic priest, was charged with child sexual abuse. In May the following year there was a high-profile trial with lots of media coverage. Steve was profoundly affected by survivors coming forward, telling their stories and, for the first time, being believed. It was "a huge moment" for him. Ryan was convicted and went to prison. It caused a revolution in Steve's consciousness. He sensed that something in the culture was changing. Although he understood how difficult historic cases of child sexual abuse were to prosecute, the Ryan case gave Steve confidence that he was not alone. There were others like him who had suffered too. They'd taken on their abusers, fought back through the courts and won. This was an absolute revelation to Steve.

But the Ryan case also took Steve right back to the past. The abuse by Parker was now again uppermost in his mind, dominating everything. If a Catholic priest didn't get away with raping kids, why should an Anglican priest like George Parker?

"I wasn't coping. Lisa wasn't coping with me, and that's understandable. I would have been hard to live with." They had had a conversation about the abuse, but Lisa did not know how to deal with it. She was a practising Catholic and their children attended a Catholic school. Steve did a lot of handyman work for the school and was president of the Parents and Friends Association. He got on well with the local parish priest, Father Bob Searle.

When Lisa came home from mass one Sunday, Steve was stirred up over the Ryan case, which was in the news. Lisa suggested he talk to Father Bob. Father Bob was kind and receptive and listened attentively. Then he handed Steve an Anglican brochure with a phone number for a "confidential helpline".

Steve thought the church might help with understanding, pastoral care, counselling … *something*. He still had what he calls a misguided hope – that, compared to the police, "through the church there would be a better understanding, or a more pastoral approach".

On 24 April 1996, just before 7 p.m., feeling desperate and emotional, Steve rang the Anglican helpline. His call was taken by the dean of the cathedral, Graeme Lawrence. Steve knew nothing about Lawrence, but Lawrence was a hugely powerful player in the Anglican Church. One bishop described him as the most influential Newcastle church man in a generation. He was a great networker and, along with the most powerful members of the Newcastle elite, frequented the exclusive Newcastle Club – a male-only, private gentlemen's club next door to the cathedral and to Lawrence's residence, known as the Deanery. Steve knew none of that. He did not know that "priests in trouble" for sexual misconduct frequently turned to Lawrence, or that there had been several complaints about Lawrence sexually abusing boys in the 1990s – or that between 1986 and 1995, Father George Parker, as assistant dean of the cathedral, had worked closely with Lawrence.

Steve had been taught since he was a little boy that God and the church were there to care for you, and that the church was where you were meant to turn if you needed help. He kept on hoping.

The Christian philosopher Simone Weil wrote that:

> At the bottom of the heart of every human being, from earliest infancy until the tomb, there is something that goes on indomitably expecting, in the teeth of all experience of crimes committed, suffered and witnessed, that good and not evil will be done to him. It is this above all that is sacred in every human being.

That was true of Steve. It wasn't just counselling or sympathy he wanted. The idea of justice had taken deep root in him in childhood. He wanted recognition of the wrong done to him. Despite everything that had happened, Steve said, he "gave the church another chance".

When Lawrence picked up the phone, the dean spoke with a cold formality, in a posh voice. Steve was distraught and found Lawrence's haughty manner off-putting. There was something condescending, even as the dean went through the motions of professing willingness to help. His formal expression of concern was belied by his chilly, dismissive tone. He was extremely inquisitive: "Who?" "When?" "What happened?" "How old were you?" Lawrence said the church would hold a thorough investigation, and that these matters would be dealt with appropriately. Steve was terribly upset throughout the conversation, weeping, while Lawrence remained coolly composed. Steve did not feel Lawrence was at all empathetic. It ended with Lawrence promising to organise a meeting with the bishop of Newcastle, Roger Herft.

Lawrence wrote a file note for Bishop Herft on 29 April. It is a formal, emotionally distanced note, describing Lawrence's conversation with a:

> man who claimed he wished to talk about an incident of sexual abuse which happened to him and another boy. He said, "I am not looking for legal redress, but I do need help." I suggested he might come to see me. Up to this point he had not given a name. He said he was dubious about coming to see me as he felt like it might be "like an inquisition". I assured him that this was not the case. He agreed to come and see me on Saturday, 27 April [1996] ... He did not come to the arranged interview.[4]

Steve did not go to the meeting for a very simple reason. He reported back to Father Bob Searle and told him that he had spoken to someone after ringing the Anglican helpline.

"Who did you speak to?"

"Graeme Lawrence."

Bob was alarmed. "Don't go near him," he said adamantly. "He's one of the bad guys."

Steve was horrified. "You're kidding!"

"Nup," Bob said. "Stay away from Graeme Lawrence." Bob was happy to talk to Steve again, but he was emphatic about staying away from Lawrence. He didn't explain in any detail why.

Steve's marriage was now breaking down. It was that downward spiral again. "It was just a really, really unhappy time." Steve left Pasminco and began working as manager of the Newcastle region of the YMCA, running the centres as well as the camps. Steve and Lisa were struggling financially, so they moved with the kids to Crangan Bay, on Lake Macquarie, living in a cabin while renting out their house to save money. Steve ran the youth camps there. But it seemed inevitable by this stage that he and Lisa would separate. They returned to the family home in 1998, but only lasted together another two months. Steve left the family home and rented a place nearby. Then Lisa moved to Port Macquarie, four hours to the north of Newcastle, with her new partner. Steve moved back into the family home to look after the children, as he had custody via a consent order.

On Christmas Day 1998, Steve drove the kids on the long trip to Port Macquarie to see their mother. When it was time for them to return, he found Lisa had withdrawn the consent order, as she wanted the children to stay with her. Steve was upset, but he decided the best way out of the impasse was if he compromised and went to live and work at Port Macquarie. He got a job in a Catholic school as a teacher's aide. "However, I was really struggling. I was just falling apart." Steve had once again reached breaking point. He tried the church one more time. He was determined to speak to Bishop Herft, "the man at the top".

Unfortunately, when he phoned, he again encountered Lawrence. Lawrence's manner was just as cold. He reproached Steve for not keeping the previous meeting. Steve grew more and more distraught during the conversation. Lawrence later described him as "very emotional" in another file note to Bishop Herft. According to Steve, "We had a very similar conversation to the last time ... I said to him, 'You guys have done nothing, you've pushed it under the carpet.'"[5] Lawrence denied it.

Steve pointed out that nothing had happened to Parker as a result of Steve's previous disclosures. He insisted that he only wanted to have a meeting with Bishop Herft, and that he would only talk to the bishop. Lawrence told him that wasn't how it worked, and that a meeting with the bishop without Lawrence wouldn't happen.

Steve told Lawrence that he was going to the police. Lawrence stiffened. He informed Steve icily that this was his right. Lawrence wrote a letter to Steve afterwards, outlining his options, and assured him there would be no cover-up.[6] The deputy chancellor of the Newcastle Anglicans, Paul Rosser QC, carefully examined the draft before Lawrence sent it.

Child sexual abuse was discussed increasingly in the media. As Steve was reminded constantly, it was a crime. He decided to take the matter into his own hands. In February 2000, "I found myself on the forecourt at Port Macquarie police station. I remember pacing back and forwards. 'Will I? Won't I? Will I?' Then I thought, 'Stuff it, I've gotta tell someone about this.' I walked in to make a complaint."

At the front desk, he told the policewoman that he wanted to report a sexual assault. She asked him, "Who?" He answered, "Me." She stared at him. It was unusual for a man to report sexual assault. Steve was embarrassed, to say the least. In the waiting room he saw people he knew. He hadn't anticipated his first serious disclosure to police about Parker would be heard in public. "So, I stood there talking to her, but eventually I said, 'Can we at least go into an office somewhere?'"

Steve was ushered into another room and a detective came in. The world-weary policeman seemed reluctant to interview him. He was "dismissive and uninterested in the extreme. It was like I was wasting his time." The policeman asked Steve who had abused him. Steve told him the name of the priest: "George Parker." The copper asked him sceptically, "Look, do you have anything? Any evidence? What sort of car was he driving?" Steve had the type of car and the number plate etched in acid in his memory. He rattled it off: a white Galant station wagon; the number plate was GKD 999.

"The detective looked at me like I was an idiot." However, he went off and checked the name and number plate.

"Jeez, you're right. It's his car." Then he took Steve's statement.

The detective's initially dismissive manner had profound and lasting consequences. Steve felt it impossible to tell the whole humiliating story to such a person. *He is not going to believe me*, Steve thought. Hundreds of rapes? Forced oral sex? Anal rape? All of it? Over years and years?

No way.

Steve now made a fateful snap decision. He decided to tell the detective only about the last incident: the sexual assault at the Gateshead rectory.

PART TWO
TEAM CHURCH

CHAPTER SIX

TEAM CHURCH

PROTECTING EVERY DARK network of paedophiles is a "grey network" of protectors. After Steve made his complaint to police about Parker in February 2000, the Newcastle church machine went into overdrive. Steve was dealing with an institution with a track record of protecting paedophile priests and the reputation of the church. Moving a priest on to another diocese without disciplining him or reporting him to the police was so common it had entered Anglican folklore. It was known as "throwing a dead cat over the fence". There is every likelihood that Parker was a dead cat hurled over the Victorian border to the diocese of Ballarat. Reverend Roger Dyer met Parker at a clergy conference in about 1996 in Victoria, where Parker was bitterly complaining about being "forcibly removed" by Assistant Bishop Richard Appleby from Newcastle.[1] Parker appears to have left Newcastle hurriedly and without a send-off.[2]

At Port Macquarie police station, Detective Lysaght was scratching his head over what to do with Steve's complaint. It was notoriously difficult to get a conviction for historical child sex offences. Moreover, this complaint was against a *priest*. To an outsider, the church was a mysterious institution. How did he find out where Parker was now? When had Parker been the rector at Gateshead? Did the church have any records? Whom should he ask?

Sensing the detective's lack of interest, Steve had not reported all the sexual assaults going back to when he was ten: only the events at the Gateshead rectory. He could not remember the exact date of this abuse, just that it had occurred in 1974 or 1975, shortly after Parker moved to Gateshead. He remembered the intense relief and jubilation he'd felt on learning that

Parker was leaving Edgeworth – only to have his hopes dashed when his mother agreed to her boys staying over at the rectory.

It was crucial for police to find out exactly when Parker's move to Gateshead had occurred, and where he was now. On 7 February 2000, Detective Lysaght rang the Newcastle Anglican registrar's office. The receptionist, Ms Brown, on discovering he was investigating a sexual assault, told him to contact Lyn Douglas, the chair of the Diocesan Committee for Allegations of Sexual Misconduct (CASM).[3] Brown told the registrar, Peter Mitchell, who was George Parker's close friend. Mitchell, on learning of the inquiry, did not contact the police to tell them Parker's whereabouts now, despite knowing full well where his friend was, nor did he inform them when Parker was at Gateshead. The detective's first inquiry, then, drew a blank.

Two days later, Lysaght rang the office of Dean Graeme Lawrence, asking to speak to him about "a sexual abuse case".[4] As Lawrence was out of the office, his secretary, Teresa Kerr, took the call. At first, she confused Parker with someone else and told him Parker was dead. Lysaght said, "Oh, in that case it solves everything,"[5] revealing the reluctance with which some police approached historical cases of child sexual abuse in that era. Then, Kerr realised she had made a mistake: Parker was still alive, she told Lysaght, but no longer in the diocese. She suggested he contact CASM or the registrar's office. But he had already tried the registrar and got nowhere.

When Lawrence returned, Kerr told him about the phone call and gave him the name of Lysaght's station. Lawrence later claimed that he thought the call was a "hoax", so did not follow it up. Given Steve had told him in 1999 that he was likely to go to the police, this seems implausible.[6]

Another police officer, Mick Lang, now took over the case, but did not know what to look for.[7] In the absence of clear information from records readily available from the diocese, he too was puzzled and frustrated, trying to find out when Parker was at Gateshead, and whether the charges should be for 1974 or 1975. No wonder he was confused. Only a church person would have known what records to look for and where to find them. As he later explained to a DPP solicitor:

> the OIC [Officer in Charge] … rang the Diocese for exact records – told they didn't have any. Left it at that. OIC had said he was told GP [George Parker] was likely or could have been at G [Gateshead] in '74. Framed charge to cover 74.

"Didn't have any" was an outright lie. Both Mitchell and Lawrence had exact records, and they knew where to find them. The past and present parishes of all licensed priests are recorded in diocesan yearbooks, which meticulously cover the whole of Australia. These were held in the registrar's office. The detective wasn't told about these yearbooks. Nor was he told about a second record that would have provided the information he was looking for: the parish register of services. All priests fill this out on a weekly basis. The register records all services held in each parish, including the time of every service, including those specially held for the altar boys. Yet when the detective asked, no one in the Anglican Church told him of the existence of these records. In the absence of this readily available information, he was preparing to frame the charges for 1974 – the wrong year.

On 17 February 2000, Parker's solicitor, Keith Allen, one of the church lawyers, wrote to Mitchell, asking for a list of Parker's past licences. Mitchell wrote back, outlining all the places in Newcastle where Parker had officiated between 1970 and 1980. The letter clearly states that Parker was licensed for Gateshead on 30 April 1975.[8] However, the detective was not informed. If the charges were framed for 1974 and they could prove Parker was not at Gateshead that year, it was game over. The charges would be dropped.

It is customary in sexual assault cases to include a wide range of possible dates in the charges, especially when, as so often happens, the complainant is very sure *what* occurred but unsure exactly *when* it occurred. Trauma research shows that sexual assault victims frequently remember emotionally salient – often horrifying – details of the crime, such as physical sensations, sounds, smells, what was said, the pain, or humiliating details, or their fear. Research also tells us that it takes survivors decades, on average, to come forward. Unsurprisingly, if it was a long time ago, the exact date or even the year may not be precisely recalled.

This is what happened, at first, with Steve. A quarter of a century after the abuse occurred, he wasn't sure if the Gateshead incident had been 1974 or 1975. By now police had contacted his younger brother, B, who confirmed the events of the night at the rectory and told them he had been sexually assaulted too. He joined the case against Parker. B thought it might have been 1974.

When the police did finally locate Parker, through his car registration, in Ararat in central Victoria, he refused to answer any questions. In August 2000, a week before Parker was charged, the officer in charge of the investigation again contacted the dean of Newcastle's office and requested the dates when Parker had been the priest at Gateshead parish. Although Parker's defence team had been in possession of these dates for six months, the dean's office told the police that it was "unable to assist".

A committal hearing was held in May 2001. By then, Parker's instructing solicitor, Keith Allen, had known since 17 February 2000 that Parker had been in Gateshead in 1975 rather than 1974. No one on Parker's defence team did anything to correct the error at the hearing, because it gave Parker a welcome alibi. In cross-examination, the lead lawyer, Paul Rosser, kept trying to pin Steve down to 1974. Steve refused, saying, "I wouldn't fall off my chair if it was a year either way."

The magistrate at the committal hearing deemed that there was sufficient evidence for the matter to be tried at the District Court. The trial was due to start on 13 August 2001. At this stage the indictment was still for 1974. However, Steve did an internet search and found the entry in the yearbook which confirmed the correct date that George Parker arrived in Gateshead. It was 1975. Steve immediately faxed a copy to the Office of the Director of Public Prosecutions on 8 May 2001. Keith Allen wrote to the ODPP on 31 July, finally informing them that "the accused was not appointed to the parish of Gateshead until 30 April 1975."

A few days before the trial started, the DPP solicitor rang the police at Port Macquarie and spoke to Mick Lang. Lang explained that the police had rung the diocese trying to get "copies of licences". They were fobbed off with another lie. When he asked if it could have been 1974, they said that "could be right". He was told of "records in the archives" but he "understood" these did not include licences or appointments.[9] In a scrawled file note, the frustrated solicitor wrote and then crossed out: "What was needed? I didn't know what?" On 13 August, the trial was briefly adjourned, and the detective again rang the diocese and asked for details of Parker's time at Gateshead. He noted that they "stated that [19]75 was probably correct", but that "because of the age of the matter he was not surprised to be told records didn't exist". The detective "took it no further believing [it] to be a useless exercise."

But the records did exist! The defence team had already been provided with them as early as 17 February 2000.[10]

In April 2001, Parker's solicitor had a subpoena served on the diocesan registry office, asking for "Any notes, letters, correspondence or copy in possession of the bishop or diocese relating to any complaint of sexual misconduct by any person against Steven Smith" and his brother. On 26 April 2001, the registrar, Peter Mitchell, sent copies of relevant documents. He produced a list of all the documents held by the diocese in relation to Steve's complaint. They included the confidential file notes written by Graeme Lawrence in 1996 and 1999 summarising his phone conversations with Steve, and details of Steve's time in psychiatric hospital, which he had confided to Lawrence.

However, Mitchell's list of documents did not include his letter to Allen of 17 February 2000, in which he had listed the parishes where Parker had held a licence, and which showed that Parker had been at Gateshead in 1975, not 1974. The letter undoubtedly should have been produced under the subpoena. This had the effect of concealing the dates when Parker had been at Gateshead and allowing the erroneous date to stand.

There was another seriously odd thing about this subpoena. It also asked Mitchell to produce the membership rolls of the diocesan synods (that is, the annual meeting of the Newcastle church) for the years 1973 through 1984. On the subpoena, someone – we don't know who – has changed 1973 to 1978, by simply altering the 3 with a few pen strokes to make it an 8. This meant the subpoena was for an entirely irrelevant time frame, which excluded the dates of the Gateshead abuse whether it took place in 1974 or 1975.[11]

In the lead-up to Parker's trial in August 2001, Team Church had also been busy obstructing the DPP prosecuting solicitor's access to another crucial piece of evidence: records of the special church services held for altar boys known as servers' guild meetings. On these occasions, a solemn "high mass" was performed, usually on a Saturday. The altar boys, fully robed, received holy communion, followed by a morning tea provided by the women of the parish. Steve and his brother both remembered that Parker had driven them to stay overnight at the rectory, but their recollections of the mass that weekend differed. Steve thought they had stayed at Gateshead on a Saturday night, in order to help out at a Sunday "welcome" service for Parker, who as yet had no altar boys. His brother, however, thought they might have gone to Gateshead on a Friday night, in order to attend a servers' guild service on the Saturday. Both remembered a morning tea after the service.

Steve's and his brother's accounts of the timeline meant that three facts were important to prove their case: when Parker had arrived as the new priest at Gateshead parish; whether there had been a server's guild meeting on the Saturday; or, if it had been a Sunday service, whether Parker would have had time for morning tea after the service, or would have immediately had to travel to other churches in the parish. Just before the trial started, the prosecuting solicitor wrote to Mitchell, asking where and when servers' guild meetings had been held in the years 1974 to 1976. Mitchell replied that there were no records concerning the guild services. He confirmed they were held on Saturday mornings but said: "We are not aware of the status of the guild. We cannot find any evidence that it was a part of the diocesan structure. We are therefore not aware of any records of when and where services or meetings may have been held."[12]

It is inconceivable that any church official, let alone the diocesan registrar, would not know of the servers' guild and where its records were kept. There were records of servers in the registry book held at every parish. The church's responses to the police and DPP had been deliberately obstructionist throughout.[13]

There were also serious issues of conflict of interest in how the church went about defending Parker. Keith Allen, Parker's solicitor, was a leading member of the laity who had senior governance roles on several diocesan committees, which meant he also had responsibility for vulnerable parishioners – including survivors such as Steve. Allen was also a close friend of Parker's. During the trial, Parker stayed with Allen at his home on the NSW Central Coast.

Meanwhile Paul Rosser, Parker's barrister, was also the deputy chancellor of the Anglican Church in Newcastle. This was another clear conflict of interest. When Rosser accepted the defence brief, he was working as a solicitor for Many Rivers Aboriginal Legal Service. That meant the "cab rank" rule, which requires a barrister to take cases on a first come, first serve basis, as long as they are free to do so and the matter is within their knowledge and expertise, did not apply.[14] Rather, Rosser had gone out of his way to defend the priest.

Peter Mitchell, another close friend of Parker, provided the priest with a glowing character reference. Allen drafted the reference and sent it to Mitchell on 3 July 2001. Mitchell was happy with the draft; it was close to identical to the one that went to court. It describes how Parker spent every Christmas with Mitchell's family. It says that Mitchell had left his children with Parker on many occasions, without any concerns, and that Parker was the godfather of Mitchell's daughter. It states that Mitchell had never heard Parker tell an untruth, and never heard rumours or innuendos about him. Mitchell even says, "I have the care, custody and control of the records of the Diocese of Newcastle, and I know of no complaint of a sexual nature ever made against George Parker."

This was an astonishing false claim given Mitchell had seen the records of Steve's conversations with Lawrence and had sent them to Parker's defence team.

What else was Team Church capable of? On 26 July 2001, just before the trial, the defence team sent another church lawyer, Robert Caddies, a very time-specific subpoena for records from a date range intended to capture Steve's confidential conversations with Lawrence, during which he had told Lawrence about being hospitalised at the Mater Psychiatric Hospital. Caddies delivered the records to the District Court of Newcastle the same day.[15] The church was getting ready to use Steve's psychiatric history – a direct result of Parker's sexual abuse – against him in court.

Bishop Herft had regular weekly meetings with Keith Allen and Peter Mitchell about Parker's upcoming trial and kept in contact with the priest.[16] The church also hired a public relations firm to liaise with the press, prepare the bishop's media statements and manage the church's image during the trial. Tracey McKelligott, its PR person, even prepared two different press releases, to be ready if Parker was found guilty or innocent. The church newspaper, the *Anglican Encounter*, was ready to cover the trial. The church paid for Parker's lawyers.

In contrast, no one in the Anglican Church reached out to Steve or his brother as survivors. They were on their own.

CHAPTER SEVEN

MISCARRIAGE OF JUSTICE

ON THE MORNING of the trial, Steve was extremely nervous. He rose at 3 a.m. to shave, "to look as tidy as possible". He wore black trousers, highly polished zip-up black boots, a long-sleeved, collared blue shirt and a dark blue tie. His hair, newly cut, was shorter than usual. The spring weather was clear and sunny after a cool, crisp night. When he arrived at the courthouse, B was also looking smart, wearing good jeans and a collared shirt but no tie.

The brothers were anxious about what was going to happen. The old courthouse was intimidating. Built in the Italianate style of the Victorian era, it was one of the grandest buildings in Newcastle. It was in the posh end of town, just a little way down Church Street from the elite quadrangle of Christ Church Cathedral, the Newcastle Club, Newcastle Grammar and the dean's residence. Steve and B walked through an ornately carved portico into a large, arched tower, the foyer for the central courtroom.

The courts felt like a foreign world for a working-class man. "It was nerve-racking," Steve recalls. "I had no idea what to expect ... The officer in charge [Mick Lang] had been out on the turps with some other cops and turned up a bit dusty [hungover]. We were in Court 4. The same court I had sat in for the 1979 inquest into Mum's death. We had no pretrial conference or heads up. It was horrible."[1]

The Anglican diocese did not send anyone to support Steve and his brother. In contrast, the church was out in force to support and defend Parker. It was the first time Steve had laid eyes on Keith Allen, who was a shortish, square-shaped man with heavy white John Howard eyebrows and wisps of grey hair folded over his balding pate. Archbishop Herft later described Allen as "a difficult person and a busybody" who had a finger in every church pie, serving on multiple committees including the synod, the diocesan council and the powerful board of trustees, which dealt with church finances. Allen frequently acted as the church's lawyer and boasted he had "big church connections"[2] and the ear of several bishops. He was the self-appointed Mr Fixit of the diocese and had already successfully defended priests accused of child sexual abuse.[3] Greg Thompson, a former Newcastle bishop, thought Allen, a suburban solicitor from the Central Coast, tried to gain "social significance" and status through his role as the legal protector of Anglican clergy.

Rosser, who led in court for the defence, was a gruff, imperious man with a deep, booming voice. An accomplished advocate and QC, he could be intimidating in court. In 1997 he had successfully defended a lay preacher, Jim Brown, who had preyed on boys from the St Alban's orphanage. Phil D'Ammond, an Indigenous boy from St Alban's, was sexually abused by Brown over many years. In court, Rosser went after D'Ammond so aggressively that D'Ammond fled the witness box in the middle of the cross-examination. "Rosser hammered me," Phil told me.[4] It was a humiliating and traumatic experience that triggered Phil's downward spiral into a twelve-year struggle with drug addiction, crime and depression. Brown was eventually imprisoned in 2012, sentenced to twenty years for multiple sex crimes against children.

The powerful dean of the cathedral, Graeme Lawrence, was also in attendance to support Parker.

When Steve looked at George Parker in the dock, the man who had abused him for so many years, he felt sick. It was the first time he had seen him since the shock of finding him presiding at his mother's funeral. Parker looked ominously confident and stared at Steve throughout the trial, "smirking from the dock", unnerving him.

The judge was Ralph Coolahan.[5] Steve saw a man with the bulbous nose and mottled cheeks of a heavy drinker, glowering down at him from the bench. After he died in 2010, the *Newcastle Herald* obituary observed that "Coolahan ... was at the heart of a social scene where long lunches often evolved into late nights and chamber parties were frequent ... after the parties, paper cuts bled red wine."

Although Coolahan came from a Catholic family – his brother, Monsignor Frank Coolahan, was a senior figure in the Newcastle Maitland Catholic diocese – the judge had a connection to the Anglican church, having acted for the diocese in a disciplinary hearing of a priest. Keith Allen was concerned enough about this to write to Rosser before the trial, noting the potential conflict of interest and asking, "Is it an issue that we should raise?"[6] There is no evidence that either Allen or Rosser did raise the issue, and Coolahan did not recuse himself.

On the first day of the trial, 13 August 2001, the DPP suddenly changed the date of the crime for indictment from 1974 to 1975. Exactly why it had not done so earlier, since it had found out courtesy of Steve's fax in May, is something of a mystery. Perhaps it was overlooked in the busy prosecutor's office.

In response, Rosser began aggressively, complaining that the "goal posts have changed this morning". "Time was of the essence," he argued – it was of prime importance to the defence case when the offences were alleged to have occurred. He criticised Steve and B for not making the new date clear at the committal hearing in early May, although they were not sure of the correct year until Steve's internet search later that month. In fact, at the committal Steve had refused to be pinned down to 1974.

Rosser asked Judge Coolahan to refuse the Crown leave to amend the indictment to 1975. He told the judge, "Now we are going to be treated, I suppose, to the spectacle of witnesses … swearing that all these things took place in 1975, when the evidence has at all stages been that it was 1974." Coolahan listened respectfully and sympathetically to Rosser, allowing him plenty of time to make his case against the date change.

Sarah Huggett, the young prosecutor, began to explain why the dates had changed: "Your Honour, the complainants will be called to give evidence—"

Judge Coolahan rudely interrupted her: "Well, I would have thought so." His tone had abruptly transformed from silky agreement with Rosser to one of aggressive impatience.

Huggett continued: "And no doubt my friend can cross-examine them—"

His Honour again interjected, cutting roughly across her: "No, no, no. You're not going to get away with turning up here this morning and filing a fresh indictment, contrary to the one to which the accused has already pleaded not guilty and over which a committal has run … I don't give a hoot about … cross-examination."

Huggett tried to explain how the incorrect date had come about, point-ing out Steve's uncertainty at the committal hearing. She said the key facts hadn't changed, the boys were quite specific that the offences occurred at Gateshead shortly after Parker arrived there, and all their allegations were exactly the same. It was only the year that was different.

Coolahan demanded to know how long the DPP had known about the new date. Huggett conceded that they had been informed by 31 July.

> Coolahan: So, from 31 July until today, was any contact made with the representatives of the accused to indicate that the indictment would be amended?"
> Huggett: No, Your Honour.
> Coolahan: Why not? Just take them by surprise, is that the attitude of the DPP?
> Huggett: Not at all, Your Honour.
> Coolahan: Well, it is starting to look like that.

Coolahan swung his attention back to the accused priest and his de-fence team. He asked sympathetically, "As I understand it, Mr Rosser, you're taken by surprise?"

> Rosser: Yes, we certainly are.

Coolahan then put words into Rosser's mouth: "And prejudiced by it?"

> Rosser: And prejudiced by it.
> Coolahan: What do you say to that, Ms Huggett?

With a judge like Coolahan, Parker hardly needed a defence team. All these criticisms of the prosecutor and the complainants were made in front of the jury.

"What about all the investigation that has gone … [into] providing … an alibi or ascertaining the whereabouts of the accused in 1974?" Coolahan asked indignantly. "That all goes by the wayside, and Mr Rosser could have perhaps an hour to work out what he was doing in 1975?"

Huggett pointed out that the prosecution had never been notified that the defence was using an alibi. In New South Wales, if defence lawyers are intending to use an alibi, they must notify the prosecution team with an alibi notice, at least fifty-six days in advance of the trial. Grudgingly, Coolahan withdrew his comment about the alibi. Huggett suggested an adjournment to investigate what the accused had been doing in 1975.

"The [prosecution] will be paying the costs," Coolahan shot back. Then he exploded:

> These allegations are twenty-six years old. The fact that a fresh indictment is presented today is nothing short of a complete disgrace on the part of the DPP and those who investigated the allegations. The fact that someone is brought to trial twenty-six years after an alleged offence is in itself a disgrace, but to present an indictment today for a trial that has been listed for some time which is different to the indictment presented when the accused pleaded to it, and contrary to what the witnesses said on oath in committal proceedings, which then laid the ground work for the accused's preparation of his case in the matter, makes it even more a disgrace. It makes the whole thing a real farce ... There's one person who seems to have been forgotten during the whole of your argument and that's the accused, who sits here presumed to be innocent and has allegations made against him that are twenty-six years old and dates have been changed on the morning of the trial.[7]

Father Parker, far from forgotten, had the full might of the church supporting and defending him. And now the judge seemed to be on his side.

Huggett's tone was conciliatory, placating the furious judge – "Witnesses can make honest mistakes, Your Honour" – but Coolahan was still seething.

> Coolahan: You know, when people turn eighteen, the law places upon them enormous responsibilities. How old are these complainants?
> Huggett: Thirty-eight, I think, Your Honour.
> Coolahan: Thirty-eight.
> Huggett: Thirty-eight and ... thirty-six, Your Honour ...
> Coolahan: So, they have waited years since they attained their majority ... well, that is just ridiculous. It is truly ridiculous.

What we know, of course, from the Royal Commission into Institutional Responses to Child Sexual Abuse, is that on average, Anglican victims of institutional abuse come forward twenty-nine years after the offences; for Catholic victims, the average is thirty-three years. Even in 2001, it was understood that child sexual abuse victims can take considerable time to come forward. Since 1986, judges in New South Wales had been required to direct juries that even though many years had passed since an alleged sexual assault, it did not mean the allegation was false. Coolahan was doing the exact opposite.

Steve felt ambushed. He had expected the defence lawyer to go in hard, but he had not expected the judge to denounce him before the trial had even started. He was scorched with humiliation. "The judge was using the power of the bench to slap me down. If I'd known the way I was going to be treated I'd never have walked into the courtroom ... He was basically calling me a liar in court, that I was fabricating it. I remember thinking, somebody say something."

Coolahan's attack on the brothers before any evidence had been given realised Steve's worst fears. He had always dreaded that no one would believe him, that he would be shamed for coming forward, and that the authority of the church would prevail – that Parker's denials would be believed while Steve was branded a liar. Now, right there in the courtroom, that was exactly what was happening.

Eventually, Rosser agreed to an adjournment to give both parties time to look at 1975 as the new date for the allegations. The trial would recommence on 10 September 2001. Steve, deeply shaken, now knew what he was facing.

*

The transcript of the ensuing trial makes painful reading. It shows a clever and aggressive barrister given free rein by a biased judge. Rosser continually tried to confuse or trip up Steve and B. Rosser's savaging was met with few objections; the inexperienced Huggett seemed intimidated by his bluster.

In our adversarial legal system, every judge has a legal obligation, under section 41(a) of the 1995 *Evidence Act*, to make sure the rules of evidence are upheld. That means not allowing harassing, demeaning, misleading, confusing, repetitive or irrelevant questioning, and stepping in on behalf of vulnerable witnesses. Judge Coolahan was very lenient towards Rosser. Rosser repeatedly questioned Steve and B about the change of date, despite the matter being settled, attempting to cast doubt on the veracity and reliability of their memories. Steve often became confused and distressed, with no intervention from the judge.

For Steve, the most devastating aspect of the trial was Rosser going in hard over his psychiatric history. The brochure for the Anglican helpline said the service was confidential, and Steve had trusted this meant what it said. During his phone calls with Lawrence, Steve had broken down in anguish and disclosed details of the abuse, his marriage breakdown, the collapse of his mental health, his suicide attempts and his stints in psychiatric hospital. Lawrence had handed the records of these confidential conversations to Parker's defence team. Rosser then got the Mater hospital records, where the treating psychiatrists had dealt with Steve's drinking – a symptom – rather than searching for reasons why he drank so much. Because of feelings of shame and humiliation, Steve did not disclose the sexual abuse to the treating psychiatrists. Rosser pointed to this as evidence that no abuse had occurred. It took until 2002 before Steve was able to disclose the sexual abuse to a therapist, and many more years of therapy before, in 2014, he could disclose the full extent of it, including the penetration.

It is common for survivors of child sexual abuse to suffer anxiety, depression and PTSD. Steve's admission to a psychiatric hospital could have been interpreted as evidence that he had been sexually abused. Instead, it was used to undermine his credibility. He was "mad", it was implied, his testimony unreliable and not to be believed. It was a form of gaslighting, where the mental illness caused by the abuse was used to damage him.

Judge Coolahan behaved as if everything Rosser and the church said was true. Rosser interrogated Steve aggressively about Graeme Lawrence's claim that he had found no record of Steve's mother having complained to Bishop Shevill about Parker's abuse of her son. Yet this was the diocesan modus operandi. Records of child sexual abuse were not kept, or were inadequate, or were falsified or "disappeared". When they were available, senior church representatives such as Lawrence and Mitchell were perfectly capable of denying their existence.

Records were also unlikely to exist because of the hostility expressed towards anyone making a complaint, which discouraged people from putting their complaints in writing. Steve's mother, usually quite stoical, had left her meeting with Bishop Shevill sobbing uncontrollably.[8] I found in my research that this behaviour, aimed at shutting down complaints, was typical. One clergyman reported that if anyone complained about child sexual abuse, Shevill "blasted them from one end of Bishop's Court to the other".[9] A church worker, Noelle Freeman, said that when parents came forward about Canon Harold Marshall's abuse of two little girls, Shevill's response was that "This would be bad for the church", "We must never speak of it again", and "We must protect the good name of the church."[10]

While Steve was denigrated in court for having been a psychiatric patient, the church was assumed to be beyond reproach. In 2001, few expected representatives of a Christian institution, purportedly committed to the Biblical commandment "Thou shalt not bear false witness", to lie or to conceal evidence. There was a reservoir of trust and goodwill towards the church.

Rosser grilled Steve repeatedly on why he had not disclosed the abuse sooner. Having been silenced by shame, he was now blamed for not disclosing. During the trial, Steve described telling his mother about the abuse as they drove home from Gateshead. "I was upset. I was scared too, I guess. I was scared to tell Mum." Steve didn't tell his father but trusted his mother to do so. It "wasn't something to be talked about, I don't think. I assumed Mum had taken whatever action was necessary. It wasn't my place."

Steve's lack of disclosure to his father was held against him. It "would've been a hard thing for me to speak to Dad about", he explained. Steve did recall a conversation with his dad in 1984, when, over a beer in the garage, Steve made an oblique reference to Father Parker "having bad habits with little boys". He also told the court that he had disclosed the abuse to Father Bob Searle at his kids' school.

As Rosser interrogated him over and over, constantly tripping him up, Steve began to sound exhausted. At one point he answered wearily, "I'm sure you will tell me", because nothing he said seemed to count. Steve remembers looking pleadingly at the DPP solicitor and the judge, hoping they would stop it.

The brothers had outlined a clear timeline: the night at the rectory when the sexual abuse occurred, and then, the next day, the service followed by morning tea. Strangely, the whole trial came to hinge not on the night when the assaults took place, but on the question of whether Parker had attended the morning tea or had needed to rush off to another service. It was the defence's intention to cast doubt on the morning tea, and thereby on the brothers' truthfulness. If they got that wrong, the defence logic went, what else had they misremembered? The sexual abuse?

In his cross-examination of the brothers, Rosser focused on the morning tea. When B mentioned it during cross-examination, Rosser smoothly changed every subsequent reference to it from a "tea" to a "meal" – a much longer repast. He was trying to establish that Parker had no time for a "meal" before heading to the next church, so either the brothers' memories were wrong, or they were lying. Rosser admitted later that he wanted to "lock the [brothers'] story in in front of the jury"[11] before he produced new evidence to contradict it – the Gateshead Register of Services.

After the Crown changed the date of the indictment from 1974 to 1975, the defence could no longer claim that Parker was not at Gateshead when the offences occurred. They needed a new alibi. They immediately held a conference between Allen, Parker and Rosser, and it was agreed they would get the Gateshead Register of Services, presumably in hope of finding a new alibi. The very next day, on 14 August, Keith Allen had telephoned Reverend Sonia Roulston, who was now the local parish priest at Gateshead. He asked if he could come that evening to look at the Register of Services for 1975. According to Roulston, Allen told her that he wanted to check the Register for the accuracy of a claim supposedly made by Steve and B that the bishop had attended the service the day after the sexual assaults. This was entirely untrue – neither Steve nor his brother ever made such a claim. It was just a ruse to get a look at the Register. Roulston obliged, and Allen visited with his then wife. Roulston gave him the relevant Register and left to do household tasks elsewhere in the rectory. Allen and his wife were left alone with the volume for about five to ten minutes.[12]

When the trial recommenced, Allen asked Roulston to bring the Register to court. Her memory is that she brought it on a Friday, during the trial. Rosser would later tell the royal commission that Peter Mitchell brought the Register into the foyer of the courtroom the following Tuesday.[13] This meant it likely that Mitchell had been left alone with the volume over the weekend.[14]

Steve's memory is that he was sitting in the witness box, weary from the repetitive badgering by Rosser, when he noticed Mitchell carrying in a heavy, official-looking book and thumping it onto the table. It looked like the defence had something up their sleeve. Keith Allen kept moving the book around conspicuously on the desk, and the Crown solicitor looked nervously at it. Allen later boasted that he had been "fidgeting intentionally through the books" as a tactic, "messing with the Crown's mind".[15] Steve observed that Parker was smiling expectantly. Suddenly, the defence team approached the bench with the book. The Crown lawyer joined them in a huddle before Judge Coolahan. After they had conferred, the trial ended for the day. The book was handed to Huggett, the DPP solicitor, who took it away to be examined overnight.

At the time, Steve didn't understand what was going on, but the register allegedly contradicted the brothers' account of the morning after the abuse. It was treated like an alibi for Parker. So much hinged on it. Steve's life hinged on it. It was, Rosser claimed, "devastating" for the prosecution's case.

The book contains a series of orderly chronological entries, recording the names of parishes, their priests, the dates and types of each service, the number of people in attendance and the money collected. Few entries are worthy of comment. There are no crossings-out or corrections in the entire book – except on the page relevant to Steve and B's allegations. On that page, the chronological order suddenly changes. The services are out of order and are recorded in different handwritings. Some entries are crossed out and some dates have been changed. The records of money collected at each service have been altered and are written in red ink – a different colour from the other entries – and are scrawled over the top of other, earlier entries. They look as if they were written hurriedly.[16] The "collections", which represent the number of people attending, were originally recorded as all having been at the same church – consistent with Steve's memory of it being a special, larger service, with parishioners from all three churches gathering at Gateshead to welcome Father Parker. However, the first set of numbers for the second and third churches are crossed out, and the larger figure from Gateshead is transposed and redistributed to the second church of Mount Hutton and third church of Windale respectively. These changes makes it seem that Parker attended all three churches. (Later, during the royal commission in 2016, there was fierce cross-examination of both Peter Mitchell and Keith Allen over these alterations to the register. There was no doubt that it had been altered, but the commission did not make a final judgement as to who had made the alterations. There is no suggestion Mr Rosser had any knowledge that the register was altered.)[17]

Some sections are left blank in the register, meaning entries could be added or amended later. It is unclear when the entries relevant to Steve's case were filled in. Anyone could have added to the columns recording Parker's attendance at Mount Hutton and Windale, making it seem that Steve's memory of a morning tea after the Gateshead service – and by implication his allegation of sexual assault – was false. There are blank sections around the same period, suggesting there were not always services at Windale and Mount Hutton.

The Register was only a starting point to help determine Parker's movements, and it was never an alibi for the abuse the night before. Even if Parker had gone on to the Windale parish after the Gateshead service, as the Register seemed to suggest, it was only four minutes by car. If mass started at 8 a.m. and ran for forty-five minutes rather than the full hour, Parker could easily have enjoyed a leisurely morning tea of twenty or thirty minutes with parishioners before heading to the next church. Had the police and prosecution lawyers been told of the book's existence when they first asked the church for information in early 2000, they could have scrutinised it more carefully, investigated the travel time between churches, and interviewed parishioners to see if they remembered the morning tea. There was no cross-examination by the prosecution to verify the contents of the Register or its meaning. Instead, they had just one night to examine the book; and on the face of it, it seemed to contradict the brothers' account.

After examining the book overnight, Huggett met Steve and B outside the court the next morning. Her news was grim. She was kind, but she told them that the new evidence meant the prosecution could not proceed. She advised the brothers to accept a "no-billed" case – meaning charges would be withdrawn but Parker would not be acquitted. If they proceeded with the trial and Parker were acquitted – which the Crown thought would be the likely outcome, given the supposed alibi – the case could never be reopened. If they accepted a "no-billed" result, however, the case could return to court if further evidence were to come to light. Huggett also said, however, that in practice such cases were almost never reopened.[18]

Steve was dumbfounded by this sudden turn of events. He asked in anguish, "Do we have a choice here?" Huggett said that no, they didn't really. The brothers were gutted.

*

The ordeal was not yet over. After the trial ended, Judge Coolahan gave the brothers and the prosecution what Steve described as "another bollocking". Coolahan told the court that he would have directed the jury to find Parker not guilty, and questioned the propriety of Steve, his brother and the DPP in bringing the case at all. "I really had some concerns about yesterday's trial of Parker," the judge said. He asked Rosser if the registry book was an ordinary record kept by the church. "They were records kept in the custody of the rector of the particular parish," confirmed Rosser. "Yes, that's so."[19]

Coolahan asked: "And they were readily available had anyone issued a subpoena?"

Rosser now uttered the most telling line of the entire trial: "Well, if someone knew what to look for and where to look, yes." That is, it would have required insider knowledge of the church. "There does not appear to have been, so far as we are aware," Rosser added, "any investigation prior to charging him to check the accuracy of that date."

As I have shown, this was patently untrue. The police and DPP had made multiple requests to the diocese for the records.

Rosser then noted that "Mr Allen, who instructed me in the matter, has some connection with the church. He knew precisely what sort of records to look for and where to look for them. He approached the rector at Gateshead and obtained a copy of the Register of Services ... [which] records every service that is conducted in that parish." This was the very information the police and prosecution had needed before the trial. As Rosser now observed, the Register of Services "became of absolutely critical importance ... I don't think it's putting it too highly to say that it was completely destructive to the Crown case". Its significance, Rosser claimed, "really [be]came clear only when it was clear to us what the witnesses were going to say ... I think it is fair to say that the significance of that book has only been to the forefront in the last month." That wasn't true either. The question of Parker's movements on the day of the alleged abuse had been "at the forefront" since Steve first made his complaint to police in January 2000.

Coolahan thanked Rosser for his explanation.

Huggett responded to Coolahan with a spirited defence of the DPP, pointing out the multiple times that police and the DPP had investigated Parker's whereabouts only to be told by the diocese there were no records. They had also inquired about records of the servers' guild services, again to be informed there weren't any. Yet Huggett's sharp eye had spotted records of services for altar boys; "they were actually in the suddenly produced Register of Services", contrary to what her office had been told.[20]

Coolahan returned to his theme of how old the allegations were:

> But what concerns me is that the Director [of Public Prosecutions] had before him allegations which were totally unsubstantiated and which at one stage were twenty-six years old, at one stage twenty-five years old, and that it appears that absolutely no investigation was made by him to gain any evidence which might substantiate those allegations. Instead, Father Parker was dragged from Victoria, placed before a judge and jury, and it was only when a record was produced, which in my view ought to have been obtained by the Crown before any trial took place, that established conclusively it seems that what the complainants in this case were saying, was false … it seems to me that it's an abusive process.

Steve reeled. His bringing a case against Parker was "abusive"?

*

As they filed out of Courtroom Four, Steve was shattered. What had just happened? He felt his attempt to get justice had resulted in being taken by the scruff of the neck and his face rubbed in the dirt. Parker had watched with a smirk on his face; "he was enjoying seeing me beat up".

The judge's words – "complete disgrace", "truly ridiculous", "a real farce", as though it had been a malicious and mischievous suit against an innocent man – echoed in Steve's head as he made his way outside. He was already fighting with his brother, who blamed Steve for bringing the case in the first place. Their relationship never recovered.

Standing outside the Grand Hotel, opposite the court, he looked across the road and saw Team Church – Lawrence, Rosser and Parker – "standing there on the courthouse steps … They stood there laughing at us." All that was left to Steve were his fists. "I took off and headed across to give them a hiding … Dad grabbed my shoulder and said, 'Not here and not now.' That was his advice to me, and I just threw my hands in the air and just said, 'I'm going home.'"

It was 11 September 2001. The twin towers of the World Trade Center had been blown up by terrorists, an inferno of fire, blood and bodies. Everyone was talking about it. "The train ride home to Port Macquarie was one of the worst four hours of my life. I got home and contemplated suicide. I'm not ashamed to admit that."

CHAPTER EIGHT

THE FIGHTER

STEVE PLUNGED INTO deep despair after the trial fell over. In just a few weeks, however, by early October 2001, he'd picked himself up and decided to fight on. It is important to understand Steve's character. He is courageous. Like a bareknuckle fighter, even when on the ropes or the canvas after what seemed a knockout blow, however beaten, bloodied and broken, he got up and had another go. Over the coming years, Steve never gave up, even though he did not really expect to get anywhere. Miserable, living alone in Port Macquarie, he made an important decision. It was to "punch on ... If you want a blue, I'll give you one."

He just didn't – yet – know exactly how to fight them.

The first thing Steve did was to write an anguished and angry letter to Bishop Herft. He wanted to know how information about his stints in psychiatric hospital, taken from his confidential conversations with Lawrence, had come to be used in court to discredit him.

> I am writing to express my disappointment and dismay at the attitude of the Anglican Church toward me ... My main concern is the fact that confidential conversations I had with Dean Lawrence, were transcribed (albeit inaccurately), and provided to Parker's defence counsel ... The breach of confidentiality completed the betrayal and abandonment of myself by the church.[1]

Steve asked for assurances that "any further approaches to the Anglican Church, by myself, in search of counselling or support, will be treated confidentially".

The day he received the letter, Bishop Herft, who was going away for two weeks, wrote to Peter Mitchell, asking him to reply on his behalf. Herft told Mitchell that it was "vital to obtain some good legal advice about how to proceed, although I do wish to include that I am concerned for him and want to assure him of my prayers".

Mitchell workshopped the letter with the diocesan lawyer, Robert Caddies, who prepared a draft "in response to your concern that there may be ongoing legal consequences and care should be taken not to make any admission which could constitute an admission by the Church".

Mitchell sent his letter to Steve on 16 October. Defending the use of the confidential information, he explained that "The Diocese and the Dean were subpoenaed to produce records at the trial." He said that the diocese had sought "legal advice on whether the confidential conversations" were "privileged", like confessions, but discovered they were not. "The Church did not in any direct way provide records to the Reverend George Parker's defence except through compulsory Court processes ... the church was bound to produce records to the court."[2]

This claim was false. There was nothing "compulsory" about the defence deciding to use Steve's hospital records against him and deliberately organising subpoenas designed to get them. Allen told Rosser in a letter on 12 June 2001 that they were issuing subpoenas for "Lawrence and the Hospitals".[3] Later, in July 2001, the diocese was sent a very specific subpoena from Parker's defence team, carefully designed to elicit the records of Steve's confidential conversations with Lawrence, and Caddies delivered the requested records to court. What is striking is the easy facility with which Mitchell lied about it.

Mitchell reassured Steve that "confidential support" and "counselling" provided by the church "will be treated confidentially", then immediately contradicted himself. "The Church cannot, if litigation arose, guarantee that records brought into existence may not be the subject of any compulsory procedure by law to produce such communications to a Court." So, it's confidential – except it isn't. Not if the church needs it in a trial to defend a priest.

At the end of the draft letter, Caddies included a cold little placeholder line: "[ADD RELEVANT COMMENTS OF PASTORAL NATURE]". In the final version, Mitchell squeezed out Bishop Herft's "concern for your wellbeing and an assurance of his prayers for you".[4]

The Anglican Church had not quite finished with Steve. His father brought him the October edition of the diocese magazine, the *Anglican Encounter*. "Graeme Lawrence had actually signed the thing and shoved it under Dad's door." Steve's father, no longer an active member of a church, had moved, so they must have gone to considerable trouble to find his current address.

The magazine included an article by Peter Mitchell entitled "Confusion over False Action".[5] It was a report of the trial and proclaimed Parker's innocence. Mitchell had workshopped it with Keith Allen straight after the trial.[6] In a tone of pious injury, Mitchell claimed that Parker's trial had "created confusion and concern among many in the Diocese and the greater community. Rumours and fears that the matter had not been fairly dealt with are unfounded." "The reality," he went on, "is that the Crown did not have a case against George Parker and was heavily criticised by the Judge for attempting to bring action against him under these circumstances." Mitchell denied claims made by the regional TV station, NBN, that the dean's office had been uncooperative with police. "These claims were strenuously denied by Dean Graeme Lawrence." Mitchell wrote that "several options for making a complaint were given to the complainant, including both the Diocese's sexual harassment process and the civil process." He said that Steve had not kept appointments to see Bishop Herft and Dean Lawrence. (As we've seen, Steve had been warned by Father Bob Searle against having anything to do with Lawrence.)

Mitchell described the late change of date and wrote that as a result of "the information contained in the Service Registers, the Crown withdrew all charges, and the Judge discharged the jury, as there were no facts for them to consider. The facts show the Crown did not have evidence to bring any action against Father Parker." In a tone of confected sorrow, he observed: "Sadly, this seemed to become apparent to them only when the matter had been taken to court and covered by the media."

Then, he offered a boast:

> If a positive can be taken from this tragic incident, it is the effectiveness of the Diocese's Sexual Misconduct Principles and Procedures in dealing with allegations of sexual misconduct ... The community should be reassured the Diocese of Newcastle has, for some time now, required rigorous

psychological and physiological profiling designed to ensure that those seeking ordination are suitable for the position they hold.[7]

The "Sexual Misconduct Principles and Procedures" amounted to a few meagre brochures dealing with sexual misconduct and sexual harassment against *adults*. The protocols for dealing with child sexual abuse, Herft would later admit, were "hopeless".[8]

Mitchell ended his article with a sanctimonious flourish, highlighting Parker's magnanimity:

> George Parker is a free man, with no criminal record and many years of dedicated service to the community behind him. While he cannot comprehend the actions of the complainants, he bears them no ill will. Our prayer is now that the community will pray for George Parker, his accusers and all who are wounded.

It made bitter reading for Steve. He feared that if his family, friends and acquaintances read the article, they would think he had made the allegations up. He thought, "When is enough enough for these people? And that was the moment ... I read it ... I thought, all right, you blokes want a fight, I'll give you a fight. And that's how it started ... I went from broken to just angry. I didn't feel broken any more. There was a purpose to the whole thing."

At first, however, "There was nothing to fight. [It was] like you are fighting ghosts. I didn't know the connections between various people in the church, Rosser and Allen, how tight they were in the church, Lawrence and his involvement, you just couldn't put it together."[9]

Immediately after the trial, the diocese of Newcastle had released one of its two pre-prepared media statements, with the headline "Reverend Parker acquitted of all charges". Claiming that Parker had been "acquitted" was, of course, false. In the statement, Bishop Herft called for respect for the court's decision. "I would ask people of the Diocese [of] Newcastle to pray for Reverend Parker as he travels through this difficult stage in his life. We should also ask for prayers for his accuser."[10]

On 13 September 2001, Dean Lawrence sent a threatening letter to the NBN news service. He was indignant about a report by journalist Helen Kapalous, which stated matter-of-factly that "the DPP had defended its actions in bringing the case", and that the Crown claimed that "when they first approached the Dean's office to confirm dates and records they were told [the dean's office] were unwilling to assist them". Kapalous had misquoted the transcript of the DPP's words, replacing "unable" with "unwilling". However, as we have seen, the NBN report was accurate. But Lawrence took umbrage at the suggestion he was unwilling to assist, even though it was quite true. In his letter to NBN, he claimed falsely that "No request was received by myself or my staff from the DPP for any information regarding Father Parker." He claimed the NBN report had caused him "considerable personal distress" and threatened a defamation suit, which clearly did not have a leg to stand on.

Peter Mitchell was busy too. On 3 October, having already written his article for the *Anglican Encounter*, he wrote an indignant letter to the NSW director of public prosecutions, Nicholas Cowdery QC, to protest at the case having been brought at all. He claimed insufficient investigation was made into the allegations before the trial, and reiterated Lawrence's indignation at the implication he had been "unwilling to assist".[11]

A DPP solicitor, drafting a reply on Cowdery's behalf, pointed out that:

> The DPP were told directly by the registrar that there were no records about the Guild Services. Mr Rosser conceded at court that the parish records were available if one knew where to look. Mr Allen had the advantage of being a church goer. I can only speculate how long he knew beforehand about that record.[12]

Quite so. In a conciliatory but firm tone, Cowdery pointed out all the investigations undertaken, and drew Mitchell's attention to the fact that these records did exist. Cowdery quoted Rosser's comments at the trial that "Mr Allen 'had some connection with the Church' and 'knew precisely what to look for and where to look'." In contrast, despite the DPP's "Reasonable efforts … to ascertain if records were available", it had been left at a loss. "[W]ithout knowing what to look for or where to look, other than with the Dean's Office and the Registry – already contacted without success", "the vital record, the Register of Services, was not obtained" until the defence suddenly produced it at the trial.

Cowdery finished by commending Steve and his brother, who "attended three conferences in total" and "On each occasion … impressed the Crown Prosecutor and respective solicitors as truthful and honest".[13]

Soon after Parker's trial, Keith Allen wrote to Bishop Herft, thanking him for the "consideration and care that you have shown to Father George in the past months".[14] This was in contrast to the complete absence of pastoral care for Steve and his brother. While a great deal of energy was expended pursuing the DPP for costs, threatening NBN with defamation and writing sanctimonious articles for the *Anglican Encounter*, nobody from the church had exhibited the slightest concern for how Steve and his brother were faring.

Just at that moment, a new scandal broke in the diocese. The pious registrar, Peter Mitchell, was charged with fraud.

*

In January 2002, five months after Parker's trial, Mitchell, one of the two people who had the opportunity to alter the register of services, was discovered to have been defrauding the diocese for over nine years. He had stolen nearly $200,000.

In contrast to Bishop Herft's "do nothing" approach to Steve's allegations in 1996 and 1999, his response to Mitchell's embezzlement was swift and decisive. Herft had just returned home from overseas when he learned about the missing funds. Herft immediately demanded Mitchell's resignation. The police were notified, and audits of church accounts organised. A special meeting of the Diocesan Council was called the very next day, on 24 January 2002.

It was held at Bishopscourt, Herft's grand seven-bedroom home. Built in 1929, it had been donated by a wealthy benefactor for the Anglican bishops of Newcastle to use as a residence in perpetuity. Bishopscourt reflected the power and prestige of the church in Newcastle. Situated in the "dress circle" suburb of The Hill, it boasted an ornate timber staircase, wood panelling and leadlight windows. Although in the centre of town, it was situated on over an acre of manicured gardens, with a beautiful view over the city, towards the sea and the lighthouse at Nobby's Head.

The diocese had been investigating Mitchell for some time. Tim Mawson, then diocesan secretary, had noticed Mitchell "actively looking to discard files of financial relevance".[15] But at the Diocesan Council meeting, many were shocked to learn of Mitchell's theft. Mitchell had "tendered his resignation with immediate effect". Herft, for once, did not prevaricate or dither. "The Bishop indicated that the facts were clear and that there was no doubt about the matter." The council asked that pastoral care be made available to Peter Mitchell and his family.[16]

Herft's treatment of Reverend Rod Bower, a close friend of Mitchell for almost twenty years, was revealing. Bower is now a high-profile radical priest at Gosford, known for his incendiary comments, displayed on a billboard outside his church, defending the LGBTQI community or advocating for refugees. In 2002, however, Bower had a senior role as archdeacon of the Central Coast. Bower decided he would be Mitchell's "soul friend" "in his hour of need". By supporting Mitchell, he believed he was giving expression to an ideal, deeply embedded in Christianity, to "pity the wrongdoer", recognise their pain, remorse and shame, and offer pastoral care.[17]

On 11 March 2002, Herft wrote to Reverend Peter Lord, "I commend [Bower] for this Christlike and honourable action." Then Herft sacked Bower, who felt treated like a leper and sidelined from senior leadership positions for the rest of Herft's reign.[18]

Mitchell pleaded guilty to fraud. The *Newcastle Herald* reported that the judge found he had engaged in "multiple and complex deceptions" to "milk various church trusts" in order to live a "comfortable and materialistic lifestyle". Weeping, Mitchell was led from the dock "with a tearful uncertainty". He was sentenced to twenty-one months' imprisonment, with a non-parole period of seven months.[19]

So, theft from the diocese was resolved speedily. Mitchell was forced to resign instantly, police were involved immediately, the Diocesan Council was informed, audits were organised, and there was a trial, conviction and prison sentence, all within a year. Justice was done.

In contrast, decades on from 1971, when the sexual abuse had begun, Steve still had no justice. In June 2002, he approached a law firm, Stacks, about making a claim under the NSW government's *Victims Compensation Act*. Steve agreed to a psychologist's report for the purposes of that claim.[20] Gary S. Grant completed the report. He interviewed Steve for an hour and a half. The psychologist described Steve as a "very hurt and sad man of forty-three years". Grant noted, however, that prior to Parker's abuse Steve had no psychological symptoms, and had a happy childhood in a close, church-going family.[21]

Steve still could not bear to disclose all the abuse, just the last incident at Gateshead. Grant outlined how Steve had found "the attempted sodomy" "very disturbing and confronting". And he "struggled to make sense of the assault … why a man of God would take advantage of a young altar boy". "Mr Smith felt confused, alienated and resentful as a result of Father Parker's sexual assault" and the "betrayal of trust and respect". Steve told Grant he was "haunted by intrusive flashbacks and he would think about it again and again".

The psychologist noted a "high level of severity of symptoms", as Steve had been at a very young and vulnerable age when the assault took place. In the 1970s, "the concept of sexual assault of a man on a boy was not a very acceptable concern to explore."

Steve told Grant: "The Church laughed at me, the elders scorned me, and I felt devalued as a person." His life after the assault had been "like a ship without a rudder". Grant diagnosed him with depressive disorder and several symptoms of PTSD.

However, the psychologist found many positive characteristics in Steve.

> Mr Smith impresses as a caring and compassionate person whose life experiences will assist him in a teaching career. Mr Smith has been very courageous in his efforts to stand up to the Church and confront what he perceives as "an injustice." He has developed a healthy outlook on life and will make every effort not to hold grudges or resentments.

The psychologist finished by describing Steve as "a caring and resilient man who exhibits common sense and integrity".

Steve was granted $8250 in compensation. It was next to nothing for what he had suffered, or for the income and opportunities foregone by leaving school early, but it was a start. However, the church still refused to recognise the wrong done to him.

*

Every symbolic occasion, such as Christmas, brought home to Steve how shattered his life had been by Parker's abuse. On Christmas Day in 2002, he went to the cathedral.

It was desperation ... I needed help, I was in a bad way. And I just really needed someone to care. All I'd seen from them was "We don't care." It was almost like a symbolic thing in my mind. I hated the cathedral with a passion. I had served there as an altar boy as a kid, but I hated the place.

Christmas Day and a church triggered old trauma memories.

I've been raped on Christmas Day, and I've been raped at Easter time. I hated Christmas Day, and I hated Easter ... I would be in my altar robes aged ten, eleven, twelve, and knowing full well what would happen afterward. Parker would be at the pulpit that my family donated, standing there preaching about love and kindness and goodness, and as a kid I was thinking, "Are you kidding? I know where we are going from here."[22]

Just to walk into the cathedral on Christmas Day "took an enormous amount" from Steve. But he did it. He had hopes of seeing Bishop Herft, hopes for some kind of simple expression of compassion and care. It was, after all, Christmas, when the celebration of Christ's birth was meant to foster a spirit of giving, reconciliation, mercy and Christian charity.

Instead, he encountered the dean, Graeme Lawrence. When Steve said he wanted to talk to him, Lawrence was:

ice cold, like rolling his eyes. "Oh, not you again." He was just so dismissive, like, "I'm far too busy, I haven't got time for you, and I want you to leave." The arrogance of Lawrence, like waving a peasant away. I was being cast out of the place like I was the one who had done something wrong.

Steve got angry at the rude dismissal and there was a heated exchange of words. Steve said that one day he would see Lawrence in prison greens. Lawrence angrily turned away, sweeping off in his grand robes towards the altar, to sermonise about the Christmas spirit.

After this encounter, Steve was "crushed".

I remember thinking, "How can you people talk as you do when you do what you just did? In that state of mind, I could easily have thrown myself off the cliffs of Newcastle Beach. I was in my darkest moments. My marriage had ended, I had to hand my kids over to my ex on Christmas Day ...

with all this Christmas spirit running around … I wasn't thinking about money but pastoral support … I needed someone to say they cared about me and what was happening to me. It was a cry for help.

Steve did not, however, give up. Back at Port Macquarie, in the new year of 2003, he was still determined to fight back. Although he often felt like he was pointlessly bashing his head against the splendid brick walls of the cathedral, he was in fact making headway – but with no thanks to any Christian charity on the part of Lawrence, Herft or anyone else in the Anglican Church.

CHAPTER NINE

LAWYERING UP ON HIS WAY TO CANTERBURY

SOMETIMES A REVOLUTION occurs in a distant place, but, like the reverberations of an earthquake deep in the tectonic plates, the tremors are felt far away from its epicentre. For the Anglican Church, such an earthquake occurred in the Brisbane diocese, causing the very public downfall of the then governor-general, Peter Hollingworth.

Hollingworth was a highly regarded Anglican minister who had headed up the Brotherhood of St Laurence. In 1989 he was appointed archbishop of Brisbane. In June 2001, Prime Minister John Howard made him governor-general – the first time a Christian priest had occupied the position. Hollingworth received many honours during his career. He was made a member of the Order of the British Empire in 1976, was Australian of the Year in 1991 and was awarded the Companion of the Order of Australia in 2001.[1] He had a long way to fall from that pinnacle of community regard.

In December 2001, a scandal erupted over Hollingworth's failure to respond appropriately to child sexual abuse complaints against a teacher at the Anglican Toowoomba Preparatory School during the 1990s. The Brisbane diocese had to pay out $834,800 in damages to the female victim.[2] Hollingworth, under great public pressure, eventually apologised to the victim, but the apology came too late to save his reputation. From there, things only got worse.

In February 2002, he made a disastrous appearance on *Australian Story* on ABC television. A woman, Beth Heinrich, had made a complaint about his handling of her sexual abuse by Reverend Donald Shearman, later a bishop. As archbishop, Hollingworth had allowed Shearman to continue his ministry for six years, even after Shearman confessed to Hollingworth that he had had sex with Beth Heinrich when she was a minor. On *Australian Story*, Hollingworth said:

> The genesis of it was forty years ago and it occurred between a young priest and a teenage girl who was under the age of consent. I believe she was more than fourteen and I also understand that many years later in adult life their relationship resumed, and it was partly a pastoral relationship, and it was partly something more. My belief is that this was not sex abuse, there was no suggestion of rape or anything like that, quite the contrary. My information is that it was rather the other way round.[3]

There was a furore. A great many people were outraged, especially survivors of sexual abuse. Hollingworth was clearly blaming the victim, who was only fifteen when the sexual offences started. It was a crime, not a sexual "relationship" – being underage, she could never be correctly described as the initiator. The sharp public reaction showed the profound cultural transformation – the moral quickening – that had occurred in attitudes to child sexual abuse by 2002. Blaming the victim and exonerating powerful male perpetrators were no longer socially acceptable.

Then, in February 2002, Rafael Epstein reported on the ABC's *A.M.* program that another alarming case had surfaced. Hollingworth had dismissed sex-abuse claims against a clergyman, Ross McAuley, after McAuley denied the allegations. Hollingworth later appointed McAuley to the church's Cathedral Sexual Abuse Committee; when the committee had to deal with fresh allegations against McAuley, they were not told of the earlier complaints.[4]

Hollingworth said, "He gave me an absolute, unconditional promise that it was not him, that he did not do it, he had no knowledge of it, and I accepted what he said, and I believe it." Hollingworth justified not telling the other committee members about the previous allegations: "Well, what was I supposed to tell them? That we've had what would seem to be an unsubstantiated allegation from someone who's in a bad way? We couldn't possibly establish it one way or the other and there is no case to answer."

Support for Hollingworth, even from his stalwart defenders such as Prime Minister Howard, now waned. Howard described the accusations as "very nasty allegations" that "should be placed under a very powerful magnifying glass".[5]

On 19 February 2002, Hollingworth's replacement as archbishop of Brisbane, Phillip Aspinall, announced the establishment of the Board of Inquiry into Past Handling of Complaints of Sexual Abuse in the Anglican Church, and an inquiry into the Brisbane diocese's handling of child sexual abuse, including Hollingworth's behaviour.

The Brisbane inquiry's conclusions, tabled in state parliament by Queensland premier Peter Beattie in May 2003, were damning.[6] The inquiry concluded that Hollingworth had also allowed another known paedophile, John Elliot, to continue working as a priest. In 2002, Elliot was convicted of many sexual offences against boys, beginning early in his career and continuing over many years. As early as 1993, as archbishop of Brisbane, Hollingworth had become aware of child sexual abuse allegations against Elliot. When Hollingworth met with Elliot that year, Elliot admitted to the abuse but claimed "there had been no other wrongdoing on his part". Hollingworth accepted his protestations.

Despite Elliot admitting to the alleged offences, Hollingworth did not report his serious crimes to police and allowed Elliot to remain in his ministry, citing the financial difficulties Elliot would face if he lost his licence. Elliot's victims included a nine-year-old boy whom he had abused on a regular basis at Brisbane's Church of England Grammar School, in the local parish and at Church of England Boys' Society camps. Elliot also abused the boy's brother. When the parents later met with Hollingworth, he told them he had not removed Elliot because "it is better to upset one family than a whole parish". Removing a priest would damage the church.

The Brisbane inquiry found against Hollingworth in the case of Elliot.[7] Hollingworth's position as governor-general had become untenable. In May 2003 he resigned, and his role as governor-general was revoked. He was completely disgraced. By 2003, a cultural revolution in our understanding of child sexual abuse had occurred. Mishandling of sexual abuse had brought down not just an archbishop but a governor-general. The Anglican Church had been put on notice.

*

The Brisbane inquiry and Hollingworth's downfall sent shivers down the spines of Newcastle Anglicans, including Bishop Herft. Originally from Sri Lanka, Herft had enjoyed a meteoric rise in the Anglican Church. According to some Newcastle clergy, he was so highly regarded that he might one day even become the Archbishop of Canterbury, the head of the whole Church of England.

Herft was a small, even dainty, man, and was regarded as a dynamic preacher. He was reflective, intelligent and talented. He could also be fussy, prickly and timid. He was known to be extremely ambitious, a quality many also observed in his wife, Cheryl. Some people whom I interviewed were unflattering about Cheryl, seeing her as a social climber. One clergyman's wife described being "cut to ribbons" at a social gathering by Cheryl, who then walked off looking for someone who was "somebody" to talk to. Bishop Farran, who succeeded Herft as bishop of Newcastle, told me, "I think people's social standing was very important to them."

Herft liked being on the international stage, he was away from the diocese a lot ... Lawrence once said to me, Herft's management style is to get things off his desk as quickly as possible onto somebody else's desk ... He was a pretty prickly person, and I think he felt he was culturally misunderstood sometimes, because he was from Sri Lanka.[8]

Reverend Canon Paul Robertson thought that Herft was concerned for the reputation of the church and for his own reputation.

Herft was very ambitious ... most bishops think [Newcastle] is a premier diocese [i.e. if you had made it to bishop of Newcastle, you had got to the "top"]. But Herft was looking forward to becoming an archbishop, and he didn't want to have anything in the public domain that would interfere with that. Truth could be a casualty. Someone said to me, "Saving face was more important than truth, in his culture." And that governed his behaviour. You might deny something and tell a lie, to save face.[9]

Some clergy I spoke to still held Herft in high regard. Colvin Ford recalled his kindness. Herft always remembered people's names and had a gift for storytelling.

He was childlike ... with a kind of innocence about him. When he would
come to confirmation, he would love telling the story of his Sri Lankan
childhood ... [about] someone in his early life who prayed for him all the
time, and he would tell the kids how important it was to know that someone was praying for you.[10]

Herft was dominated by and afraid of one of his archdeacons, Peter
Rushton. Rushton was an Anglo-Catholic so violently opposed to women's
ordination that he refused to allow Herft to give communion in his church,
as Herft's hands had been "tainted" by consecrating women. Astonishingly, Herft didn't discipline Rushton, but submitted to this indignity
and disobedience.

Herft was also afraid of Graeme Lawrence, the dean and powerbroker
of the diocese. Rod Bower told me:

Roger was afraid of Lawrence ... He was afraid of his ecclesiastical power.
His ability to manipulate. I once heard it said ... that Graeme Lawrence
was worth thirty votes at synod. So, if you had Lawrence on side, once
Lawrence got up and spoke at synod that was kind of the end of it.
You knew.[11]

Lawrence had a pithy way of describing his power over Herft. Referenc-
ing his roles as a gay icon in Newcastle and the power behind the throne,
Lawrence was heard to use a chess analogy: "Queens have more power than
bishops!" No appointment was made without Lawrence's input and control.

Ambition itself is not a hangable offence, and most of the higher-
ranking clergy would have harboured personal ambitions. However, if
ambition means the bloody-minded protection of oneself, of other clergy
or of the institution, or if it means turning a blind eye to reports of child
sexual abuse, it can be wicked. If ambition means the only "risk management" you are concerned with is reputational damage, rather than
managing the risks posed by predator priests to children, then it is a
disaster. Such ambition also surely violates any true Christian ethic. If
self-interest involves lawyering up, bullying and threatening survivors
rather than giving them pastoral care and compensation, it surely violates the biblical injunction to care for "the least and the lost", as Herft
himself put it.[12]

Herft was concerned enough about Steve as a reputational problem that between Parker's trial in 2001 and June 2004, when Herft left Newcastle to become archbishop of Perth, he held a number of meetings with senior personnel and forwarded Steve's many emails and letters to the diocesan lawyers for advice before replying.

The Hollingworth inquiry report of 2003 also worried the wily church lawyer Keith Allen, George Parker's solicitor. On 28 April 2003, Allen wrote to Herft, expressing concerns that given "sexual harassment" [child sexual abuse] was receiving media attention, claims such as Steve's allegations against Parker might "resurface":

> Out of the Parker matter, in my view, there are other issues of risk management that perhaps need to be reviewed. The documents subpoenaed from the Dean of Newcastle, the diocese and the parish, in my view, raise other issues that should be of concern to the Diocese. The Year Books of the Diocese provide an exact public record which may produce problems in connection with the documents produced under subpoena.[13]

This suggests that there were conflicts between what the yearbook said about George Parker's appointment to Gateshead and his movements, and the Registry of Services suddenly produced at the trial. Allen clearly knew there was a problem and was drawing his bishop's attention to it.

Allen was also worried that Steve and others might sue for civil damages, which have a lower threshold of proof than in a criminal trial. He raised with Herft the issue of "risk management of all insurance claims". Allen claimed, incorrectly, that "the criminal issues have been dealt with", but "the civil issue has never been dealt with and having regard to the Brisbane Report it may surface again." Allen wanted to set up a meeting with Herft and the diocesan business manager, Bruce Hockman, and secretary, Tim Mawson, to discuss the Parker/Smith matter, "to talk through what I believe the perceived problems may be for the Diocese in the future". He apologised to Bishop Herft: "I am sorry to raise this issue with you, however there is no good time to raise these sort of issues."

Events in Brisbane and the possibility of Steve suing the diocese for damages were also clearly weighing on Roger Herft. A payout to a complainant like Steve would open the floodgates to other Anglican abuse survivors and create a blot on his "blemish-free" record of having almost no successful cases against the diocese for child sexual assault. This had been achieved by doing nothing when he received a complaint, unless the complaint was in writing and the complainant was prepared to be named or had legal representation[14]. He hardly ever reported complaints to police and had on occasion threatened those reporting abuse with defamation. Up until now, clergy did not rise in the church by reporting allegations to police, offering compensation or apologies to victims, or admitting their church had a problem with child sexual abuse.

By 2003, however, Hollingworth's disgrace presented a new kind of threat. Now, the time-honoured path of doing nothing might end in a public scandal. By March 2003, Herft was concerned enough about risk management to tell the diocesan manager and secretary to notify the insurer that "Two clergy and two laypeople who have links to this Diocese are under investigation for complaints surrounding child sexual abuse". He added that the diocesan lawyer Robert Caddies "has also asked me to raise with you the need for us to keep our old policies in respect of insurance, as there could well be a claim again against them if the case went back in time".[15]

*

Two years after the trial, Steve was still struggling in its aftermath. He sent a fax to Herft in April 2003, describing the anguish he had suffered during the trial and upon reading the account of it in the *Anglican Encounter*. "The author of the article is one Peter Mitchell, a man now well known for his honesty and integrity," Steve wrote sarcastically. Steve described the article as "an attack on my credibility and state of mind. I find this somewhat incredible given the nature of what happened to me. I stand by my allegations and hope to further pursue this action in the future."

Steve continued:

> I have recently spoken to a person who's [sic] son was also interfered with by Parker and she recalls my late mother speaking to her in regard to the incident involving my brother and myself. My mother also told her that she had been to the Bishop of the day about this.
>
> I had hoped for some sort of closure in regard to this matter, and some support from the church. All I have seen up until this point is the

churches [sic] determination to discredit me and my family. You might contact some of your senior clergy and find out exactly what my families [sic] contribution was to the church over many years. My family has been scarred to the point where my father (who is suffering from a serious illness) has insisted that the Anglican Church has no part in his Funeral arrangements. This is one of the great tragedies of this whole affair.

Much of this pain and suffering could have been avoided by the Church apologising for what Parker did and Parker himself acknowledging that he had done something – terribly wrong.[16]

Steve had never forgotten his childhood lessons about justice. He wanted Bishop Herft to bear truthful witness to what had happened to him, and to respond to the injustice of it. He wanted Herft to respond with what the philosopher Raimond Gaita calls "a serious, lucid responsiveness to the moral significance" of Parker's terrible crimes.[17]

Two weeks later, on 1 May 2003, Herft replied: "I note the pain and distress in your letter," he wrote, but he told Steve the courts had "dismissed" the case. He defended Mitchell's *Anglican Encounter* article, saying that media coverage of the trial had created widespread community interest. He reminded Steve that "the Dean and I made ourselves available for you to meet with me – the appointments were not kept … At a pastoral level I am still open and available to meet with you."[18]

Steve's letter obviously worried Herft. He wrote to Allen on 6 May 2003, saying that it was "quite critical" that he, Dean Lawrence, Simon Cotterill from the diocesan solicitors, Jean Sanders as the chair of CASM, and the diocesan business manager Bruce Hockman:

meet in the not too distant future to consider the risk aspects and the channels of information sharing regarding the sexual harassment matters concerning the clergy within and outside this Diocese. I do believe that the matters that are now before us within the findings of the enquiry in Brisbane will also create further tensions in terms of how we operate as a Diocese.[19]

As always, Herft had a keen eye for possible legal issues. When he wrote of "risk aspects", he did not mean risks to children from predatory priests. He meant risks to the diocese and to his reputation, and the risk of Steve suing for compensation.

On 13 May, Keith Allen wrote back to Herft, pointing out that if Cotterill, the diocesan lawyer, were to be present at the meeting, it would be important to make "clear in my view, that this is an informal discussion. The difficulty would be that the Diocesan Solicitor will bring into existence documents which may not be privileged and that may impact". He suggested meeting without Cotterill, to which Herft agreed.[20]

Why was he so worried about the discussion not being under privilege? Likely, he was concerned that if Steve were to sue, his lawyer might subpoena documents from such a meeting, which could implicate the diocese in covering up child sexual abuse.

Before agreeing to a meeting with Steve, Herft sought advice about this question of privilege from the lawyer Robert Caddies. On 3 June, Caddies faxed some information about "Statements made without prejudice" to Sanders and Herft. Caddies told Herft to make sure any meeting with Steve was done on a "without prejudice" basis, meaning that statements made at the meeting could not be used as evidence in any legal proceeding without the consent of both parties. However, Caddies warned:

1. I don't think "without prejudice" would have any legal effect in the case.
2. It would undermine your credibility and the relationship you have established with the person concerned.
3. It would have demonstrated a "Cover Up" mentality.
4. It would have demonstrated an absence of care and concern.[21]

During 2003, letters and emails flew back and forth between Herft, Bruce Hockman, the lawyers Robert Caddies, Keith Allen and Simon Cotterill, Jean Sanders of CASM, and Dean Lawrence. At one point there was a memo expressing concern about using Steve's name: "thinking of sending a copy of yr letter to the folks re arranging a meeting – however perhaps not a good idea, as names are named, i.e., Smith." This anxiety over naming names is another example of how the diocese was preparing, in the event of a civil case brought by Steve, not to admit anything by naming him in its correspondence.

After one meeting, the "privileged and confidential" notes show that after prayers, concern was expressed about the process so far, risk management issues, how records should be kept, who could access them, who had possession of the two keys to the filing cabinets where the secret files were kept, and the implications of new legislation from the General Synod (the governing body of the whole Anglican Church). The concerns were all about legal risks, about protecting the church's reputation and its coffers.[22]

There was one glaring omission. What was entirely missing was any discussion of pastoral care for Steve Smith.

*

Why were these leading Newcastle Anglicans so worried about a man whom they had defeated at trial? Partly, because Steve simply would not go away. Any time Steve wrote to Herft, even if he marked his often anguished letters and emails "Confidential", the bishop quickly forwarded them to the lawyers to advise on a risk-free form of wording for his reply. The diocese racked up thousands of dollars in lawyers' fees over the problem of Steve Smith in 2003 and 2004.

Steve wrote many times requesting a face-to-face meeting with Herft. As well as wanting the church to take responsibility for what Parker had done, more deeply, Steve wanted to connect with Herft, one human heart to another:

> All they were panicking about was legal action ... I thought, no. I kept think-
> ing, I'll give these blokes a go, try and do the right thing, and I thought,
> the change may happen within the church ... And if I could force them to
> change how they did business, it [would] have a bigger effect.[23]

However, Steve said, "It was like getting into the Super Max. They just didn't want to talk to me." But Steve kept at it.

Finally, he succeeded. Herft agreed to meet Steve on 13 June 2003. Despite Lawrence's unwelcome presence at the impending meeting, Steve was tremendously buoyed, as he'd been trying to meet with Herft since 1999. Immediately he thanked Herft, reassuring him, "I have no axe to grind."

> I am simply seeking to resolve an issue that has been the primary focus
> of my life for over 25 years. I have a great desire to begin the process of
> regaining my faith and filling the void that has existed in my life for so
> long. My firm belief is that you are a good man, with a firm sense of justice,

and I trust that with your assistance I can finally turn my back on this
episode of my life and forgive those people who have treated myself and
members of my family so badly.[24]

The meeting began at 11 a.m. and finished at 12.30 p.m. At the meeting,
Steve was struck by how Bishop Herft kept looking nervously at Lawrence, as if not knowing what to say. It was clear that Lawrence ran the
show.

> I met with Roger Herft … we were across this big table. He sat in the
> middle and Lawrence sat on his side and Roger Herft couldn't answer a
> question without referring to Lawrence. I found it quite amazing. I was
> upset, and I'd say, what about … why hasn't this happened … and he would
> look at Lawrence … Lawrence controlled Herft, no question of it. [Herft
> was] terrified of him.[25]

Steve could still only bring himself to talk about the last incident at
Gateshead. Herft and Lawrence admitted nothing and deferred to the trial
result. Steve spoke about his family, their strong faith, how much they had
done for the church in Edgeworth, the devastating pain of Steve's loss of
belief, his difficulty in ever attending church again. He talked about the
destruction of his schooling and his employment prospects, and his difficulties in relationships, including the end of his marriage. He told them
about his mother's complaint to Bishop Shevill, and how he had complained to Bishop Appleby in 1984 but that nothing was done about Parker.
That his younger brother had also been abused by Parker, as had another
altar boy he knew, who had later committed suicide. He told them that the
2001 trial had fallen over on a technicality. While Herft and Lawrence took
no responsibility, no doubt primed by the lawyers, in a non-committal kind
of way they seemed to acknowledge that Steve had been in pain, that he
had gone through *something*. Herft later admitted that at this meeting it
occurred to him for the first time that Steve was telling the truth.[26] However, as what followed shows, that realisation did not change his behaviour
towards Steve one iota.

By the end of the meeting, Lawrence agreed to meet and talk with Steve's father and stepmother. On 15 June 2003, Steve wrote to Herft:

Although the outcome may not be what I had hoped for, the very fact that a simple man like myself, had the opportunity to meet with a man of your standing in the community, and had the chance to press my case, is a great credit to you personally. To you and Dean Lawrence, I can only wish the greatest of good fortune and hope that you will remember my children and myself in your prayers.[27]

Herft perked up at the mention of prayers, which would cost him precisely nothing. He wrote back: "it was most helpful to listen to you speaking to us. I hope too that you are now able to move forward, slowly perhaps ... Hopefully, the Dean's commitment to speak with your parents will also help the healing process ... I hope in time you will relearn to pray."[28]

Herft forwarded a print-out of Steve's grateful email to Lawrence. On the margins, next to Steve's expression of gratitude for the meeting, Herft purred: "This is nice, isn't it, and very moving", says the hand-written scrawl. It looked like the troublesome "problem of Smith" was now resolved.

It wasn't.

Steve is an intelligent man. Over the next month or so, he kept thinking about the meeting and the parlous state his life was in. He realised that despite nice-sounding words from Herft and Lawrence, nothing had actually been done. Lawrence had not visited his father and stepmother as promised. A single dad, Steve was still confronting the economic disadvantage caused by Parker's abuse. He loved being a teacher's aide, but it was a low-waged job. Steve had a strong sense of duty to provide for his children.

On 10 August 2003, he wrote again to Herft. His tone had changed. "I have given much thought to my situation and have come to the conclusion that I should be compensated by the church for their negligence. Do you have any thoughts on this matter?"[29]

On 19 August, when he had received no answer, he wrote again. "I was disappointed that I did not receive any reply to my message. I am assuming that you have been away or that I sent to the wrong address."

On 20 August, the bishop finally replied. His tone was cold, brisk and irritated. Why was Steve not moving on? "The sentiments expressed in your email of 15 June 2003 suggested that the meeting on 13 June 2003 had helped you to move on. The dean has made efforts to contact your father but has not met with success."[30]

What efforts, Steve wondered? Lawrence had found his father easily enough when he wanted to stuff Peter Mitchell's odious *Anglican Encounter* article under the door. Did Herft think that one meeting would be enough to resolve Steve's pain and help him "move on"?

Herft advised that Steve, a poor man, would "need to seek independent advice regarding the matters you raise concerning compensation". In other words, get a lawyer. On 21 August, Steve fired off another email, telling Herft:

> I have sought independent advice re this matter and was advised to proceed through the legal system. I was also advised that I would have a strong case to present. I asked for your thoughts in an effort to avoid putting myself through more heartache in regard to this matter.

On the same day, Herft forwarded Steve's email to Caddies, asking, "Please advise how I should respond to the email below." There is a confidential file note on Caddies' response, written by Herft the next day: "Caddies ... advised that my correspondence with Steven should be in hard copy rather than email."[31]

In Herft's next reply to Steve, any warmth towards him has dried up.

> Sadly the matters that have been alleged have pain and heartache attached to them and to those involved no matter what action is envisaged. As I indicated in my letter of 20 August I am unable to comment on the legal course of action for which you have received advice.[32]

On 1 September, Steve wrote back to Herft expressing his despair. "I must now consider what is best for mine and my children's futures. To be abandoned by the church yet again has caused me enormous grief."

Herft's response to Steve's heartfelt letter, on 5 September, was clinical:

> [I] note the contents within it. I am sorry you express a feeling of abandonment yet again by the church, but as I indicated to you in the process of meeting with the Dean and myself, given that you appear to have exhausted all the legal ways in which this matter could be resolved ... our response could only serve in being present to you in a listening capacity.

On 15 September, Steve again wrote to Herft, describing his anguish as a father to see the fallout from the sexual abuse affecting the next generation:

> The problem that I now face is that I am trying to raise 3 children on my own and am faced daily with the limitations that have been placed on me by the behaviour of a priest in the employ of your church. I have lived with this for 28 years and have never received assistance from anyone. I attend Mass on a weekly basis with my work at school, and often hear reference to struggle and inequity. I also sit and listen to sermons advocating the need for Christian behaviour and compassion. I feel that I am in need of compassion and assistance, if for nothing else, for the sake of my children. They are now paying the price for my mistreatment. They will have limited opportunity due to my limited means and will never have the opportunity to study further. It could have been very different if Parker had kept his hands to himself. Once again it is the innocent that suffer. I am sure that God didn't mean things to be this way.

Herft replied by telling Steve that as Parker had been acquitted, he could only respond in a pastoral way. Steve wrote back correcting the bishop: "Parker was not acquitted. The case was no-billed ..." That meant the case could be reopened. "If I have my way, this will happen."[33]

By the end of September, Steve was in a state of angry despair. Late one Saturday night, on 27 September, he fired off another email. "Your lack of response leaves me with little choice. I will now pursue every legal avenue available to me against your church. I thought that we could resolve this matter in a civilised manner. I have nothing to lose in this matter." Herft wrote on his copy, "no need to respond as this begins to canvas the legal issues".

In the new year, on 7 January, Steve wrote to Herft: "I trust that the Christmas season has been joyful for you. I have suffered the usual despair that comes with this time of year. I am not sure that I can cope with this anymore."[34]

Steve sounded close to suicide and Herft must have known that he had attempted this before. Yet Herft's reply was cold and brief. "Greetings for 2004. I am in receipt of your e-mail. I am not sure how else we can be of help to you or to your parents." In the margins of the draft, Herft had written, then crossed out, "given your negative ...", before continuing:

"I am sorry that genuine attempts to make contact with your parents have proved unhelpful to them."

Herft sounded fed up with Steve. As though one meeting with the bishop and the dean should have been enough to set Steve's life to rights, and he should make no further demands. Why did he think "attempts" – as opposed to an actual visit – would be helpful to his parents?

Six months later, on 12 June 2004, Steve wrote to Herft again.

> Bishop, Just a short note to let you know that my life is worse than ever. The actions of one of your priests has certainly left its mark. I can only hope that Parker is paying even a small percentage of the price that I (and my children) have payed [sic] for his depraved actions."

Herft forwarded Steve's agonised email and a draft reply to the lawyers. In his reply, he again claimed that Parker had been acquitted. In his draft, workshopped with Caddies, he also claimed therefore Parker would be protected by the principle of "double jeopardy", which, Herft wrote, meant that "someone could not be charged twice for the same or substantially the same offence". Caddies advised Herft to delete this reference to double jeopardy, and warned that Steve could still bring a civil case against the diocese. In a civil case, the standard of proof would be lower; Steve would be required to prove his allegations "on the balance of probabilities, not beyond reasonable doubt as in a criminal matter".[35] Caddies also advised the bishop to add a line at the end: "I do acknowledge your distress whatever the facts of this matter are and the Dean and I of course remain available etc."

Why did the bishop require a lawyer to remind him to write a few words of care?

In early October 2004, Herft was promoted to archbishop of Perth. Despite Herft's legalistic approach entirely lacking in compassion, Steve responded with typical generosity and on 12 October congratulated him.

> I believe that you are a good man ... You have given me a fair hearing and I will be eternally grateful for your consideration. It is unfortunate that we did not resolve my issue, but I believe that the church has moved forward and is far more aware than it was in the past. If what I have suffered has contributed to this awareness, then perhaps it was not all for nothing.

Once again, congratulations, and I believe that you are headed for great things within the church. Please do not waste your talent for conciliation and compassion.[36]

Herft replied with a much lengthier email than usual, sounding buoyed by his promotion. "Your contribution to our awareness of difficult issues that the Church must face up to is appreciated, though I recognise that the outcome you had hoped for was not realised."

By the time Herft flew to Perth, he and the diocese had offered Steve no recognition of what he had suffered, no compensation and no apology. Steve's life continued its downward spiral. Herft continued onwards and upwards.

PART THREE
A NEW REGIME

CHAPTER TEN

A NEW REGIME

AFTER HERFT LEFT for Perth, Brian Farran was enthroned as the bishop of Newcastle in 2005. Farran would never have been installed without the approval of the influential Graeme Lawrence and the support of all the votes he commanded at the synod.

Lawrence and Farran were old friends. They had been young priests together in the NSW Riverina district, where they had shared a house. Farran had met his wife, Robin, in the parish of Griffith, and they had four children. Describing the experience of sharing a house with Lawrence, Farran told me that it always felt like Lawrence's house, in which Farran lived. Whatever Lawrence wanted to happen, happened. If Lawrence was displeased, he could "make something a Something".

At St John's College, Morpeth, while training as a priest in the early 1960s Farran had joined the sporting crowd, and one could imagine him emerging from a scrum, triumphant, with the ball. As bishop, he had a toughness quite different from the hypersensitive, prickly, timid but ambitious Herft, who had darted all over the world, networking, while leaving Lawrence to run the diocese. In contrast, Farran was more action-orientated, with what some thought was a "crash-through or crash" style. He could be abrasive and insensitive, but he also had a softer side, born of losing his father early and growing up poor with a struggling mother in a housing commission flat. If someone shared his mother's vulnerability, it could trigger a great rush of emotion and he would respond with empathy. He was intelligent, having completed a Bachelor of Arts at the Australian National University, followed by a PhD in ministry studies from the Melbourne College of Divinity, before training as a priest.[1]

Farran came to power as bishop after a quiet revolution had occurred in the Anglican Church. Following the Brisbane Inquiry and the Hollingworth scandal, in 2004 the national General Synod passed some innocuous-sounding legislation, the Professional Standards Ordinance. It was a dull name for a radically new approach designed to put the investigation of sexual misconduct on a rigorous professional footing. Newcastle adopted the Ordinance in 2005.

Before the adoption of the Ordinance, child sexual abuse complaints in Newcastle were handled by the amateurish Committee for Allegations of Sexual Misconduct (CASM). It was a hopeless framework, as Herft later admitted, emphasising "conciliation" and conflating sexual harassment of adults with child sexual abuse. Since taking over as chair of CASM in October 2001, Jean Sanders had tried to improve the lackadaisical record-keeping. When she began in the role, files on sexual misconduct were kept haphazardly in an unlocked filing cabinet in Peter Mitchell's office. She organised them into yellow envelopes and placed them in a locked filing cabinet to which only she, the bishop and the registrar held keys. Bishop Herft also had file copies. On the outside of each envelope was the accused priest's name, the parish, the date and the victim's name. Sanders also instituted a protocol that she was to be notified by email whenever anyone accessed a file.[2] This was a step up from the previous "system" consisting of a little black book containing a "caveat list" of dodgy priests suspected of sexual misconduct, which was apparently passed around discreetly but was frequently kept in the bottom of a bishop's filing cabinet.[3]

Sanders estimated that about thirty complaints of child sexual abuse were reported to CASM from 2001 to mid-2003, each tucked away in a yellow envelope. She was frequently telephoned by distressed mothers who accused Peter Rushton, in particular, of sexually abusing their boys. They usually did not want to leave their names. "I was told by other priests that Rushton was a serial abuser of boys, but no-one lodged a complaint with police," she said.[4] When she checked the files, astonishingly, there was no envelope for Rushton, despite the multiple complaints. Disastrously, complaints were only taken further if they were made in writing, and many victims, their relatives and other informants were too frightened by defamation threats to identify themselves in writing.

The CASM committee included three lawyers – Robert Caddies, Keith Allen and Jim Hellman, who were also all lay members of the church – as well as Sanders, Bishop Herft and other clergy. Every so often at a meeting, a file would be taken out and discussed. The yellow envelope containing the allegations, facts, evidence and any interviews would be put on the table but left unopened, like an unexploded bomb. After an oblique, roundabout discussion, it would be put back in the cabinet.

There were multiple occasions during his period as bishop when Herft should have contacted police about allegations of child sexual abuse but did not do so. The entire budget for CASM was $2000, a derisory sum for such a crucial committee. Sanders later admitted that it was a tokenistic response to child sexual abuse.[5]

The new National Professional Standards Ordinance, however, was a root-and-branch revolution. There were to be no more unopened envelopes and stunned mullet committees gingerly looking at the explosive files before hiding them away in the filing cabinet and doing nothing. No more dithering bishops. Under the ordinance, there would be a salaried director to undertake independent investigations into allegations of sexual misconduct by clergy. The new system did not rely, as Herft's regime had, on complaints being put in writing.

When Newcastle adopted the ordinance, it established the 2005 "Faithfulness in Service" Code of Conduct, which instructed clergy very clearly on what constituted sexual misconduct:

You are to be chaste and not to engage in sex outside marriage ...
You are not to:
　　Sexually abuse an adult
　　Sexually abuse a child
　　Engage in prostitution
　　Visit brothels and other places associated with the sex industry ...
　　View, possess or distribute restricted material containing sex or nudity
　　　　without legitimate purpose
　　View, possess, produce or distribute any form of child pornography ...
Sexual exploitation refers to any form of sexual contact with an adult,
　　with whom there is a pastoral or supervisory relationship, whether
　　or not there is consent and regardless of who initiated the contact or
　　invitation ...
　　Children are entitled to be safe and protected ...
Ministry where children are involved requires absolute trustworthiness ...

Clergy and church workers have authority over children because of their
position and power, because of their greater age, maturity, physical
size, and life experience. Abuse arises from the misuse of authority
or power.

Any form of child abuse is always wrong.

Due to the inherent imbalance of power, children are incapable of giving
valid consent to abuse.

You are not to abuse children.

If you know or reasonably suspect another member of the clergy or church
worker has abused a child, you are to report this to the appropriate
civic authorities and Director of Professional Standards.

Most importantly, the Ordinance placed at the very centre a separation
of powers: professional standards investigations and decisions were to be
completely independent of the bishop. The new regime had three key elements: a director, a committee and a board, all responsible for different
tasks. The professional standards director was responsible for investigating allegations. Evidence about complaints would be examined by a
Professional Standards Committee, selected by the Diocesan Council and
consisting of at least five members, preferably a roughly equal number
of men and women, either clergy or people with experience in law, child
protection or social work. If a case was deemed serious enough, the committee would send the evidence to a Professional Standards Board, which
held hearings into priestly misconduct. Both respondents and complainants could give evidence and have legal representation, which in some
circumstances the diocese would pay for. Any priest accused of misconduct must be given the allegations in writing in a timely manner before a
hearing and offered pastoral care. The board would give a "determination"
on each case and where appropriate would recommend penalties, including, potentially, deposing a priest from holy orders (defrocking).

The Ordinance also spelled out clearly that any failure to report sexual misconduct on the part of clergy or church workers was an offence.
Conduct of a criminal nature, including child sexual abuse, was to be
referred to the police and/or to the Department of Community Services
by the bishop.

The Ordinance broke the conspiracy of silence on child sexual abuse.
Board hearings and judgements were to be made transparent by being held

in public. The media could attend. The board was so independent that it wasn't even obliged to tell the bishop before making its decisions public.

The reason for the separation of powers, Bishop Farran told me, was to put a stop to the Team Church mentality. It was now recognised that for far too long bishops had acted, with their legal and other advisers, to defend the interests of clergy and protect the reputation of the church at any cost. "Mates protected mates," as a later bishop, Greg Thompson, put it. The rights and needs of complainants – the victims of child sexual abuse – were simply not on the radar, except as a problem to be hushed up.

*

By 2005, there were an increasing number of media stories about child sexual abuse. The Catholic Church had been reeling since the 1990s, lurching from scandal after scandal, as priest after priest was convicted of child sexual abuse, including the notorious Gerald Ridsdale from the Ballarat diocese in Victoria, and Vincent Ryan and Jim Fletcher from the Maitland-Newcastle diocese. Joanne McCarthy began investigating and reporting abuse in the Catholic Church for the *Newcastle Herald*, which became the famous "Shine the Light" campaign, often credited with eventually sparking the Royal Commission into Institutional Responses to Child Sexual Abuse.

The public scandal over child sexual abuse in the Catholic Church, however, obscured the fact that the Anglican Church also had a serious problem. With the Hollingworth affair that began to change, and cultural change over child sexual abuse – recognising how widespread it is and the damage it does – was underway.

When Farran arrived in Newcastle in 2005, he had very little experience of dealing with child sexual abuse. The only case he could remember, he told me, was: "In the Riverina, one time, there was a guy at Deniliquin … the police came to the bishop and said, 'If you're getting him out tonight, nothing will happen,' and he just disappeared." That was how, in that era, it was handled. Another dead cat over the fence. Farran told me he had no inkling of a problem of child sexual abuse in Newcastle: "Oh, absolutely none, none at all." His predecessor, Herft, told him nothing whatsoever about the many complaints against Peter Rushton, or about

Steve's complaints against George Parker, or about the multiple complaints against Graeme Lawrence.

Lawrence had been a leading voice in passing the Professional Standards Ordinance at the Newcastle synod in 2005. Farran thought that no
one in Newcastle at that stage quite realised the radical implications of
the new system. He was right. Despite passing the Ordinance, the events
that followed showed that many clergy, prominent laity and parishioners
expected business to continue as usual. Many clergy expected Farran to do
what bishops Herft, Holland and Shevill had always done. The old guard
of the laity – lawyers Robert Caddies, Keith Allen and Paul Rosser, as well
as cronies of Lawrence such as former lord mayor and Labor Party heavy-
weight John McNaughton – were all still in positions of power.

Farran told me that when he arrived in Newcastle, "There was a culture ... of absolute deference to the bishop ... I was trying desperately
hard to help people see that I was an ordinary human being and that they
needed to have an adult relationship with me." However, Farran thought
the deference was:

> two-faced as well ... one long-time serving clergy, a Newcastle person, said
> Newcastle people always hate their boss ... there was a kind of dualism
> going on, really, about the bishop and authority. But people ... couldn't
> believe there was now a separation of powers ... [they] were wanting me
> to intervene [in sexual misconduct cases] and just sort of say, "Well, they
> did the wrong things, but we'll forgive them."[6]

They expected the bishop to hand out forgiveness as Santa Claus hands
out sweets on Christmas Day, without considering the perspective of the
victim. Farran was expected to look after his clergy, in a culture that saw
child sexual abuse as a little sexual misdemeanour to be indulged, one that
did not outweigh a priest's other "good works". This notion of forgiveness
was solely about the priest's sin and the state of his soul. There was no
emphasis on reparation to the victim. It was as though the human being
they had abused did not exist.

Some of the more powerful laity, especially those close to Graeme
Lawrence, also expected to control the bishop. They had dealt with weak
bishops for decades. Keith Allen expected Farran to maintain the existing hierarchies and keep the church's reputation clean. As Farran told me:

> In the case of Keith Allen, he and I fell out pretty quickly, actually. At the
> very first synod, when we passed the Professional Standards Ordinance,
> Allen was Chairman of Committees and he kept trying to tell me what to
> do. I said to him, "Who do you think is running this show, me or you?"[7]

It was the first real fissure and a sign of what was to come. The new regime
was clashing with the old.

The new professional standards framework required a strong bishop.
He needed to be confident enough to let the Professional Standards Committee do its work in complete independence, and to face down criticism
should action need to be taken against a priest.

It was a new regime all round. Gwen Vale was appointed as chair of
the Professional Standards Committee, replacing CASM and Jean Sanders. Vale was a kind person and in correspondence with Steve showed
real concern for his welfare. A very different culture was beginning to
be established.

There was also a new registrar, or business manager, John Cleary, appointed in 2007. The appointment of Cleary turned out to be pivotal. Cleary
was not an Anglican. He was an outsider in another way, too; he had previously worked as a credit analyst in the banking industry, which had been
grappling with the 2001 collapse of the giant insurance firm HIH. The director of HIH, Rodney Adler, was jailed for two and a half years for breaches
of his director's duties. Cleary told me: "ASIC turned up at our office because
we managed his affairs for the bank, and they wanted to see everything ...
any interaction we had with him, we'd file a note ... So, I learnt that discipline of writing notes."

Cleary's habit of writing detailed file notes immediately after meetings was to later prove invaluable in exposing how the church operated.[8]
Farran liked Cleary and thought highly of him; he was dependable, quiet,
conscientious and careful. Farran also thought Cleary was quite an anxious person. Cleary's brother had been a policeman who worked on
child sexual abuse cases, and had committed suicide. Farran thought
this had been hugely influential in forming Cleary's zero-tolerance attitude to child sexual abuse.

After Cleary's interview for the job, one member of the selection panel observed that he was an impressive candidate, but wondered if he
was too mild-natured to cope with what the panellist described as the

"nest of alligators" he would encounter in the church. The phrase would prove prophetic.

Cleary was hired, and two weeks later there was a lunch for him at the prestigious Newcastle Club. The club was the place to be seen for the city's elite: the wealthy, political powerbrokers, influential professionals, the lord mayor, the headmaster of Newcastle Grammar and captains of industry. The bishop, the dean and the business manager of the Newcastle diocese all had automatic membership. Lawrence lived next door and dined there frequently. A supreme networker, he enjoyed mixing with Newcastle's elite. He was often seen, Rod Bower told me, "working the room, and it was very clear who was in charge there. People deferred to him."

The club was originally an all-male bastion modelled on the old British clubs, and locally on their Melbourne and Sydney iterations. Women had only been allowed as members since 2002. The club rooms are wood-panelled and plush, with a mahogany staircase and heavy Chesterfield sofas. Bower described it as a "dusty old gentlemen's club. High-backed leather chairs, private dining rooms, the whole catastrophe". Stepping into the lift, you encounter pictures of early coal-mine managers with their names written underneath. In this predominantly working-class coal town, those managers were men of consequence. The club sits high on a hill beside the cathedral, looking down on the city, with its pulsing smoke-stacks and sepulchral gleam of industry. Its view takes in the Hunter River, whose wide mouth enables a busy harbour of large coal ships and the tug-boats which ferry them out to sea.

When I travelled out to Cessnock, Kurri Kurri, Aberdare, Bellbird and Edgeworth, the places where children had been abused, the poverty was striking. Tiny workers' cottages with few amenities housed large families. It could be a harsh life. In these towns, the rectory of the local Anglican church was usually the best building in the street. Steve came from this world of the working-class poor. Most of the abused children did.

The Newcastle Club is a world apart from this poverty. From the bar with panoramic views, you feel truly above everything in Newcastle; you are looking *down* on the city. There is a whole room devoted to whiskey, and a library of dusty books which looked like they had been donated from a boy's school in the heyday of the British empire: histories of World War I, and the works of Rudyard Kipling, Mark Twain and Noel Coward.

However, in one respect this impression is misleading. The Newcastle church was much more progressive than the evangelical Anglicans of the Sydney diocese. Cleary told me:

> they did embrace women into the priesthood, they did embrace homo-sexual clergy, and I guess it was during the eighties HIV epidemic ... from what I understand, [Graeme] Lawrence created the cathedral as a bit of a safe spot for gay people to come and worship, and it's obvious that there were other like-minded clergy around him, so he wasn't just a sole voice.[9]

Lawrence was also admired because "people say he was a very fine pastor and a very caring man".

However, Cleary quickly learned:

> you would never want to get on his bad side ... Pell-like in a way ... Pell, from what I understand, ran services immaculately and you know, every-one had to be in a straight line and step at the same time and everything was choreographed. Lawrence was the same in the cathedral here, and he was very intimidating to people that he didn't like ... so [there was] a fear of him ...

*

Early in John Cleary's time in Newcastle, in late 2007, Steve Smith rang him. Cleary listened with shock as Steve outlined what had happened, and what he thought had been covered up, including Rushton's and Lawrence's roles. Cleary believed Steve and went to the bishop. "I raised some of it with Far-ran," Cleary recalls, "and he replied, 'John, you are about to be subjected to a very dark era of the church.' I thought, 'What am I getting into there?'" It was the beginning of "a long association" between Steve and Cleary.

Steve was not the only victim to come forward. The new Pastoral Care and Assistance Scheme (PCAS) meant survivors could get compensation from the church without going to court. Cleary felt caught between two cultures: the new, which supported victims, and the old, which still advo-cated lawyering up, admitting nothing and paying nothing. "I think people [were] getting their head around paying the redress while the old guard was still there, thinking, 'Well, people usually just make this up, or, [we should] protect them [the priests] [and] it will all go away ... You know, it was just a whole shift in mindset."

There was a telling moment during a meeting of the Board of Trustees, which governed the church's finances. A board member asked Cleary, "Why are we advertising [for survivors to come forward]? Because we're only, you know, lowering the church's reputation and having to pay out money?" When Cleary hired an ex-policeman to be the professional standards director in 2009, he faced more questions. "It was almost like the criminal saying, 'Who dobbed me in?'"

This period was the beginning of a huge transformation in Steve's life too. The new professional standards framework, and the arrival of new people in the diocese, changed the dynamic between survivors and the church hierarchy. Steve was one of the first to be given compensation from the church, initially a modest amount. At this stage, he had told nobody of the extensive abuse. But for Steve, the compensation was still an important admission of responsibility.

Steve sought and received financial assistance under PCAS in order to move to Perth to be near his daughters. He reflected to me that he had again hoped that with a change of scene, he could leave the "horrible past" in Newcastle behind. In January 2008, Steve wrote to Cleary, telling him that as:

> this matter has cost me career prospects as a young man, my marriage, a great deal of distress and my faith, I think that consideration should be given to a resolution up to the maximum amount. If I was compensated adequately I could resume my life in Perth with my family and finally put this matter behind me.

Steve then thanked Cleary and the church. "There is not much more that I can say except that I wish my parents were alive to see the Church acting in such a responsible and caring fashion."[10]

Gwen Vale carefully read the large documentation file Steve sent to her as part of his application under PCAS. In the file was the offensive eulogy that Parker had delivered at Steve's mother's funeral.[11] Vale wrote to Steve with kindness and respect about his distress over the eulogy. She noticed empathetically that he was "feeling down", so she offered six counselling sessions and finished, "I wish you well."

Canon Paul Robertson was a member of the Professional Standards Committee in 2006 and 2007, deciding Steve's case.[12] He was a pastor of a different ilk to the Anglo-Catholics who had predominated in Newcastle. Quiet, thoughtful and upright, Robertson was from the minority evangelical tradition in Newcastle and had written a well-regarded book on the subject. He believed Steve and told me he thought a serious moral wrong had been committed against him. He supported his claims for counselling and an award under the PCAS scheme of $30,000, to improve on that given to Steve by the state of New South Wales under the *Victims Compensation Act* in 2002. Robertson had been uneasy for a long time about Herft's indulgence of Peter Rushton and was relieved at the arrival of the new regime.

On 15 February 2008, Gwen Vale wrote to Brian Farran that the Professional Standards Committee had:

> reviewed reports from Steve's psychologist and we are satisfied he has a legitimate complaint against this Diocese. He has already received victim compensation through the courts ... We are concerned that Fr. Parker's involvement in this matter not go unrecorded ...

The committee suggested that Bishop Farran "contact the Bishop of Ballarat and issue a caveat against George Parker". Farran did so.[13]

Vale also points out that the committee was very concerned about the conflicts of interest involved in Paul Rosser and Keith Allen representing Parker, and Graeme Lawrence as a court supporter, while also senior members of the Diocesan Council.

> The spiritual and psychological damage to Steven Smith is considerable. The PSC strongly recommend that members of the Diocesan Council think very carefully about their duty of care for both complainants and respondents before they agree to act professionally for either.[14]

What a difference to what had gone before!

However, the new system did not get everything right. In February 2008, a very insensitive "healing service" was organised for Steve. No one from the senior leadership – neither Bishop Farran nor Dean Lawrence – turned up. The service was performed in an almost empty church, attended only by the priest, Reverend Ann Watson, Gwen Vale, Steve's

friend Rachael (whom he would later marry) and a nun. Far from "healed",
Steve felt:

> So betrayed … we did this little church service thing, and I just sat there
> rolling my eyes and at the end of it they gave me this candle, with shit
> written all over it, and … I took it home and threw it in the dam. Like, the
> first thing I did when I got home, I took it up the back and hoicked it in
> the dam. That's what I think of your candle.[15]

Steve suffered another blow when he tried to interest Joanne McCarthy
at the *Newcastle Herald* in his case, and in child sexual abuse by Anglican
clergy. She had been writing articles about abuse by Catholic clergy. However, she blew him off. McCarthy told me she had been preoccupied by
the Catholic cases and was pouring all her energy into that. She couldn't
fathom – yet – Steve's astonishing story of corruption in the Anglican
church. She also told me she feared investigating further because of the
potential effect on Steve's then fragile mental health. Had she taken up
Steve's case, as she did with many Catholic survivors, it would almost certainly have made a huge difference to him.

By 2008, Steve had received his first compensation payout of $30,000
from the Pastoral Care and Assistance Scheme. Although it helped him to
go to Perth, he couldn't escape the past. He kept reading newspaper articles about child sexual abuse by Catholic priests. By 2009, he had decided
to return to Newcastle and fight on. He just wasn't quite sure how. Then
the answer walked through his front door.

CHAPTER ELEVEN

AN ALLY ARRIVES

ONE DAY IN 2009, Steve, by now back in Newcastle and feeling very depressed, heard a knock on his front door.

"I said, 'Who are you?' And he said, 'Michael Elliott. I've just been appointed professional standards director of the Anglican Church.'"

Elliott was a plain-looking man with a serious expression. He carried no extra weight, so his face was angular, even gaunt, with deep crevices lining his cheeks. His eyes were deep-set under heavy brows, but their expression was surprisingly soft. He spoke quietly. Elliott came inside and held out a heavy volume for Steve to consider. It was the 1975 Register of Service for Gateshead parish, which had provided the alibi for George Parker.

Elliot had been examining old cases. "He'd apparently gone into the [archives], going through old files and cases, and this thing was sitting in my file. He couldn't even work out why it was there."

Steve grabbed the book and leafed through it. Ever since the 2001 trial, he had wanted to examine this register containing Parker's supposed alibi. Elliott asked him what its significance was.

> I said, "Here's three or four hundred entries without alteration, but on these pages, there's two entries that are altered, and that's the entries in relation to my matter." And I said, "They're not even in order of date, they've been added along the page." I said, "No one even noticed that."
>
> Elliott looked and he said, "Jeez, yeah."
>
> I said, "It's clearly been added to the page."
>
> "Look," he said, "that date's out of order, and this is crossed out. This is wrong."[1]

Steve had long suspected there was something wrong with the register suddenly produced at the trial. He had even written to Bishop Herft about it, casting doubt on its veracity. But he had never been able to examine it, until now. He spotted the irregularities immediately.

Elliott asked why it mattered.

Steve explained that the case being dismissed – "no-billed" – hinged on whether Parker could have stayed for morning tea after the service, as the boys remembered, or had gone straight to another service, as the register seemed to show.

Elliott was incredulous. "Do you mean the trial fell over on the basis of *this*?"

"Yep."

"Wasn't it examined and cross-examined by the lawyers for the DPP? Did the judge look at it?"

"Nope."

Elliott could hardly believe it. But he got it. Straightaway. From that point, Michael Elliott and Steve became good mates.

Elliott was a former policeman and was not an Anglican. He had been hired by John Cleary as the first full-time director of professional standards. Cleary identified Elliott's qualities in an interview. For the first time, someone with a forensic cast of mind, unclouded by church loyalty and with an understanding of the law, was in charge of investigating sexual misconduct by Anglican priests. As a former police officer, he had no problem recognising paedophilia as a crime, not a minor misdemeanour, or in recognising what the clerical collar might conceal.

For Steve, after Elliott's arrival, everything changed. "Michael was the first ally I'd ever had."

Elliott was on a steep learning curve about a very dark network of paedophiles who had operated unimpeded in the Newcastle diocese for decades. He was on a similar learning curve about the grey network of clergy and lay protectors who had been assiduously covering up the abuse. His independence from the church hierarchy was underscored by the fact that initially he worked from an office in a separate building, and later from a separate floor of the Anglican offices in King Street.

Bishop Farran gave Elliott access to the yellow envelopes of confidential files but did not examine them himself. Elliott found that some files were empty or contained little information. Like George Parker's. Apart from the register which Elliott found in the filing cabinet, despite the complaints by Steve's mother in 1975, and by Steve himself in 1984, 1996 and 1999 and the 2001 trial, Parker's file was almost empty, apart from a one-page form with a tick beside "Acquitted".[2] Which was, of course, untrue. In 2003, Keith Allen had told Bishop Herft that he was going to hand over a "large file" on George Parker to the diocese.[3] So where was it? Either someone had taken all the documents or Allen had never handed them over.

Steve and Elliott formed a productive alliance. Elliott was working alone without any staff to assist with the huge task confronting him. He would often ask Steve to help him find information. They would meet for coffee, and Elliott would ask Steve about priests – who were the bad ones? – or ask Steve to look something up in the Newcastle Library. Steve spent hours going through microfiche in the library, finding information on priests. He had by now amassed a huge knowledge of offenders in Newcastle and those who had protected them. He proved to be a natural sleuth.

I'm pretty good at finding people ... I'd use online things, social media, and find people for him. I gave him a lot of intel. He didn't know anyone in the church, and he would ask, "Do you know Father so and so?" And I'd say, "Yeah, I know him. He's a grub." There was a lot of stuff about Rushton he didn't know, so I filled him in ... there was never a week that went past that Michael was not asking me to find out something ... We shared a lot ... I got to trust him, and that was beneficial for both of us.

Elliott found the church's files on sexual misconduct alarmingly sketchy. Many were incomplete, with pages missing. But gradually, thanks to more survivors of abuse coming forward under the new regime, Elliott started to map out those who were, in police language, "persons of interest". His files kept growing and growing. So did his awareness of how these crimes had been covered up. He had begun working with the Catholics at Zimmerman House, the diocesan child protection unit and professional standards service established by the Maitland-Newcastle diocese in 2007. He knew from this experience that the Newcastle Catholics were very bad when it came to child sexual abuse and cover-ups. But he gradually formed the view, based on evidence, that what had gone on in the Newcastle Anglican Church was actually worse – more organised, with abusing priests often aware of, and co-operating with, one another.

Between them, John Cleary and Michael Elliott – both outsiders to Anglicanism – discovered a culture of denial, where the values and thinking-as-usual constituted a web of deceit and self-deception. The diocesan council, the synod and the various church committees were all shaped by the Team Church mentality. There was far too much psychological identification with priests who were seen as superior to their flocks and more important than their victims and were protected without question. Cleary had an apt phrase for this. He called it a "pro-respondent" culture – where the respondent was the accused priest – in which, he explained to me, the interests of the accused priest were defended at all costs. Their reputation and above all the reputation of the church must be protected. All sympathy in this culture gravitated, in an unquestioned way, to the accused priest. Cleary thought the leading lights in this culture were tone-deaf to survivors, to the point of being anti-survivor. The ideals of justice and restitution for survivors, at this point in Newcastle, had only just begun to find support.

Elliott realised the sexual misconduct went further than the clergy. He began to believe that other men were involved. One survivor fled the office, crying out when he saw a powerful member of the laity there, "He's one of them, he's one of them!" Who had abused boys at St Alban's Boys' Home? They weren't all priests, according to survivor Paul Gray. So, who were the others? The clergy's misbehaviour acted as a portal, an invitation to a highly pleasurable world of sexual transgression, enabling others to live out a darker version of themselves.

As an ex-policeman and a non-Anglican, Elliott was not only an outsider to this culture of denial. He was also implacably opposed to it. Elliott was absolutely clear that paedophilia (sex with children) and hebephilia (sex with underage teenagers) were crimes. It was black and white, no shades of grey. There was no normalising, minimising, fudging or covering up.

That straightforward understanding of the criminal aspect of paedophilia meant Michael Elliott was like a hand grenade thrown into a vicar's garden party. Elliott had another incendiary quality. He saw things not from the point of view of the perpetrator or the institution but from the point of view of the survivor. There had been an extraordinary lack of empathy for the victims of child sexual abuse – a trivialising and minimising of what the experience meant for the child. The culture in the church had been to think they were lying or to ask, "Why don't they move on?" Bishop Farran and John Cleary both paid tribute to Elliott's rapport with survivors. And as Elliott built up trust and encouraged survivors to come forward, more followed.

For Steve, the work Elliott asked him to do was empowering. He wasn't paid, but psychologically he had swapped the role of powerless victim for someone who had agency. He was now the pursuer, the investigator, coming after the perpetrators. And he was good at it. Elliott was piecing together an astonishing subterranean culture of sexual transgression involving children, committed by networks that had been rife and unchallenged for a long time. Abusers had been put in positions of power on committees investigating sexual misconduct, keeping the whole sick and seedy culture going.

Elliott and Steve were of one mind about what had gone on in the Newcastle diocese. But while Elliott's views were consistent with widespread community norms, they created an extraordinary amount of conflict within the church. In a diocese where the bishop was seen as someone who should defend the interests of his clergy, giving complete independence to someone like Elliott, with his uncompromising moral clarity, was explosive. Elliott could be blunt, laconic, even dour. Bishop Farran described him as "austere". Steve summed up Elliott's style as an investigator as "determination. Like he'd just go down the rabbit hole and keep digging. He just wouldn't stop." And he was hated for it. It caused pandemonium in the Newcastle church and then an ugly backlash, including vandalism and intimidation.

The number of files Elliott held grew from 100 to about 1000, representing both known offenders and persons of concern. Almost all these files related to child sexual abuse, ranging from minor unverified intelligence to criminal convictions.

Among the many shocking cases Elliott uncovered was a racket of underage male sex workers, known as Troy's Boys, allegedly run by an Anglican priest in the late 1980s from Church Street, one of the main streets of Newcastle. Bishop Holland was in charge of the Newcastle diocese at the time. The connection was uncovered when a concerned citizen, Peter Matthews, noticed that the phone number in newspaper advertisements for Troy's Boys was the same as that of a local priest. Matthews wrote to Bishop Holland, alleging that one of his ministers was "running a male escort agency from his unit at 5/37 Church Street".[4]

Now, in 2009, Elliott tasked Steve with finding the advertisement for Troy's Boys. Steve spent hours in the microfiche room of Newcastle Library, painstakingly reeling through old copies of the *Newcastle Post* and *Newcastle Star* from 1986 to 1988. Finally, he found it, in the last six months of 1988: "We offer you the hunkiest young studs at their best. Straight and gay services for your demand, we never close. Ph 7 days".[5] The ads for "Troy's Boys" included the priest's Church Street address and his phone number.

At the time, the priest had been questioned by Bishop Holland, who replied to Matthews on 26 October 1988:

> I have taken up the matter with [the priest] who has informed me that these advertisements appeared without his knowledge and had been placed with malicious intention by some unknown person wanting to smear his reputation.[6]

Holland accepted this denial, although he told Matthews to contact him if he had "any further evidence" and to mark any such correspondence as "Private and Confidential".[7] A new notice about "Troy's Boys" appeared in the *Newcastle Post* on 8 and 15 November 1988, informing patrons that the brothel:

> Has temporarily closed down whilst moving premises. We expect to reopen in the near future, bigger and better than before. Please watch this space for our new phone number.[8]

In 2009, Michael Elliott and Steve went together to look at the block of flats where Troy's Boys had once operated. They realised it was brazenly operating close to the backyard of Bishopscourt, the bishop's residence, at 34 Brown Street.

This was just one of the stories unfolding through Elliot's investigations. His files now contained not only Steve's case, but testimony from survivors including Paul Gray, Phil D'Ammond and others who had come forward to describe their experiences at St Alban's Boys' Home. Gray told of being taken by Rushton to the "Fucking Room", where multiple men raped him and other boys. This suggested to Elliott that there was an organised ring. Another St Alban's boy told Elliott that he had been taken out of the orphanage and sexually abused by a number of Anglican priests.

Elliott also learned of allegations that Graeme Lawrence ran "Men's and Boys' Parties", where homeless teens would be picked up, plied with alcohol or drugs and abused by priests. The number of perpetrators that Elliott was aware of just kept growing. Among them were the lay worker Jim Brown, priests Michael Cooper, George Parker, Father James Brown, Reverend Stephen Hatley Gray, Robert Ellmore, Eric Griffith, Allan Kitchingman, Walter Ogle, Peter Rushton and the trainee priest Ian Barrack.[9]

As Elliott uncovered all this, he kept investigating Parker.

*

There was one key new discovery about Steve's case. On 30 September 2009, Elliott rang and interviewed Tim Mawson, a former diocesan archivist, and discussed the letter from Keith Allen to Herft which noted a discrepancy between the yearbook and the Gateshead register that might cause trouble for the diocese if Steve brought a civil case in court.[10] Elliott read Mawson the Allen letter and told him it "appeared suspicious". Mawson then told Elliott:

> that he suspected the former Diocesan Registrar Peter Mitchell and Solicitor Keith Allen instigated a situation that resulted in confusion around the identity of Parker as the offender when [he] appeared in court (by destroying /falsifying documents).

Elliott questioned Mawson as to why he thought that.

> Mawson indicated he had heard Allen and Mitchell joke about the matter on two occasions, once whilst travelling in a vehicle with them when they joked "yeah it's funny how those documents went missing isn't it".[11]

In another file note, Elliott summarises a conversation with Mawson not describing documents as going "missing" but being altered.

> Tim Mawson told Michael Elliott in a phone conversation that he had overheard Mitchell and Keith Allen joking about the parish registers that

turned up during the George Parker committal trial indicating an alibi for Parker. Mawson got the impression that the two had been involved in some form of fabrication or amendment of the registers.[12]

Elliott's discoveries kept Steve fighting. His isolation was replaced by camaraderie, as he and Elliott engaged in a collegial enterprise in uncovering the truth. Instead of denial and dismissal, he was receiving confirmation and respect. A new sense of agency and confidence began stirring in Steve's soul. But everything he discovered was triggering, too. He still struggled, and at times during these years he was homeless. It was several steps forward, then several steps back.

Elliott cared about Steve and became his advocate in the diocese. In February 2010, Elliott was so worried he sought out Ian Smith, Steve's elder brother, to ask whether he thought Steve was at risk of suicide. Steve had been homeless, sleeping on the beach or in the park or with acquaintances. He had asked Elliott for money and was spending much of his time at the Newcastle Mall.

Michael arranged for more counselling sessions to be paid for, and these allowed Steve, for the first time, to begin to disclose the extent of the horrific sexual abuse he had experienced, although he still couldn't disclose the full extent of the anal rapes. The psychologist diagnosed him with severe PTSD, depression and anxiety.

Whatever Steve's mental state, he kept on fighting the church.

> I kept agitating, I just kept on going, going, going, going … I was annoying the Christ out of them … I was so determined to call these people to account, and I was learning a bit more about Lawrence and what they'd been up to, because Michael was filling in some gaps for me … These are the people who were protecting Parker, and they're a bunch of crooks. And I was getting angrier and angrier.

CHAPTER TWELVE

THE OMERTA CODE AND THE FAKE CELIBATES

"I DID NOT have sexual relations with that woman," Bill Clinton famously declared after having a sexual affair with Monica Lewinsky, which involved not intercourse but oral sex. Clinton simply reinterpreted "sex" very narrowly to mean vaginal intercourse. He rationalised and minimised his actions. He was not "really" being unfaithful to Hillary. He was not "really" lying. He had not "really" done anything wrong.

When I was researching an essay on the Catholic Church and child sexual abuse for the human rights journal *Right Now* in 2013, I was shocked to discover that for some Catholic priests, "celibacy" might be interpreted in a very Bill Clinton kind of way. It did not necessarily mean what ordinary worshippers thought it meant – that celibate priests has no sexual relations with anyone, in order to give themselves entirely to their Christian mission.

Notwithstanding the many Catholic priests who live according to their difficult vows of celibacy with honour, I was not far into my research before I had a growing file documenting cases of sexually active priests. It kept growing. It was the same all over the world, in the USA, Ireland, the UK, Italy, Australia, South America, even the Vatican. There were many priests who lived with women and fathered children, and priests who were actively gay. Richard Sipe, a former Benedictine monk, has estimated that up to half of Catholic priests in the USA are sexually active. Not since I read *My Secret Life*, the sexual memoirs of a Victorian-era gentleman writing as

"Walter", had I encountered such a double world: a public world of piety and punitive prudery, coupled with a shadowy sexual underworld of private libertarianism.

My concern in this book, however, is not with those who had sexual relationships with adults. It is with a very different category of priests: those who engaged in child sexual abuse but who maintained it wasn't really breaking their celibacy vows. Patrick Parkinson, when he was professor of law and child protection at Sydney University, outlined in a 2013 lecture what a survey of clerical offenders found:

> Some priest-offenders rationalise their abusive behaviour on the basis that sex with boys is not a breach of their celibacy vows, whereas sexual relations with a woman would be … Indeed, a high number of respondents described offenders they knew as having a strong commitment to celibacy.[1]

Although Catholic Canon Law 1395 forbade sex with other men and children, by far the greatest emphasis and energy in Christianity has been expended on controlling women's sexuality and reproduction. And not just in the Catholic Church, but in all churches. Hence sex with women is considered the greatest sin. There is even a biblical foundational story – of Eve as the temptress of Adam.

Those attitudes shape the "cognitive distortion" Parkinson outlines, which "may well be an important factor in sex offending against boys … If priest-offenders have a strong commitment to celibacy, then sex with women or girls will not be permissible". But sex with men, teenage boys and younger children can be "rationalised" as "either not being a breach of their celibacy vow at all or a sexual peccadillo which will be tolerated in the Church and forgiven by God". The word "peccadillo" means the breaking of a minor rule, defined as "something small" or an "unimportant sin or wrongdoing".

Although Parkinson was talking about Catholic priests, he could have been describing a number of Anglo-Catholic "celibate" offenders in Newcastle. Peter Rushton was a leader of a group of Anglo-Catholic priests – including George Parker, James Brown and Michael Cooper – who wanted many aspects of Catholicism restored within the Anglican Church, including celibacy. All these men were later exposed as child sexual abusers and were precisely the kind of fake "celibate" that Parkinson talks about. The group held to the line that celibacy was the highest calling for a priest. For them, celibacy had a very particular meaning. It meant no sex with *women*. If sex with women was regarded with disgust, sex with other men, and with boys, was not only justified, as Parkinson argues, but also treated as a priest's entitlement. They were extremely sexually active with one another and did not morally distinguish between sex with adult men and sex with minors.

There is another aspect of Newcastle Anglicanism to be considered. Many in the dominant Anglo-Catholic faction, like Catholics, held to the view that priests were "ontologically different" – transformed into a higher being above ordinary mortals – after ordination. Bishop Farran told me that "Rushton certainly had that view, very strongly. He talked about that publicly … there were lay people in the diocese who were quite acquiescent to that culture as well." This elevated the clergy and distorted how parishioners thought about their priests, amounting to a kind of hero worship.

Bishop Herft, like Bishop Holland, "had a very high view" of priests; "those who were ordained were of a very high moral and spiritual integrity." That meant no one challenged their behaviour. The "specialness" of the priest, his mystical, elevated status above ordinary mortals, was reinforced by all the trappings of the Anglo-Catholic tradition: calling priests "Father" rather than "Reverend"; the liturgy; the elaborate lace frocks; the incense. Canon Paul Robertson, as an evangelical, once questioned the use of incense at the cathedral and got a stinging letter from Herft about it.

Tim Costello, a Baptist minister and later CEO of World Vision, was invited to speak at the Newcastle Anglican conference in the late 1990s. He was struck by how dominant the idea was that priests were no ordinary mortals – that they were God's representative on earth, superior to their flock.[2]

This belief in the superiority of priests allowed what is called "clericalism", but is really clerical narcissism, to flourish. All narcissism is toxic. Its crucial element is felt superiority to others. Life as a charismatic clergyman satisfied the needs of narcissistic supply: grandiosity, an excessive desire for attention, an overweening sense of entitlement to special treatment, a willingness to exploit others and a lack of empathy. Narcissism obliterates any recognition of, or attentiveness to, the Other. Children were dehumanised, seen as of lesser worth than adult male priests. As Ian

McEwan writes in his novel *Atonement*, "It wasn't only wickedness ... it was the failure to grasp the simple truth that other people are as real as you."

The former bishop of Canberra and Goulburn, George Browning, points out that Anglo-Catholicism had its roots in the "Oxford movement" of the nineteenth century, which "at its best gave enormous energy and vitality to the church ... The church took up the cause of social justice, the care of the poor and social reform. It was easy to see the gospel of Jesus lived out in this tradition." The Brotherhood of St Laurence is "the most well-known legacy of this fine tradition, ironically founded in the Newcastle Diocese in the 1930s".[3]

"At its worst," however, Browning says, "the Anglo-Catholic Oxford movement was authoritarian; it exalted the authority of the priest and made an unhealthy separation between clergy and people." Bishop Browning gives two telling examples from the Newcastle diocese. In 1974, as acting principal of St John's College at Morpeth, Browning attended the ordinations of theological students. At the ordination of a young priest at Wallsend, Peter Rushton, as rector, gave the homily. Rushton "made the extraordinary assertion that by virtue of his ordination, the young man was ontologically different. He was no longer simply an ordinary human being. His being was now different, requiring appropriate respect, loyalty and obedience from the people." Browning remembered Rushton as someone who "seemed more concerned for the vocation of the priest and the trappings associated with it than the proclamation of the Gospel of Jesus". Browning had come to the priesthood from jackarooing, and in Rushton "there was little common humanity I could recognise or relate to".

The second striking example Browning gives concerns Bishop Shevill. After a few months as bishop, Shevill gave "an extraordinary performance" at the synod. He "was clearly unhappy with the manner in which he had been received. He made a speech about his importance and how lucky we were to have him ... the message I heard was he did not want men of integrity who would be loyal and who would resolutely speak for what they considered to be right."

From these two examples, although Browning thought Morpeth College was "not in itself germane" to the "predatory behaviour", he could not help but ask himself whether "this controlling and authoritarian view of priestly activity could be fertile ground in which perverted and pernicious moral activity would find a seed bed". (Bishop Farran was blunter about Shevill, describing him to me as "a terrible narcissist".)

Clerical narcissism was also at the heart of the cover-ups. It established a hierarchy of human value in which priests mattered far more than their victims. Closing ranks and doing everything to protect the reputations of the clergy and the church was seen as a good thing. The missionary aspect of Christianity played a role, too. It seeks converts. This makes going public about child sexual abuse all the more difficult, as creating a scandal would diminish the likelihood of attracting new members.

Furthermore, many parishioners believed what they were told: that celibate priests were special creatures, changed by ordination, placed above ordinary sinning mortals. They were sexless. And, therefore, it was safe to leave children in their care.

*

Archdeacon Peter Rushton and Dean Graeme Lawrence were the two most powerful clergymen in the diocese. Rushton was a charismatic preacher with a large following of disciples. Rod Bower, who disliked Rushton intensely, nonetheless spoke of his mesmerising voice when giving a sermon. "Physically he was very short ... but very large. He was like a barrel, basically, a keg on legs ... if you saw him in the street, in plain clothes, he would be a very nondescript person." All that changed when Rushton swept down the aisle in his lace frock and stood before the pulpit. There was an

> incongruity in what you're looking at, [with] what you were hearing. He had ... a kind of sweet and mellow voice, the tenor of his voice was quite beguiling ... he was charismatic, and certainly at Wallsend, his charisma drew large congregations ... you had to get there early to get a seat. Now, I understand from my own experience, that does something to the ego. Rushton had an enormous ego, and I think [it was] fed by his success.[4]

Rushton was a High Church Anglo-Catholic, so his services were rich in ritual and liturgy, with all the bells and whistles and the waving of the thurible containing incense. Bower told me Rushton's clerical garments had lots of "lace, yes, lace and birettas and pom-poms and cassocks, red ... Rushton was attracted to the more extreme forms of ecclesiastical dress".

Bower thought it had a strong element of "self-aggrandisement. As I reflect back, he had a small-man syndrome, he was compensating for that."

To some among his flock, Rushton could be caring, but he was also an aggressive, socially dominant man, a ruthless operator who brooked no opposition and knew how to manipulate people. He was known to be very nasty when crossed. He smashed anyone who challenged his sexual behaviour with a defamation threat and verbal abuse. Such bullying can be effective, at least in the short term. Milder-tempered people fear bullies, and many people will simply avoid conflict. A number of people described Rushton to me as a narcissist. A Wallsend parishioner, Christopher Hall, said, "He gave me the impression that he felt the congregation was there to worship him rather than Christ, and he only responded to people who treated him as a demigod." Valerie Hall recalled: "He didn't show me or the other local parishioners an ounce of pastoral care. I thought of him as a woman-hater and a show pony, with all of the 'High Church' palaver he carried on with (the incense, fancy robes and so on)." Reverend Colvin Ford said that at clergy gatherings, Rushton might deign to talk to you or not.

> He inevitably went to his own group – a lot of the young clergy – and spoke with them. They all thought he was marvellous … because he was outspoken, I think – he took that high ground of "I'm right and that person's a fool."

Rushton had an arrogant, authoritative manner that some called pompous. Ford avoided Rushton wherever possible because of his sharp tongue. "It was very hard to outpower Peter Rushton in words … he would have only been a young priest … and he'd already had a column in the local *Anglican Encounter* called 'Father Peter says' … this authoritative piece that he'd write."

Bower was initially mentored by George Parker, who was part of Rushton's Anglo-Catholic faction, some of whom were sexually involved with one another and all of whom were sexually abusing children. Bower had no knowledge of that but did notice that they "assumed" he was gay because he was young, single and male. When Bower showed interest in a woman – his future wife, Kerry – he was turfed out of the group. After leaving the faction, Bower was dubious that it amounted to much theologically, but

rituals of worship were important to the Anglo-Catholic group. Bower saw
trainee priests, not yet liturgically competent, being "terribly vilified by
Rushton ... by character assassination". "When you're a student [priest],"
Bower explained, "you're the most disenfranchised group in the diocese.
You're ... no longer a lay person ... but you're not yet a priest ... so you're in
this liminal, vulnerable space. You've given up your career in many cases,
you have no income for three years."

Rushton was protected by what Colvin Ford called the Gang of Three:
Graeme Lawrence, Peter Mitchell (before he was jailed for theft) and Reverend Bruce Hoare, a long-time lover and close friend of Lawrence's. They
acted together, Ford thought, to protect Rushton from discovery. Ford was
outside the inner power bloc, which held its own meetings before the official meetings; the former was where everything was decided. "Sometimes
you might raise a point and it would be agreed to, but most of the time you
just ended up with a block. Nothing. It wouldn't get past." Rushton was
master of the put-down, as was Lawrence. Rushton was also well known
for his misogyny and implacably opposed to the ordination of women. He
once refused to perform a wedding because the bride was allegedly showing too much of her breasts.

Clergy such as Ford and Paul Robertson were concerned about the
reports of wild parties at Rushton's rectory, of men and boys – altar boys –
after Sunday services. Busloads of men were said to come up from Sydney.
They went to the local spas and bathed naked. People had suspicions about
the number of young boys observed around the Wallsend rectory. Rushton
made Paul Robertson's wife, Noreen, uncomfortable. So, there were concerns – but, as Robertson said, where was the hard evidence?

The "hard" evidence – in the form of complaints about Rushton sexually abusing boys – was in the possession of bishops Holland and Herft,
who did nothing. In 1980, five people had gone to Bishop Holland about
Rushton abusing the five-year-old son of the assistant priest at Wallsend.
The boy's mother found her little boy crying, curled in a foetal position and
utterly traumatised. Rushton had masturbated and ejaculated in front of
him and interfered with his testicles.[5] The assistant priest and his wife, as
well as parishioners Valerie and Christopher Hall, went together to complain to Bishop Holland. Holland was dismissive, did not believe them and
blamed the incident on the priest's older son. He told them, "Homosexuality is here to stay whether you like it or not," a comment which showed

a grave conceptual error, falsely conflating homosexuality with the abuse of boys. Valerie Hall remembered that Holland demanded photographic evidence, and that they had all discussed on the way home how on earth they could get such evidence. Christopher Hall recalled that he and his wife were shocked by the bishop's dismissive attitude:

> he was very defensive and seemed almost offended that the priest's wife should make such allegations against Rushton. He said that unless she had definite evidence, there was nothing he would do. I got the impression from the Bishop that if any of us were to repeat these allegations, there would be repercussions, particularly for the priest … It was a very short meeting, at the end of which Bishop Holland dismissed us like naughty school children and he gave no commitment to follow up on the matter. We drove back home together in dismay and were never contacted by Bishop Holland.[6]

When news of their complaint reached Rushton, he was furious. The priest and his wife felt a subtle but decisive shift in the attitude towards them; they felt they were being sidelined. The family left the diocese, and eventually the assistant priest resigned from the clergy, a shattered man.

Lesley Danger, another worshipper at Wallsend, also raised the abuse at a meeting with Bishop Holland, who told her: "I can do nothing as [Rushton] has threatened legal action." Rushton also found out that another parishioner, Pamela Wilson, was writing a letter of complaint to the bishop about the abuse. He telephoned her, threatening her with defamation if she did not "destroy it immediately". Afterwards she thought, "Well, evil rides around the church", and that the whispers she'd heard about Rushton's sexual abuse of children were true. Wilson, the chair of the pastoral care team, was ordered by Rushton to remove the priest's wife from the team; the priest's wife explained to Wilson that the likely reason was that another family had shared with her that their son had also been abused by Rushton. Wilson left the Wallsend parish and moved to another Newcastle parish of Waratah, where Father Ken Munns, who had been close to Rushton, told her Rushton was a "paedophile".[7] Valerie Hall consulted a good friend, Reverend Bailey, who was the pastor at Maitland Jail, who told her "that there wasn't anything he could do as it was a 'closed men's club'."

Instead of immediately reporting Rushton to the police and disciplining him, Bishop Holland promoted Rushton in 1983 to archdeacon of Maitland. Holland continued to think well of Rushton as "a competent priest, a competent leader, and I thought he would do well as an archdeacon".[8]

In 1998, during Bishop Herft's time, Rushton had faced down credible allegations of possessing child pornography by threatening defamation, by lying and by bullying. When Rushton moved from Maitland to the parish of Hamilton, a removalist, Jim Jackson, contacted Reverend Colvin Ford to report that his men had found child pornography while moving Rushton's possessions. Ford informed Bishop Herft. Ford told me, "Rushton was extremely angry with me when he saw me. If he'd had a bat in his hand, I'm sure he would have hit me. And I simply said, 'Well, Peter, it's true.' And he turned his back on me." Incredibly, Herft despatched Rushton's close friend and lawyer, Greg Hansen, to ask him whether it was child porn. Rushton's denial was accepted.

Rushton was a serial paedophile. Holland in 1980 and Herft in 1998 both missed a chance to stop him in his tracks.

CHAPTER THIRTEEN

WHERE HAVE ALL THE MEN GONE?

AFTER BRIAN FARRAN was appointed bishop of Newcastle in 2005, he was asked by a South Australian bishop whether he would take Reverend Roger Dyer. There had been some trouble in Dyer's previous diocese; he had encountered financial impropriety and had been unwise enough to say something about it.

Farran met with Dyer and liked him. "I thought he was very honest and open." Farran appointed Dyer to the suburban parish of Wallsend, where Peter Rushton had been a popular priest for a decade, before being promoted and taking up other positions.

Rushton retired in 2001 and, after a period of poor health, died in 2007. In 2006, when Dyer first arrived at the pretty grey stone church with its pale pink blossom in the spring, he was looking forward to a fresh start. At St Luke's, despite many years having elapsed since Rushton's time at Wallsend, Dyer encountered a parish still mourning Peter Rushton's departure and, in 2007, his death. It can be extremely hard for a new parish priest to follow a popular one. Loyal parishioners grieve the loss of the priest who married them, christened their children, buried their loved ones, shared their joys and sorrows. The new priest can be compared unfavourably to the old, while new ways of practising the faith can seem just plain wrong.

A decade before Dyer arrived at Wallsend, during 1996 and 1997, he'd been a parish priest in the parish of Nhill, now the parish of West

Wimmera, in the Ballarat diocese in Victoria, ministering at the Kaniva Anglican church. There he encountered a retired former Newcastle priest, Stephen Hatley Gray. Gray was a "dead cat over the fence", moved on from Newcastle after being convicted of the anal rape of a fourteen-year-old boy in 1990 and placed on a good behaviour bond. He was still a practising priest; Keith Allen had falsified Gray's resignation date to the day before the rape charge, meaning Gray had, on paper, been in good standing with Bishop Holland when he resigned, and could therefore later be reinstated at a parish elsewhere. Some Anglicans in Newcastle, who assumed Gray had disappeared in disgrace, were astonished to see him on TV in 1992, presiding over a service at Belanglo State Forest for victims of serial killer Ivan Milat.[1] Gray had also been re-employed by the Anglican Church, starting at the Willochra diocese in South Australia as a youth worker, before eventually retiring.

When Dyer first met Gray in Kaniva in 1996, he discovered that Gray had formerly been the priest there from 1980 to 1982. After leaving Kaniva, Gray worked in Kings Cross with homeless street kids and sex workers in the late 1980s before moving to Newcastle, where, in 1990, he was convicted of rape.[2] Dyer knew nothing of this subsequent history but thought there was something odd about Gray's departure from the ministry. In the congregation of Kaniva, he soon noticed that all was not right. Where were all the men? The men who'd been altar boys and young teens in the early 1980s, when Gray was the priest, were now adult men who assiduously avoided the church. They had "been affected by the paedophilic activities of Stephen Hatley Gray. I observed that men in the parish would relate to me but would not become involved in any aspect of church life", Dyer observed.[3] When Dyer did speak to a male member of a family, they would often say something like, "You'd never get me in a church again." Dyer told me: "I found out about Gray's activities from his own lips and then joined the dots as to why he had retired."[4]

When Dyer arrived in Wallsend in June 2006, he began to notice a similar pattern. According to his wife, June, it took about eighteen months to identify something deeply wrong in the parish. The Dyers found it hard to put their finger on exactly what it was – at first. Archdeacon David Simpson told Dyer that his "express role was to rejuvenate St Luke's" because parishioner numbers had declined after "Rushton had been removed", as Rushton was a "colourful" priest and things had become "hot" in the parish.[5] A priest's career can fall on the hurdle of declining attendance. Falling numbers mean falling collections, which are viewed dimly by the church hierarchy. There is a business aspect to every parish church. Is it financially viable? That is why priests sometimes cook the books to make it seem they have more congregants than they really do. Dyer was worried by the disparity between what he had been told about Wallsend and the small numbers he was seeing at Sunday worship. He felt he had been "misled".

After Rushton's death, the undertaker, John Murray, a powerful figure in the parish who had been close to Rushton and to Graeme Lawrence, approached Dyer about honouring Rushton by interring his ashes under the altar at St Luke's in Wallsend. Murray offered Dyer a glass or two from an expensive bottle of scotch: "I know when someone is buttering me up," Dyer recalled.[6] Dyer told Murray to seek Bishop Farran's permission, but Dyer also told the undertaker that "I had serious misgivings concerning Rushton's sexual conduct and I thought it inappropriate for his ashes to be placed within the church building."[7]

Dyer's misgivings about Rushton did not go down well. "That's when stuff hit the fan … It was after this conversation that things in the parish started to deteriorate, and I felt that I was being alienated and undermined."[8]

Bishop Farran knew Rushton was regarded as an eminent priest in the Newcastle church and agreed to his ashes being interred. When Dyer and his wife went away for Christmas, Rushton's mates sneaked the ashes in. Dyer was furious.

Not long after, there was an anonymous complaint that Dyer had behaved abusively at the Wallsend aged-care home. It struck at the heart of his vocation. "That devastated me … Wallsend nursing home was filled with car-crash victims, young people incarcerated in aged care … people in wheelchairs … it was powerful, unseen work."

Michael Elliott, who had by now joined the diocese as professional standards director, investigated the complaint and cleared Dyer of all wrongdoing. But Dyer was stung. He saw the complaint as payback for his refusal to inter Rushton's ashes. He felt let down by Farran, who told him privately that he had been cleared but did not say so publicly. Dyer wrote to Bishop Farran, saying he was gathering character references and testimonials from parishioners. Farran thought Dyer was being oversensitive to the ordinary slings and arrows of parish life.

At this stage, the conspiracy of silence around Rushton's sexual behaviour with underage boys had not yet been broken. There had been private complaints that went nowhere, rumours and uneasiness, but no public recognition of Rushton's criminal behaviour. At Rushton's wake, however, there had been a pall over the proceedings, as Paul Robertson remembered:

> On that day, even though there was all that lauding, there was a feeling that this guy had been a disaster in the diocese, that he had been responsible for sexual misconduct and that this was going to come out.

Dyer thought that until Rushton's crimes were confronted, Wallsend would not be able to fulfil Farran's vision of "ministering communities in mission". This vision, based on Farran's doctoral thesis, saw the church as "a community of ministers" in which "every person in the church has abilities and gifts to offer".[9] Dyer wrote a long email to Farran, arguing that Rushton's toxic legacy meant the parish could not move forward; Rushton's impact on the parish was "a festering sore".

Dyer shared his concerns about abuse in the parish with another priest, Reverend David Battrick. Battrick was widely thought to be a favourite of Bishop Farran's and was touted as a likely candidate for early promotion. He was young, handsome, blue-eyed and fair-haired. Dyer expressed his concerns to Battrick, but in mid-2009, at a meeting at which Dyer, Battrick and the bishop were all present, Battrick denied that Dyer had told him any such thing.[10] The strain of the previous few years welled up, and Dyer burst into tears. After the meeting, Farran wrote to him, expressing concerns about his "volatility". Farran admitted to me that for this reason he didn't at first give much credence to what Dyer was saying about Rushton's abuse.

After this meeting, Dyer wrote to Farran, thanking him for his "care and concern for my welfare". The assistant bishop, Peter Stuart, replied on Farran's behalf, noting that he and Bishop Farran shared a concern "that you are more unwell than you may have realised". He asked Dyer if he was taking any psychotherapeutic drugs – implying, Dyer thought, that if he wasn't, he should be.

A narrative was emerging in the senior leadership team that the problem was Dyer, not the Wallsend parish. Assistant Bishop Peter Stuart wrote to Dyer's doctor, telling him they were:

"not in a position" to let Roger undertake Sunday duties … We are concerned to ensure that Roger is doing all that would be beneficial to enable him to return to ministry … that he is addressing any underlying issues that may be triggering symptoms … As far as we can tell, the placement Roger has is not more onerous than other clergy of similar age and experience. The issues that Roger is dealing with are within the normal array of complexities that parish clergy must field.[11]

But what Dyer was coping with – the fallout from one of the worst clerical paedophiles in Australia – can hardly be regarded as "within the normal array" of parish "complexities".[12]

Dyer felt he was in a split universe. On the one hand, he had built up enough trust that survivors of Rushton's sexual abuse started to come forward, telling him horrific stories. On the other hand, he felt the leadership of the diocese, apart from John Cleary and Michael Elliott, seemed to be doubting his word and were proceeding with business as usual. Dyer did now have mental health problems, suffering from anxiety and depression, high blood pressure and constant migraines. In 2009 he had a serious breakdown and took months of sick leave under medical advice.

Dyer was experiencing the misplaced adulation for Rushton at the same time as learning Rushton had been an abuser. In brazen acts of performative disrespect, Rushton's supporters called Dyer "Boy", laughing and talking loudly to one another during his sermons. Dyer's opposition to the interment of Rushton's ashes was symbolic of a deeper issue. He was refusing to acquiesce in the "official" history of the diocese, as captured in the title of Joan Murray's hagiographical history of the Newcastle cathedral, *The Vision Splendid*. In exposing the fact that there was nothing splendid about Peter Rushton, but rather sordid child sex offences, Dyer had upset the hitherto unquestioned narrative of Rushton as a shining light of the church. By uncovering the truth about an icon, Dyer was committing sacrilege.

At the same time, more and more men began to return to the church. As they gained confidence, they told Dyer their terrible stories. Some would break down in tears while talking to him at the back of the church. Dyer would send them to Michael Elliott. Elliott was entirely open to what Dyer had to say about the Wallsend parish. By now, he had formed the view that there had been a paedophile ring and that Rushton was at the very centre of it.

Stories of Rushton's foul activities kept surfacing. Roger Dyer was told by a trusted parishioner that "because Rushton was single", elderly female parishioners "would go and clean [his] house every week. And they used to laugh about him being celibate. 'We'd find used condoms under the bed,' and it was sort of acceptable because this is what happened."

I asked, "Did they know it was underage boys?"

"It was an assumption. From what he said."

One woman told Dyer that Rushton had sent a love letter to her young son. In another family, Rushton abused all three sons but turned their father against them by alleging they had stolen something from his car. For a pious family such an accusation was devastating, and the father believed the priest rather than his sons. That alienated the boys from their father and destroyed the family. A church worker told Dyer in anguish about being groomed by Rushton and seemed in a state of deep moral and sexual confusion. Dyer felt the young man had been led into dark sexual territory by Rushton.

These stories are made more plausible by the later evidence of two other convicted paedophiles, Reverend Lindsay McLoughlin and a lay worker, Jim Brown. Both were lovers of Rushton and both felt used, dominated and controlled by him. He introduced them to abusing boys. Phil D'Ammond, who was abused by Jim Brown, said: "Jimmy was Rushton's apprentice, Rushton was the master." In 2010, Brown was charged for sexual abuse of multiple boys, with his trial set for 20 September. Just before the hearing, on 13 September, Brown rang Elliott and confessed he:

> felt groomed into a culture within the Anglican Diocese of Newcastle where sexual abuse of boys was accepted as the norm. He claimed he had a consensual sexual relationship with both Fr. Rushton and Fr. Lindsay Mcloughlan [sic] although he felt these relationships were abusive.[13]

Lindsay McLoughlin also described an abusive sexual relationship with Rushton, in which McLoughlin was exploited and manipulated.[14] He described Rushton as "a bully, autocratic and very controlling".[15] He also thought George Parker knew that Rushton was abusing boys.[16] Reverend Paul Robertson's wife, Noreen, had known McLoughlin as a boy and both thought him a promising young priest. They were terribly upset by McLoughlin's conviction in 2016 for child sexual abuse and thought that Rushton had drawn him into his dark net of sexual predation. They acknowledged, however, that McLoughlin must have had a predilection.[17] McLoughlin was jailed for sexual offences against two boys in the 1980s. The first case included fondling, oral sex and an attempt to have anal intercourse with a thirteen-year-old boy. In the second, he was found guilty of abusing another boy at Rushton's residence at Wallsend. While naked and with an erect penis, he had rushed up behind the boy before the child ran away in fright.[18]

*

In December 2009, Dyer wrote to Bishop Farran asking him to perform a "Healing Eucharist" to "assist those who have been affected in any way" by the allegations of abuse. Dyer noted that "a significant precipitant of these allegations was, without question, the disposition of Fr Peter Rushton's ashes under the pulpit of St Luke's". The resulting spiritual issues in the parish, Dyer wrote, were "an admixture of confusion, betrayal, guilt, love and anger towards Father Peter and all aspects of his legacy ... I find Shakespeare's famous line both poignant and pertinent to the situation; 'the evil that men do lives after them, while the good oft lies enterred [sic] with their bones.'"[19]

News of the healing service, which Rushton's victim-survivors were invited to attend, was an affront to the adoring coterie still defending the hallowed memory of Rushton. Clergy in the diocese began turning away from Dyer at functions, and eventually stopped talking to him. Initially, Dyer recalled:

> I could sit down at the dinner table with the former Assistant Bishop of the Diocese, Richard Appleby, and I knew him well enough to call him Richard, and I quite liked the guy [when] I didn't know anything about this stuff. In the end, he wouldn't even answer the door when I went there.[20]

At clergy retreats, "they would ignore me completely. I was persona non grata ... I would not be spoken to, and the other clergy were so frightened of this system, except for a few, like Fergus King and Colvin Ford." At one retreat, Ford knocked on Dyer's door, concerned after he'd retreated from the group with a migraine. Ford went to the pharmacist for Dyer and took him out for a cup of tea. Dyer appreciated his kindness. Ford quietly confirmed that Dyer wasn't imagining things, explaining the longstanding concerns about Rushton.

There were other important allies, including Michael Elliott and John Cleary. Dyer wrote to Elliott before the service, saying "I feel that I live in a world of denial as I still hear whispers and innuendo that abuse was widespread, yet silence prevails." In an email to Elliott in April 2010, Dyer informed him of "another alleged victim ... a man now aged 40+ who was an altar server under Rushton". When Rushton made sexual advances to him, "the boy had told his father but was not believed ... The consequences of this have had a horrendous effect on the entire family." Dyer urged the man to come forward, but he trusted no one "apart from me".[21]

Elliott wrote to the man the same day and asked Dyer to forward it.

> Dear friend, I understand you have been discussing matters of serious concern with Fr. Roger. Unfortunately the church has not always dealt with such matters appropriately. Fortunately times are changing and we are now committed to listening and supporting survivors of abuse by Clergy and Church workers. I have much experience in this area and feel I can help you and support you on this journey. I can offer you the following:
> 1) Validation – I will listen to your story and accept it.
> 2) Understanding – I understand the painful effects of abuse.
> 3) Confidentiality – Your story is treated with the highest level of confidentiality.
> 4) Action – I strive to prevent further abuse in the church.
> 5) Support – I will support you as best I can.[22]

This was exactly the kind of letter that Steve Smith had desperately needed but never received over so many years of struggle.

Another ally for Dyer was Paul Robertson, who told me he wanted to give Dyer credit for outing Rushton:

> Roger Dyer ... is the whistle-blower at Wallsend ... he was the guy who cracked the whole thing open as far as Peter Rushton was concerned ... and all they could say was he was high maintenance. They pushed him

off. I said we knew Rushton was a paedophile ... Roger Dyer was the big breakthrough. He is vital to this, he's a bit of a hero in it, in some ways ... people who had been abused came forward to speak to him.[23]

Bishop Farran also acknowledged Dyer's contribution, admitting that his perception had initially been clouded by Dyer's breakdown:

Dyer had been to see me, like, I give Dyer credit. He really was disturbed by all of this. And the trouble was, because he had previously come to me seeking support with some of his interpersonal issues within the parish, at first I found it difficult to know if this was another matter of that nature or if this was something more serious. So I tasked Michael Elliott to investigate it and it became clear it was serious. So, he and I went, one Saturday, to the [Wallsend] parish ... and there were four people who came, one by one ... to see me ... And then they went across to Michael to lodge the [complaints] ... but I was there really to hear the story and to apologise ... It was a powerful experience.[24]

In October 2010, Michael Elliott persuaded Farran to make a public apology via a media statement to the victims of Rushton's child sexual abuse over forty years. The apology led to a *Newcastle Herald* cover story by Joanne McCarthy, under the headline "Hunter Priest's Evil Child Sex Secrets".[25] There was a picture of Rushton, grinning jovially, with his distinctive goatee beard. The story reported that Bishop Farran had broken down in tears at an event the week before, where victims of child sex abuse recounted the crimes committed against them. Farran told the *Herald*, "The memories for these people are so powerful ... It is extraordinary, the devastation that's occurred."

After this story was published, Farran was completely thrown by Peter Rushton's sister coming to see him.

A really nice lady ... she was letting me know what effect it had ... on her adult sons, of the story coming out ... Of how they were being treated in their workplace ... you suddenly realise the effect on ... innocent people, their lives turned upside down ... of course I wrote to her and apologised to her.[26]

While at a human level it is awful that Peter Rushton's sister and nephews had to cope with the fallout from him sexually abusing children, Farran need not have apologised. Exposing Rushton and publicly apologising to his victims was an enormous step forward for the Newcastle diocese. Farran was the first bishop in decades to show some spine. However, his excessive concern for "secondary victims" highlights the underlying ambivalence of Farran's administration. He was definitely moving on from the old culture of cover-up. He was conscientiously implementing the Professional Standards Ordinance and respecting its independence. Real progress was being made – but at times with uncertainty and trepidation.

No wonder. There was an immediate, savage reaction against Farran for besmirching Rushton, who, it was said, could not defend himself from the grave. The backlash came from clergy and parishioners, especially those at the cathedral, and, of course, from the Newcastle Club crew.[27] Farran, accused of "defaming the dead", feared the backlash could destabilise the fragile new professional standards regime.

Dyer, meanwhile, still did not feel welcome in Newcastle, although he was now being believed about Rushton. He wrote to Michael Elliott:

> It is apparent that the institutional church is in denial of the effects of their failures at every level ... I remain convinced there is a need for a public apology and real repentance at every level of the institution for we are making a mockery of ourselves while denial remains the norm.[28]

What finally sealed Dyer's fate, he felt, was his speech at the 2010 synod. Despite the public outing of Rushton in the *Newcastle Herald*, when Bishop Farran addressed the synod about media stories "publicising serious allegations against a high-profile priest",[29] Rushton wasn't explicitly named, which angered Dyer.[30] He'd also heard that "they were about to sack Michael Elliott", and so decided to speak out. Bringing a motion without notice, he "got up and publicly said, this diocese must recognise the effects of child abuse on the work of the ministry". According to Dyer, several people tried to thwart his motion, including David Battrick (the ministry development officer), Christopher Bird, who was then the provincial master of the Society of the Holy Cross (Societas Sanctae Crucis or SSC) in Australia and Chancellor Paul Rosser, who cried out "No!" in a kind of drawn-out groan.[31] Stephen Pullin, the archdeacon of Newcastle, "attempted to physically stop me from going up the stairs to present my motion, at which point I called him 'the Bishop's boy' and pushed him to one side."

Dyer's speech caused a great commotion. There was a standing ovation. One female priest told him, "I just saw a brave man fall on his sword." June Dyer recalled, "As we [went out] ... there were people congratulating us right, left and centre. At last, someone has done something."[32] Strangely, the motion was not put in the synod minutes. Dyer's moment was airbrushed out of history.[33]

Knowing he was now unwelcome in Wallsend, Dyer sought a transfer to the parish of New Lambton, where Paul Robertson was retiring. Farran sent a cold email telling Dyer New Lambton didn't want him and that the diocese was "considering other priests for this appointment".[34] Dyer realised there was no place for him in Newcastle. This could have been disastrous – a priest without a parish has no house and no livelihood. However, to his relief, Dyer was accepted into the diocese of Bathurst, west of Sydney.

While Dyer's experiences in Bathurst are not the subject of this book, one incident is relevant. In his role at Bathurst, Dyer had to counsel an undertaker who had prepared for burial the body of a cleric who had died in a wetsuit after an autoerotic sex act. Where had this cleric trained and practised as a curate?[35]

At Wallsend parish, under Peter Rushton.

*

When Steve saw the *Newcastle Herald* article exposing Rushton, he exploded. He wrote a furious email to Bishop Farran, listing all the times the diocese had been alerted to Rushton's sexual abuse. Then he outlined his own story of abuse by George Parker and its aftermath. All the years of hurt poured out of him.

> Rushton was a predator, as was Parker, James Brown, and in later times [others]. Laurence [sic] chose to ignore this. It is obvious that these people were protected by Laurence and others ... You have protected offenders for years ... You have already stolen my youth, my innocence, my life, destroyed my family, and put a lot of effort into destroying what was

left of my life. Pursue me at your peril. (bear in mind that my first sexual experience was at the hands of a tobacco and wine smelling priest)

Whilever i still have breath in me, i will seek a public and detailed apology from your church. You have stolen 35 years of my life. Then to come out with the hypocrisy of apologising to Rushton's victims. It sickens me. If i dont receive an acceptable reply within 48 hours, i will go to every media outlet that is prepared to listen. Enough is enough.[36]

When Michael Elliott saw Steve's email, smoking with white hot anger, he wrote to Bishop Farran, saying, "I believe this man deserves a formal apology and he has never received one." Farran agreed to meet Steve.

At the meeting, listening to Steve, Farran was overcome with emotion and left the room, weeping. He told me:

I'll never forget that meeting. I was so upset … He told me how he'd been treated. The thing that … really got me going was his mother, who was a church organist … she took on Shevill, who was an arrogant bastard, actually … he's an absolute narcissist … I thought, this woman went and faced him, and he treated her like dirt. And that really set me off crying, actually. How brave she was, and how vulnerable. The sort of vulnerability of a working-class woman, going up to take on. this pontificating, terrible man.[37]

Farran described to me the shock of realising the effect of the abuse on Steve.

Terrible … [it] had screwed Steven's life up. I really like Steve; I think he's a great guy. I reckon he could have been a priest actually. He would have been a very good one … Michael was there, thank goodness too. That's when I realised … how important Michael was, the trust that he had gained from these people.

Steve also recalls how important Michael Elliott was in getting the apology. "When Rach and I went in and met him, [Farran] apologised. "Farran's an alright bloke … he said, 'What do you want?'" Steve told Farran: "'I want an apology.' And I said, 'I want it printed.' I said, 'You bastards managed to give me a kicking and now you can apologise for it.'"

Steve wanted the apology printed in the *Newcastle Herald* and the *Anglican Encounter*. In November 2010, the diocese released Farran's apology to Steve.

> I recently met with Mr Steven Smith, a former member of the church. Based on that meeting and other available information, I believe Mr Smith and his family were treated inappropriately over an extended period of time by members of the Anglican Church after he reported that he had been sexually abused as a child by a member of the Church. I wish to extend a sincere and public apology to Mr Smith and his family for this situation and the pain and trauma they have experienced as a result.[38]

The statement was published in the *Newcastle Herald*. The apology was also printed in the *Anglican Encounter* – a sweet victory after Peter Mitchell's deceptive account of the 2001 trial.

At last, after thirty-five years, Steve had an apology. He cherished it. It wasn't, though, the end of the road. He was going to fight on.

And just then, the biggest scandal of all broke in the diocese. This time, it was about Dean Graeme Lawrence.

CHAPTER FOURTEEN

THE WOLF HIDING IN PLAIN SIGHT

IN LATE 2009, the dean of the cathedral, Graeme Lawrence, was reported to Michael Elliott, director of professional standards, for sexual misconduct with an underage boy in the early 1980s. (It was not to be the last such report.)

Bishop Farran immediately suspended Lawrence. Other priests – Andrew Duncan, Bruce Hoare, Graeme Sturt and Lawrence's partner, Greg Goyette, a music teacher and church organist – were also suspended over sexual misconduct with the same person. For Steve, the shock was immense but also a revelation. "Lawrence was a child molester, and I'm ringing this helpline to talk, and he's a paedophile."[1]

The fox had been guarding the henhouse. The implications were enormous. Lawrence had been known as the kingmaker: he controlled the appointment of bishops and other senior clergy and had created a network by strategically placing his supporters so that nothing was ever done about child sexual abuse. Suddenly, the reason for his actions was clear. Lawrence wasn't just the most important figure in the protection racket; he was the perpetrator at the centre of a paedophile ring.

From 1993 to 1999, Lawrence had chaired the Board of Enquiry, which was eventually replaced by the Professional Standards Committee. Like Peter Rushton, he had been on the Panel of Triers, which was supposed to discipline clergy, from 1996 to 2001 and from 2005 to 2007. He was a member of the Board of Investigation, later replaced by the Pastoral

Financial Advice Board. Through these key governance roles and through sheer force of character, he had played a pivotal role, wielding power over each bishop he had served under.[2]

When one examines these crucial committees from 1993 to 2008, when the old pro-priest regime began to break up under Bishop Farran, one finds a roll call of clergy who were eventually suspended or defrocked for sexual or other misconduct: Bruce Hoare, Graeme Lawrence and Peter Rushton; clergy who were their supporters and acolytes such as Wayne Sheehan and Chris Bird; and laity who were uncritical supporters of Lawrence such as Keith Allen, Paul Rosser, Laurie Tabart, John McNaughton, Robert Caddies and Peter Mitchell.[3] It was like branch stacking in a political party.

When Elliott searched the yellow envelopes, there was no file on Lawrence, despite three complaints of sexual misconduct with children being made to Herft during the 1990s. The first complaint was made in 1995, by two devout Christians, Robert and Bronwyn Wall, who ran youth camps. Two boys separately complained that Lawrence had sexually abused them. Lawrence was supposed to be their "spiritual guide", and they also knew him from the cathedral. The boys wanted to remain anonymous but "were concerned about Lawrence having access to other kids".

The Walls, knowing Lawrence was going to another of their upcoming camps, consulted Brother James Howey, a Franciscan monk, who was the youth leader for the diocese. Howey promptly organised a meeting with the Walls and Bishop Herft for 10 July 1995.[4]

The Walls were shocked when Bishop Herft seemed uninterested in what they were saying. Herft told them that unless they disclosed the names of the boys, the allegations would be defamation. "He wanted to know all the details and asked for the names." As that would be breaking the boys' confidences, the Walls refused. "He indicated to us if we continued to complain about Lawrence, we would be facing legal action for defamation of character."[5] The Walls were frightened by the legal threat. They decided to take the matter no further, but after the meeting they felt Herft was frequently checking up on them. Although these allegations concerned the most senior clergyman apart from himself in the diocese, Herft kept no record of the meeting with the Walls – no file note or diary entry – and nor did he record his subsequent meeting with Lawrence about the accusation. However, that meeting certainly occurred. Herft wrote to the Walls in July 1995:

> Further to your meeting with me I have raised your particular concerns
> with the priest against whom the allegations were made and he has clear-
> ly informed me that as far as he is concerned he [was] not aware of
> any indiscretion.

A simple denial from Lawrence was enough to shut the matter down.

Herft enclosed documents which the Walls could fill out if they wanted
to take the matter further, explaining:

> If there is any foundation at all in the allegation, the Church will take
> every step to see that the matter is resolved and the offender duly dealt
> with. However, it is equally true that if the matter is all speculation and
> rumour and has no basis, then we must be conscious that we are ruining
> a person's character and integrity. I am sure the strong Christian ideals
> you hold to will recognise both elements within this case.[6]

There were two more allegations that Lawrence had abused children.
In December 1996, Reverend Brian Kelly, a rector at Engadine, wrote to
the archbishop of Sydney, Harry Goodhew, telling him he had received
complaints about Lawrence sexually abusing "young boys", although
the family of one of the boys was reluctant to press formal allegations.[7]
Kelly met with Archbishop Goodhew, who advised him to contact Bishop
Herft, since Lawrence was now in Newcastle. Kelly did so, but wrote again to Archbishop Goodhew in February 1997, telling him he'd had no
response from Herft.[8] Goodhew rang Bishop Herft, who told him that he
had spoken to Lawrence, who had "denied any wrongdoing in the past".
Goodhew's memo of the conversation notes: "I do not know if the discussion related to [any] person other than those now expressing concern."[9]
Herft did not report the serious allegations about Lawrence to police or
to the Committee for Sexual Misconduct. Goodhew thought it was Herft's
jurisdiction, so left it with him and did nothing more – much to Reverend
Kelly's frustration.

In July 1998, Goodhew received another allegation about Lawrence.
Reverend Bruce Clark told the archbishop about a conversation between
Reverend Tony Drayton and a parishioner, David Andrews. Andrews had
previously lived in Griffith, and he alleged that Lawrence had "sexually
harassed a number of families in Griffith ... I understood he had been

sexually abusing boys". Goodhew advised Clark to contact Bishop Herft, but "beyond this there does not appear to be anything else that can be done at this time". Goodhew claimed that he didn't realise he could have made a complaint to the police "even if the Griffith families did not want to press charges".[10]

Herft handled these three serious allegations about child sexual abuse by simply asking Lawrence in a private conversation whether the allegations were true. When Lawrence denied them, he was believed. No further investigations occurred. Lawrence was not reported to police, which by law he should have been, and no yellow envelope files on the complaints were created.

Why was there no yellow envelope for Lawrence? Had an envelope been created and destroyed later? Herft later admitted that he did not inform Jean Sanders of the allegations against Lawrence when she attempted to impose some order on the records of child sexual abuse complaints between 2001 and 2003. Was it that Herft did not write such notes, precisely in case they were later found? Or were they written and subsequently "disappeared"? When the bishop was away, Lawrence, as commissary, held the key to the filing cabinet containing the sex secrets of the diocese. Michael Elliott found evidence that after Lawrence retired, one of his minions had shredded large numbers of incriminating documents. They jammed the shredder and were dumped in garbage bags. Elliott got hold of the bags and passed them to Detective Jeff Little, who painstakingly put the documents back together. One was an invitation to Lawrence and Goyette to a night of "naughtiness" at a "house of debauchery" wearing only their underwear.

*

Elliott now told Steve about an entirely new case that had landed on his desk, dating from Lawrence's time in Griffith in the Riverina during the 1980s. In late 2009, a man I will call H, after his pseudonym CKH at the royal commission, came forward and alleged abuse by Lawrence, Lawrence's partner Greg Goyette, and several other Anglican clergy, beginning in 1979 or 1980 when H was fourteen.

Homophobia was widespread in Australian society – stigma and persecution of the LGBTIQA+ community were pervasive, including gay hate crimes such as the murder of Scott Johnson in 1988. A revolutionary movement had begun for one of the most important human rights struggles – gay liberation. Gay pride was exemplified by the celebrations of the Sydney Mardi Gras, first held in 1978. At that first march, there were 532 arrests, reflecting what the movement was up against. Many men remained in covert relationships because they had to. Consensual sex between men could be punished by imprisonment and was not decriminalised in New South Wales until 1984.

As a teenager, H was a devout young Christian who was trying to reconcile his strong faith with being gay, in a church where homosexuality was still taboo. The child sexual abuse started when H was a parishioner in Lawrence's parish of St Alban's.[11] Andrew Duncan, then a junior priest in the parish and a friend of Lawrence, befriended H's family. In the summer of 1979–1980, when H was fourteen, Duncan was invited to stay with the family on a river boat. One warm night, Duncan and H were sleeping out on the deck. Duncan got very drunk. He came over to where the boy was sleeping, told him he loved him and performed oral sex on him.[12] The next morning, H and Duncan held hands under the kitchen table. The teenager imagined he was in love.

Duncan explained to the boy about gay relationships. H assumed he was being initiated into the world of gay sex. Years later, he admitted that he had no idea that what was happening was child sexual abuse; "I had no understanding that such a thing existed." Duncan continued to abuse the boy sexually on a regular basis for the next couple of years, mainly mutual masturbation and oral sex. On one occasion, in 1980 when he was fifteen, H was in Duncan's bed when Graeme Lawrence knocked on the front door. Duncan got up, dressed hastily and spoke to Lawrence. The boy's bicycle was outside the house, which Lawrence observed. When Duncan returned, H said, "it was apparent that he thought Lawrence knew what we were doing." Duncan told H not to worry, as "He's part of the family."[13]

H assumed that by "family", Duncan meant Lawrence was part of a secret society of gay clergy. The secrecy and stigma surrounding being gay, a direct product of homophobia, was utterly central to what happened to H. Paedophilia needs the cover of secrecy because it is against the law. In the early 1980s, however, so too did any consensual sexual activity between men. The code of silence around being gay, particularly for clergymen, obscured for this very intelligent teenager that what was happening was child sexual abuse, an abuse of power by a parish priest, not a gay sexual relationship.

Duncan's sexual abuse of H continued until about 1985. By 1980, while still a child, H "had formed the belief that Graeme Lawrence was aware of the sexual activity" between H and Duncan. Lawrence had a clear legal duty, if he saw or suspected that Duncan was sexually abusing H, to report it to the police. He did not do so. He also had a clear fiduciary duty, as the parish priest responsible for H's pastoral care, to report Duncan immediately to the Anglican bishop of the Riverina. He did not do this either.

There are two issues here. The first is conduct which breaks the law. When Lawrence did not report Duncan's abuse of a minor, he broke the law. Until 1990 Lawrence was guilty of a common law offence called a misprision of felony in concealing the crime of child sexual abuse. From 1990, the law changed. It was now a statutory offence under section 316 of the *Crimes Act 1900* (NSW), making it illegal to conceal any 'serious indictable offence' which was punishable by five or more years imprisonment.[14]

From 1984, it was no longer illegal for two consenting adult men to have sex. However, there remains a second issue. Even after the secular law decriminalised homosexuality, the Anglican Church had strict codes of conduct around sexuality, even in a relatively liberal diocese such as Newcastle. Sexual relations, whether heterosexual or homosexual, between clergy and parishioners were clearly defined as not permissible in the Anglican Church because of the potential for an abuse of power. Even once H was over the age of consent, there was a clear power imbalance between an older priest and the boy. Duncan and Lawrence had responsibility for his pastoral care. Any priest who had sex with a teenager in their care, even if the teenager was over the legal age of consent, could be disciplined for "examinable conduct", bringing disgrace or scandal on the church and violating the "faithfulness in service" code of conduct forbidding sex with parishioners. The penalty could be suspension or defrocking.

Lawrence did not tell anyone in authority – the police or the bishop – that he knew Duncan was sexually abusing H. Instead, he started sexually abusing H himself. Not long after he saw what Duncan was doing, Lawrence visited H at home while H's parents were there. H was then sixteen years old and still a minor by law. Lawrence asked to go to the teenager's bedroom to see H's confirmation certificate. There he put H's hand against his trousers, where H could feel Lawrence's erect penis. Lawrence then unzipped his fly, exposed his penis and said to H, "You can have this anytime." The door was open and the boy's parents were nearby.[15] It was breathtakingly audacious.

A short time later, in 1981, H went to the rectory to see Lawrence, who was his parish priest, about prayer. Lawrence made a sexual overture, took H to a back room of the Four Rivers Christian Bookshop and masturbated him. H went on to have other sexual experiences with Lawrence, usually mutual masturbation and oral sex, until 1985, when H was in his second year of university. H turned eighteen in 1983. The diocesan prosecutor, Phil Lloyd, would later note, at a 2010 hearing into Lawrence's misconduct: "So if it [the abuse] ended therefore in 1985, for all but two of the years of this sad process, you [H] were a child in terms of faithfulness and service?"

"Yes."

"When I say child … in terms of physical proportions, you're not a large person now … were you smaller than average as a child?"

"Yes, I was."

At a certain point, around 1982, H was invited to the rectory for dinner with Lawrence and his long-time partner, Greg Goyette. They both sexually abused H at the same time. This occurred again on a number of occasions over several years. Lawrence and Goyette also both continued to abuse H individually.

After H came forward in 2009, it was Michael Elliott's job to investigate the veracity of his complaint. Elliott interviewed H, as well as people H had told about the sexual abuse over the years, who confirmed H's disclosures. As documentary evidence, H gave Elliott a number of sexually suggestive letters and explicit cards Lawrence and Goyette had sent him. One card depicted a naked male figure with an erection adorned with a large gift bow. Another, sent by Lawrence, featured a young male with an erection and the caption "Thank heavens for little BOYS! For Little BOYS get BIGGER Every Day." Lawrence had written: "Now isn't that true?? Thank heavens! Enjoy the Card!! Much love G."

Goyette also sent the teenager many sexually suggestive cards and letters. One showed a naked man in a shower, captioned "I like a man wet and willing." On another was a picture of a naked man performing oral sex on another naked man. Goyette had written: "I prefer the 'head' of this card." He also referred to pornography which had "some excellent 'group' shots that I'm sure you would find edifying … Love Gregory xxx".[16]

H also told Elliott about an incident of group sex involving H, Lawrence, Reverend Bruce Hoare and Reverend Graeme Sturt, at a clergy conference in Narrandera in 1984. By now, H was nineteen and at university. He had been considering becoming a priest himself. After the day's conference proceedings, Lawrence, Hoare, H, Sturt and a seventeen-year-old boy gathered in Lawrence's motel room. They all drank a lot of whiskey, and the younger boy passed out on a bed, dead drunk. Hoare and Lawrence both began to have sex with H, taking turns to perform oral sex on him. Sturt watched, stroking the lower stomach of the unconscious boy. When the lad suddenly started vomiting, H "became protective" and rushed to look after him, cleaning him up and taking him back to the room he was sharing with Bruce Hoare, where the boy went to sleep. Then Hoare and H had sex.

As H was by this stage nineteen, this incident did not break any laws. It did, however, violate the Anglican's "faithfulness in service" rules about sexual exploitation when there was a relationship of pastoral care. And it was very much the result of the grooming and sexual abuse that had begun when H was fourteen. When asked, Lawrence denied having been at the Narrandera conference, but other clergy who had attended confirmed his presence.

Elliott first handed the H case to police in the Riverina. It was given to an inexperienced junior detective in Griffith who, after many months, decided not to take it further. Devastatingly few sexual assault cases get to committal, let alone trial, even today. That police don't take a historical sexual abuse case further does not mean there is no evidence, simply that they are weighing up how likely it would be to get to committal or succeed at trial. (In 2012, the Newcastle police were willing to take the case further, but H declined.)

When the Riverina police did not go ahead, it became a church disciplinary matter. Elliott sought advice from an experienced barrister, Garth Blake SC. Blake was a senior Anglican, the chair of the national Anglican Child Protection Committee from 2001 to 2004, a member of the Sexual Abuse Working Group and chair of the Professional Standards Commission from 2005. He was instrumental in the development of the national Professional Standards Ordinance of 2004. Blake carefully examined the brief of evidence Elliott gave him. In a sober and confronting report, he described exactly what had happened in each instance of sexual exploitation. For each, he explained which parts of the Crimes Act and the Anglican Canon had been violated. Blake advised Elliott that it was likely the Professional Standards Board would "regard the conduct as sufficiently serious to bear upon the fitness of all of them [Duncan, Lawrence, Hoare and Sturt] to continue in the ministry or as in the case of Goyette, to hold an office or position of responsibility in the Church."[17]

Reflecting on his experiences, H observed: "in my experience, many do not want to believe that such ostensibly good men can be responsible for such hideous crimes." He is, of course, absolutely correct. Steve's story, and this book, are all about the denial of what "ostensibly good men" do. For H, the grooming meant he was unable to recognise what happened to him as a teenage boy:

> There is no doubt as I grew up, I had a clear notion that society would have condemned what I was doing with Duncan and Lawrence. But, at the time, I had no awareness to separate the socially unacceptable and therefore secret activity of gay sex from the socially unacceptable and therefore secret activity of sex with a minor. What astounds me now is that these abusers could believe it was okay to take responsibility for my sexual awakening and development when they had been entrusted with my pastoral care. It is acutely clear to me now that their having sex with me at that age was clearly very wrong, a gross abuse of trust, selfish and thoughtless.[18]

The secret society sheltering Duncan, Lawrence and Goyette existed in an alternative moral universe that reversed widely held community values. Puritanical attitudes to sex were bad. Sex was highly pleasurable, so any sex was good. There was therefore nothing wrong with introducing an underage boy to something so pleasurable. In taking responsibility for his sexual awakening, they told themselves, they were doing him a favour. In this secret society, sex with youngsters was treated as a priestly entitlement. Abuse was justified and normalised.

Between 1986, when the abuse ended, and 2009, when H made his complaint, he developed a growing awareness that what had happened was wrong. Watching a film about child sexual abuse, he realised with horror that he was watching his own story. He realised: "I had been duped".

The catalyst for his eventual complaint was his discovery that Lawrence, now retired as dean of Newcastle, had "taken up a locum position in my parents' diocese in Wangaratta [in Victoria]. I could not fathom Lawrence's audacity and arrogance to think that he could impose himself on my parents as though he expected us to simply keep silent about what he had done to me and how he had betrayed the trust my parents had placed in him."[19] In 2009, H contacted Claire Sergeant, the director of professional standards in Melbourne, and had many conversations with her. In October 2009, he emailed a long document detailing the abuse to the Anglican Church. After the case was sent on to Michael Elliott in Newcastle, things moved swiftly. H found both Sergeant and Elliott very helpful.

When Elliott informed Bishop Farran of his investigations, Farran immediately suspended Lawrence. This took courage. He was standing down a friend and a priest he regarded as the most influential churchman in a generation. Lawrence was high-profile, popular, charismatic and flamboyant, seen everywhere in Newcastle, but especially among movers and shakers. He had been a significant presence in the diocese for twenty-six years, and his profile lifted after he was particularly visible in his support for people during the terrible earthquake of 1989 and its aftermath. He was an assiduous networker, using his positions, such as chaplain to the Chamber of Commerce, to ingratiate himself with the powerful business sector. Lawrence was very friendly with powerful Liberal and Labor Party figures, and the influential professionals who frequented the Newcastle Club.

Lawrence's way of operating was to install his sympathisers, lovers and acolytes, or people who were otherwise under his thumb in some way, in important positions. Rod Bower told me that as a young, single priest rising in the church, he had been invited to the deanery for dinner. After dinner, Bower was propositioned for group sex with Lawrence and another young man. When he made his excuses and left, he knew his career in the diocese would go nowhere. Had Bower agreed to sex, Lawrence would have known he was part of the 'family'. Bower's career would have benefited, but he would also have been under Lawrence's power. That was how it worked. By refusing Lawrence's invitation to have sex, Bower was persona non grata from then on.

But Lawrence had another side. Among his supporters were powerful parishioners at the cathedral who had experienced his attentive pastoral care during family bereavements or tragedies. Robert Caddies, the diocese lawyer, was forever grateful for the kindness Lawrence had displayed when his mother died. When John McNaughton, the former lord mayor of Newcastle, suffered a terrible family tragedy with the death of his young daughter in a car accident, Lawrence was, according to Bishop Farran, hugely important helping the McNaughton family in their grief, going above and beyond in his attentive pastoral care. As Bishop Farran explained:

> He really did care for people, very significantly. I think people like Mc-Naughton are locked into this psychological dependence on him because of how Lawrence cared for them ... And he really, well, he would just give himself to people, that's what he was so good at ... The thing that worried me was, I wondered if he made [people] too dependent on him.

Farran thought there was a lack of supervision of priests and their relationships with parishioners in Newcastle. Psychotherapists are supervised by reporting regularly to a senior clinician to prevent any abuse of power. No such system was then in place for the clergy.

A sign of Lawrence's influence was evident in the extravagant farewell when he retired in 2008. Farran told me: "it was extraordinary, in the town hall ... everybody who was anybody in Newcastle basically was there, and there was a lot of laudatory [things] being said about him. The mayor at the time, John Tait, was there."

Once the allegations against Lawrence were made and he was suspended (although retired, he was still licensed and could operate as a locum priest), he leveraged all that influence. The best lie is the first lie. The best lie is a believable lie. And the best lie is the biggest lie. The truth of his misconduct over many years was brilliantly sidelined by the narrative coming out of the Lawrence camp, which portrayed him as the victim of a witch-hunt. In this story, Lawrence was a martyr being wickedly crucified on the cross of homophobia. That was entirely believable, since homophobia was and is real. Emotions find reasons, and supporters believed what they wanted to believe. The great love and esteem in which Lawrence was held – the effect of his unassailable reputation – paid off. Rumours and gossip swirled around: the boy was never underage; John McNaughton later claimed H was an adult, in his twenties, and had been a willing attendee at the deanery;[20] it was just gay sex, not child sexual abuse. H later said:

> I was very disappointed with the media coverage ... they missed the point. They focused more on the [group sex] incident when I was nineteen ... I found that frustrating, as I wanted it to be more about child sexual abuse.[21]

The fact that the boy was underage when the abuse began was lost in this narrative.

Lawrence's suspension caused a great scandal and schism in the diocese. On one side were clergy and lay supporters of Michael Elliott, John Cleary and the new regime of professional standards, and of course survivors like Steve. On the other were Lawrence's supporters, who disbelieved the allegations, felt Lawrence's suspension was an outrage and believed he was being denied natural justice. There was another hugely important group outside the church, who also, at first, supported Lawrence. For them, he exemplified modern, liberal attitudes to sex. Who cared if he went in for group sex? The actual age of the boy involved was obscured. Lawrence's suspension was seen as a backlash by a puritanical church against the new liberal community mores. This group was rightly opposed to homophobia, but that meant they could easily be groomed to believe the lie that Lawrence was a victim of bigotry against same-sex relationships.

Joanne McCarthy, at the *Newcastle Herald*, was at first part of this group. In her reporting of the board hearing, she was sympathetic to Lawrence, with articles describing the hearing as a "Kangaroo Court" and a "Star Chamber" – lines that came from the mouth of Lawrence's lawyer, John Woodward. McCarthy's coverage cast doubt on the legitimacy of the hearing and gave only Lawrence's perspective. Michael Elliott was protective of H, who did not want to talk to the media, so McCarthy tried but could not get an interview with him.[22] Elliott had by then recognised the hostility of the *Newcastle Herald*'s reporting and unwisely clammed up completely. That meant McCarthy's main source of information was Lawrence's lawyer.

Steve went each day to the hearing, and saw McCarthy leave after just a day and a half. He was furious when he read her article the next day, echoing the line being run by Lawrence's lawyer, and expressed his disappointment to her in no uncertain terms. (Over time, however, their initially testy relationship became very friendly, with McCarthy publishing many articles about Steve and the abuse he suffered.) McCarthy told me that there had been confusion about the boy's age at the time of the offences. I have read the transcript of the hearing and it is plain how old he was – that for all but two years of the abuse, he was still a child.

McCarthy also said that because the police didn't charge the priests, the *Newcastle Herald*'s lawyers were worried about defamation. Normally that difficulty can be solved by using the word "alleged". Lawrence's close friend John McNaughton, the former lord mayor, had a letter to the *Newcastle Herald* published echoing the claim that the hearing was a "Star Chamber" and a "Kangaroo Court". If anything, *that* was likely defamatory. The board included eminent citizens – Professor Trevor Waring, chancellor of the University of Newcastle, the widely respected Anglican minister Reverend Sonia Roulston (later one of the first female bishops) and the experienced and admired magistrate Colin Elliott (no relation of Michael Elliott). In fact, Colin Elliott did serve the *Newcastle Herald* and McNaughton with a notice of intention, the preliminary step to a defamation action, and got an apology.

John Cleary said of Lawrence, "He built up his façade, which worked very effectively for him ... Don't question me, look what I've done for this city."[23] Through his networking, Lawrence had effectively groomed a whole city. By grooming, a paedophile creates compliant, trusting people who simply won't believe accusations of sexual misconduct. Presenting oneself as a very caring priest establishes the "halo effect", a reservoir of admiration and goodwill, whereby people see the abuser as beyond reproach, enabling them to hide in plain sight. Grooming creates a network of defenders who can be mobilised when needed, and Lawrence's networks were important in what happened next.

Farran began to wonder if Lawrence, through his hospitality as dean, was "cultivating protection in some sort of way ... He was quite good friends with a superintendent of police."[24] Farran also remembered dining with Roger Brock, the editor of the *Newcastle Herald*, at Lawrence's house.

"Never cross Graeme Lawrence," Steve once told me. "That was my understanding, and I've talked to a lot of people about it. In the diocese of Newcastle, if you crossed Graeme Lawrence, you were finished."

Farran was about to discover this for himself.

PART FOUR
BACKLASH

CHAPTER FIFTEEN

TOO MANY NUTTY PEOPLE

FARRAN WAS BLUNT about this period when I asked him about it. It was a "terrible time".

Despite the publication of the story on Peter Rushton, the *Newcastle Herald* was running articles sympathetic to Lawrence and his supporters and hostile to Farran.[1] Joanne McCarthy admitted to me that at first she didn't really understand how bad child sexual abuse was in the Anglican Church. Raised a Catholic, her energies had been primarily directed to battling child sexual abuse in the Catholic Church.

She also lived on the Central Coast, about an hour and a half drive south of Newcastle. It was a different culture, where sporting grounds mattered more than churches. It was hard for her to understand the interlacing of the powerful elite in Newcastle – the politicians, lawyers, businesspeople and other professionals – with the Anglican Church, and the networks Graeme Lawrence had assiduously cultivated at the Newcastle Club. "I'm an outsider," she told me. "[the] really striking thing for me ... churches here on the Central Coast ... just did not have the role, the status ... that they do in the Hunter. It took a little bit for me [to understand]. It was only when I started really getting into it ... just the fact that ... how high buildings can be in [Newcastle] was dictated by the height of the Anglican cathedral. Now what does that say about the power of the Church?"[2]

Compared with the Catholic Church, laypeople in the Anglican Church had unusual power and could protect the clergy, something she did not initially understand. "If I hadn't been dealing with the Catholic stuff," she said, "I would probably have had more to put into the Anglican thing. But the Anglican thing was just ... so weird, right from the word go ... there were too many nutty people involved." The Newcastle Anglicans, she eventually concluded, were:

> corrupted from within ... if you look at all the positions that were held, that had any kind of power, these guys were all there. If you look back at a person like Rushton, who clearly was an odious human being, and yet, there he is, able to just throw his weight around with no checks, no anything, being supported by people.[3]

Through its "Shine the Light" series of articles about child sexual abuse in the Catholic Church, the *Newcastle Herald* ran a much-needed and long-overdue campaign for a royal commission and is often credited with achieving that goal. Prime Minister Julia Gillard would later write to Joanne McCarthy, thanking her for her contribution to the "Shine the Light" campaign and saying how much it had influenced her decision to establish a royal commission. Meanwhile, however, equal or even worse abuse was occurring in the Anglican Church and was flying under the radar.

Michael Elliott and John Cleary certainly had supporters. They received grateful emails, and some clergy, such as Canon Paul Robertson, were deeply relieved when Rushton was finally outed as an abuser. The president of the Professional Standards Board, Colin Elliott, was a highly respected former magistrate and an unequivocal supporter of the new regime. So was Geoff Spring, the chair of the Professional Standards Committee. But these were hardly the most powerful voices in the diocese. Loudest were those whom McCarthy characterised as "too many nutty people".

Farran told me that there had been a "sort of ... subterranean resistance" to the introduction of the professional standards regime, "there, in the background", all along. But that mood of sullen hostility now gave way to a virulent, resentful rage. Michael Elliott was particularly hated. Lawrence's supporters saw him in the same way the aristocracy regarded Robespierre or Danton during the French Revolution: as a fanatic, a cruel ideologue prosecuting harmless sexual peccadillos, sending innocent clergy to the guillotine.

Farran had been elected bishop thanks to the large bloc of votes controlled by Lawrence at the synod. If Lawrence withdrew that support, Farran could lose his job. All it would take was for a complaint to the National Episcopal Standards Board, which oversaw the appointment of bishops, to be upheld.

The diocese was split between the old and new regimes. Survivors were coming forward and, for the first time, being believed by senior figures in the diocese. Compensation and counselling sessions for survivors were being paid for under the Pastoral Care and Assistance Scheme. Public apologies for child sexual abuse were starting to be made. The board was disciplining priests for sexual misconduct, but each case brought controversy and unrest. The new regime was precarious. Farran thought that in 2010, on the diocesan council "there were eight people out of twenty who I think probably were very ambivalent about professional standards – that's quite significant".[4] The mounting opposition meant the new professional standards regime could come tumbling down, and with it Michael Elliott's position. Farran felt Elliott's very strengths – his tenacity and determination – had led to things being on the brink of blowing up entirely. Farran told me that Elliott had no feel for the nuances of Anglican politics. Farran called him "austere". He was blunt and got some clergy's hackles up. As a consequence, Farran often sidelined Elliott, fearing the fallout if he was present. Although tiptoeing around the church culture might have made Elliott's life easier, his achievements were possible precisely because he was an outsider.

Elliott and Cleary both thought Farran was vacillating and were suspicious of the influence of his prior friendship with Lawrence. Meanwhile, Farran faced mounting pressure to intervene in the decisions of disciplinary hearings. He was struggling to maintain the independence of professional standards. On 23 November 2010, he wrote to all the Newcastle clergy, explaining that the independence of the whole professional standards process was imperative, and that as bishop he must not interfere in any way.[5] His letter had no effect. At the same time, however, Farran was also trying to appease the opponents of the new regime. His administration was a transitional and uncertain one, with an ambivalent bishop who often did the right thing but sometimes vacillated. McCarthy later described him as taking "one step forward, three back" but admitted that through her hostile reporting, she "was a party to that".

Some of Lawrence's supporters emphasised the Christian idea of for-giveness. Farran told me that a senior priest in the diocese:

> wrote me a letter, saying … a significant number of clergy in the diocese
> would support me if I forgave Lawrence and Hoare … Because they had
> done so many good things in their ministry … It's extraordinary. There's
> sort of no idea that, "Hey, they committed serious crimes."

*

In December 2010, the Professional Standards Board upheld all the charges of "sexual misconduct" and "examinable conduct" and recommended that Lawrence, Hoare, Duncan and Sturt be defrocked, and Goyette banned from having any lay role in the church. The decision caused an uproar. The backlash was no longer rumbling and subterranean. It became extreme. Lawrence's supporters were baying for blood. Now it wasn't just Elliott they wanted sacked, but Farran.

Lawrence and Sturt immediately challenged the board's decision in the NSW Supreme Court. Lawrence got financial support from the New-castle elite to help fund the legal challenge.

Farran's heart sank.

> I knew Lawrence was litigious and he had money to back him all the time.
> It was terrible … Dealing with it – it was just … scary, in a way … it really
> threw me, because here's the Supreme Court, and … Lawrence is a very
> tenacious person. I think Sturt just went along for the ride. He was eas-
> ily led.[6]

Colin Elliott, the president of the Professional Standards Board and an experienced, no-nonsense magistrate, was always confident that the Supreme Court would not find against the diocese because Lawrence had been a leading voice in supporting the 2004 Ordinance and its acceptance in Newcastle in 2005. "And then he goes to the Supreme Court and says the Ordinance is invalid. So why wouldn't I be confident?"[7]

John Cleary thought it was vital to win the Supreme Court action. "We had to win that to break the back of the culture. We often talk about the royal commission doing it, but we kind of had our own little commission-like matter, and it was the Supreme Court. They challenged the integrity of the whole system and with it, I guess, the integrity of us."[8]

Newcastle is a small place. Not long after the board's decision, Cleary and his wife went to have a quiet dinner at the Newcastle Club. At nearby tables, Lawrence's supporters were hostile, pointing him out and talking loudly about him:

> They were [lay] people that were movers and shakers in the diocese and supporters and protectors of other people that I knew who were of concern ... two or three of the more vocal persons of concern were up in the bar ... they had particularly loud voices, quite deliberately were saying, "Oh, that's him over there ... he was the one who caused trouble in the diocese, and everyone knows that Farran and Cleary were the real problems" and all sorts of garbage. I was playing in their back yard there.[9]

*

"All that is necessary for evil to triumph is for good men to do nothing."

That was the dramatic subject line of an email sent to Farran in December 2010, just after the board's decision. It was from Christopher McNaughton, a leading Lawrence supporter and son of the former mayor John McNaughton. Astonishingly, the "evil" he was talking about was not child sexual abuse. Rather, it was the Professional Standards Board, and the "good man" standing by and "doing nothing" was Farran.

> I am writing to you to make sure you know what at least one sinner in the Anglican flock thinks. While I may not be a good man what is happening with public statements from the Professional Standards Board and actions are evil. It is never too late to do the right thing and I pray that God will bless you with the courage to confront and end this evil.[10]

Over decades, there had hardly been a squeak of protest against the do-nothing bishops despite multiple complaints about Rushton, Lawrence and other perpetrators. Now, when the church was at last taking action, there was a savage backlash.

As part of this backlash, the diocesan council appointed a committee to reform the Ordinance in Newcastle and review professional standards processes. Paul Rosser QC, the formidable barrister who had defended George Parker in Steve's case, was leading the charge throughout 2010. Rosser was accustomed to the cut and thrust of cross-examination in criminal trials, and he seemed to make everybody quake in their boots. Geoff Spring was one of them. As the chair of the Professional Standards Committee responsible for investigating sexual misconduct cases and granting compensation to survivors, Spring was trying to enact the Ordinance "faithfully and sometimes painfully ... as it is written". He complained to Bishop Farran that Rosser was continually interfering, was "abrasive and aggressive", behaved in a "rude and arrogant manner" and frequently "berated" him as well as Michael Elliott. "We are just appalled at the way in which the Chancellor has treated us and our work ... [he] seems hell bent on trying to destroy those who are trying to carry out their given tasks and I have no idea why."[11]

Cleary was immediately alarmed by the absence of Michael Elliott from the committee and objected to Farran. Elliott was, after all, the expert on professional standards and would have to implement any changes. His omission was no accident. Cleary felt what was going on was nothing less than a counter-revolution. Elliott was furious at being sidelined.[12]

The draft Ordinance of early 2011, which Rosser had been reworking, proposed that hearings of the Professional Standards Board should no longer be open to the public or the media. "There is not the slightest reason why these hearings should be conducted in public," it said.[13] This was a radical departure from the transparency emphasised by the 2004 Ordinance and would allow the accused priest to control who came to the hearing – including whether a survivor of alleged abuse could attend. In practice, that meant if Steve were to make a complaint under the new protocol about George Parker, it would be up to Parker whether Steve was allowed to attend.

Steve was outraged when he heard this:

> I remember blowing up at Michael Elliott and saying, "It's up to Parker whether I'm there or not? If you think for one minute that my appearance is going to be at the behest of him, you're out of your mind. If I want to be there, I'll be there ... I'll kick every door down in the joint until I find the tribunal hearing."

Elliott was entirely in agreement with Steve. He thought the change was a dreadful backward step towards the old protection racket.

Under the proposed new rules, a bishop was unable to act until the accused had been given a reasonable opportunity to show why the board's recommendations shouldn't be carried out. The bishop was no longer bound to implement the board's decision, but should instead form "his or her own opinion as to the appropriateness of the recommendation", and could override it. He could decide, for example, not to defrock Lawrence.

The 2005 Ordinance was designed to stop sexual misconduct cases being handled "in house", with bishops protecting the church and predator priests. The backlash against these reforms in the Newcastle diocese had brought furious complaints that Farran was abdicating, passively submitting to the board's decisions rather than acting to defend his priests. The draft Ordinance asserts confidently: "This proposal addresses the risk that the Bishop just seems like a rubber stamp on any decision" made by the board. In reality, the proposed changes risked reducing the board to a rubber stamp, attacking the independence of the board and transferring power back to the bishop.

Then there was the "get rid of Elliott" provision. Despite Elliott's strengths in gaining the trust of victims, and being thorough in investigations, Farran knew "there were people gunning for him". The diocesan council, demanded "an investigation of the process of John Cleary appointing him," Farran recalled. "Michael didn't realise ... I knew that they were out to get him".[14]

At the synod in late October 2010, a leading Lawrence supporter and opponent of professional standards, Reverend Chris Bird, raised multiple questions on notice about its operation and questioned the legitimacy of Michael Elliott's appointment.[15] Rosser also queried it at the meeting.[16]

In response to such concerns, Rosser proposed a "specific provision for complaints against the Director and Professional Standards Committee". In an email on 31 August 2010, to Bishop Farran, Assistant Bishop Peter Stuart and John Cleary, Rosser noted that his version was milder than it could have been. "There is still, I believe, a body of opinion that the Ordinance should be repealed in its entirety."[17]

Farran was increasingly troubled by what he called Rosser's "forcefulness".[18] Rosser's role as chancellor was meant to be a purely advisory one, utilised only if the bishop sought his legal advice. However, throughout the reform process, Rosser was taking an activist role. On 2 September 2010, Farran reproved him for overstepping. He pointed out that a chancellor is the bishop's "legal adviser – it is a 'reserved role' not an activist role ... My understanding is that the Chancellor is not an initiator but an advisor ... [not] an activist operating in your own right".[19]

Then, in late 2010, while this reform process was still underway, Rosser – despite being chancellor of the diocese – agreed to act as defence lawyer for Jim Brown, the church lay worker, whom he had previously defended in 1997. Back then there was only one complainant, Phil D'Ammond. Now, Brown faced sixty-eight charges of child sexual abuse, from twenty men. D'Ammond joined their case. Brown was convicted of twenty-seven charges and sentenced to ten years in jail, which was extended to twenty years on appeal in 2012. Farran told me that Rosser's decision to represent Brown was the death knell for their relationship. "We fell out because it was my view that he couldn't see he had a conflict of interest. I was unbelievably surprised that he couldn't see that."

At a meeting of the diocesan council in late 2010, Farran raised the conflict of interest issue. Rosser resigned shortly afterwards, on 26 November.[20] He claimed to Farran in an email that he "could perceive no such conflict" and was leaving merely to "put behind me a chapter of my life that was disillusioning".[21] It is astonishing, but no one in the diocese had considered this issue before. The diocesan chancellor could not represent an accused church worker, Brown, while also being responsible for care of his victims. It was a terrible message to send to survivors. It was exactly the message that had been sent to Steve and his brother in 2001.

*

The angry discontent over the disciplining of Lawrence was still bubbling. Rumours were rife that he and the others had been denied "procedural fairness" and "natural justice". Every one of these claims, after careful examination of the documentary evidence, was untrue.

According to the Universal Declaration of Human Rights, the three main requirements of natural justice are: the right to have allegations clearly outlined and to be given adequate time to respond to them; the right to be heard at an impartial tribunal and to have legal representation; and the right to be treated without bias. All of these conditions were met in the lead-up to and at the tribunal hearing. Lawrence and the other accused were given notice by Michael Elliott of the complaint, the charges were made clear, they were told when the hearing was to be held, and they were able to have legal representation.

When Elliott wrote to Lawrence and the others about the forthcoming hearing on 11 August 2010, he attached the "preliminary allegations" and requested that they respond to them in writing by 4 p.m. on 19 August. "You will have further opportunity to give a detailed response throughout and at the conclusion of the investigation process," he noted. His letter is formal but courteous and offered counselling and pastoral support.

> I understand this situation would be distressing to you, if you feel that you may require counselling or any other form of support, please don't hesitate to contact me (or the Rev'd Jan Deaves – Chaplain to respondents) so that this can be arranged. If you wish to discuss the matter please don't hesitate to contact me.[22]

Lawrence had multiple opportunities to respond to the allegations, he had legal representation, and he was welcome to attend the hearing and put his case. The board was not biased. It was made up of highly respected professionals with good reputations and no axe to grind.

Lawrence, Duncan, Hoare and Goyette chose not to attend the hearing or to give their side of the story. Sturt only attended briefly. Instead, they gave their "evidence" about being denied natural justice in the public realm through their influential supporters and a sympathetic newspaper. Their refusal to attend the hearing was a tactical decision, intended to cast doubt on the legitimacy of the proceedings.[23] Supporters of Lawrence such as John McNaughton and Robert Caddies later told the royal commission that they did not attend the hearing long enough to hear the evidence against Lawrence.[24] Instead, they simply accepted his denials.

Given all this, Lawrence and the others could hardly accuse the board of denial of "natural justice", or of "procedural unfairness". In truth, these were phrases used as slogans in a political campaign to besmirch the reputation of the professional standards regime that had found them guilty of sexual misconduct.

The attempts by the opposition to overturn the independence of professional standards and the board from the bishop had not yet succeeded.

It operated so separately that Farran was not even informed before the board's recommendation to defrock Lawrence was publicly announced.[25] Farran was driving with his wife along the long highway to Taree to attend a school speech night when he suddenly heard it reported on ABC radio, followed immediately by an angry Chris McNaughton ringing him to "rave on", shouting about the "outrageous trial!"[26]

Soon after, on 24 January 2011, Farran complained plaintively to the president of the board, Colin Elliott, about not being told ahead of the public announcement: "this places me in an unnecessary and unfortunate pressured environment."[27]

Colin Elliott gave Farran short shrift. He reminded Farran that the board's independence from the bishop, and the transparency of public hearings, was paramount. He scoffed at the "unfortunate pressured environment" and suggested it "would not be as seriously unfortunate had the Board proceeded in secret as you suggest". He was scathing about Farran's problem of "agitated parishioners".[28]

What Colin Elliott was saying to Bishop Farren was: stand your ground.

*

The former coal city of Newcastle is unexpectedly beautiful. Away from the industrial areas are surf beaches, stretching from the old lighthouse at Nobby's Head down to Merewether. Surfers dot the waves alongside dolphins and the occasional pluming spout of a whale. The white sand of Newcastle Beach curves lazily around from the ocean baths to the kiosk, where holiday makers eat fish and chips. On the other side of the promontory, an attractive grassed waterfront is dotted with seafood restaurants before the Hunter River sweeps out to the sea.

It was here, in early 2011, that the National Bishops of the Anglican Church held their annual conference.[29] And it was here, at beautiful Newcastle Beach, that the head of the Anglican Church in Australia, Primate Phillip Aspinall, suggested Farran resign.

All week there had been articles in the *Newcastle Herald* with pictures of the embattled bishop looking frazzled. Farran thought his opposition – especially the cathedral parishioners – had timed things to perfection, feeding stories to the *Herald* to cause him maximum embarrassment.

The *Newcastle Herald* was running all these sort of stories – "The Diocese Is in Crisis", "Cathedral Wrangle; Clergyman Conceded Concerns in Diocese",[30] all this sort of stuff. Whilst all the national bishops were here in Newcastle.

Farran was humiliated in front of his colleagues. As well as the Supreme Court challenge, he now had to contend with three formal complaints against him to the Episcopal Standards Commission, the body which had the power to remove him. The complaints came from three of Lawrence's supporters, Christopher McNaughton, Laurie Tabart and Simon Adam. The Episcopal Standards Commission's complaint form included a tick-the-box list of quaint sins such as drunkenness and unchastity. McNaughton's complaint placed a cross on those boxes. Instead, he accused Farran of "Conduct ... which would be disgraceful ... productive, if known publicly ... of scandal or evil report". He complained the board hearing the complaints against Lawrence was an "illegal" tribunal that the bishop "allowed to act without regard to the rules of natural justice", and where "untested hearsay" and a "disgraceful statement" was broadcast.

After Primate Aspinall met with the disgruntled cathedral gang, he had coffee with Farran and told him, "Look, they're not going to go away. They're not going to give you an easy time. It's certainly hard for you. It might be better if you retired."[31] Farran's fear that the whole Professional Standards regime would collapse, taking his bishopric with it, was in danger of being fulfilled. He felt "pretty anxious":

> I was rocked by Aspinall's letter ... I had a walk along the beach with my best episcopal friend, then the bishop of Bendigo, Andrew Curnow, and we talked about it. I decided I'm not going to give way to this sort of stuff, you know, it's ridiculous.[32]

Farran decided to tough it out.

*

In late April 2012, the beleaguered bishop finally had welcome news. Justice Sackar of the Supreme Court of New South Wales found against

Lawrence and Sturt and in favour of the diocese.[33] His judgement found nothing whatever wrong with the way the Professional Standards Board (PSB) had conducted itself. Sackar pointed out that:

> ample opportunity had been afforded to the plaintiffs to prove their version of events ... I see nothing untoward in the approach adopted by the PSB. They evaluated the evidentiary materials as in my view they were entitled to do. The material before them clearly permitted them to reach the conclusions that they did.[34]

In June 2012, the Episcopal Standards Commission found in Bishop Farran's favour and dismissed all the complaints against him. However, he still faced the dilemma of whether to follow the board's recommendation that Lawrence should be defrocked. Now, faced with defrocking his old friend, Farran dithered. The ghost of Peter Rushton's sister and other "secondary and tertiary victims" who would be hurt by Lawrence's disgrace hovered over his decision-making.[35] "I really do feel very much for those other victims ... Other people's lives get ruined, when all this comes out, and they're all innocent and then who cares for them?"[36]

Most crimes could be said to have "secondary victims", yet we never assume that reducing their distress is more important than justice for the primary victims. John Cleary was sceptical; he thought concern for "secondary victims" was a polite way of sounding high-minded about reputational damage to the Anglican Church.

H wrote to Farran, expressing concern about the delay in defrocking Lawrence. Farran decided he would meet with H and explain why he couldn't do it. Michael Elliott, who had an excellent, trusting relationship with H, insisted on going too. They flew down together and met H and his family. Farran told me:

> I explained to H what I wanted to do, because I was worried about these secondary and tertiary victims. Rushton's sister was very much in my mind, and I was worried about – not the people at the cathedral so much, but people who Lawrence had married and baptised, hundreds of babies ... what effect that might have on those people, that he was a paedophile.

H became very angry. In no uncertain terms, he told Farran "what [the abuse] had done to his life". Farran told me:

> Honestly, I was devastated by the effect it had had on him. He was a really intelligent man whose life had just been screwed up by Lawrence, I just remember being suddenly so overwhelmed by the sense of what this guy had suffered at Lawrence's hands ... being degraded.[37]

Seeing the ravages of the abuse on H, Farran wept and left the room for a time. When he returned, he agreed to defrock Lawrence. "I realised I had to do it, no matter whatever comes out of it." He announced the decision in September 2012.

High winds delayed the flight home, so Farran debriefed with Michael Elliott at the airport; "it was a very emotional day."

*

After Rosser's resignation, Assistant Bishop Peter Stuart, whom Farran described as having "a good legal mind", had taken over drafting the Ordinance reforms, along with Canon Stephen Williams, who had been a critic of professional standards. By late October 2012, at the annual synod, a dramatically weakened Ordinance was passed and ratified by Bishop Farran. It was clearly orientated to appeasing the opposition, overturning the independence of the board and giving power back to the bishop. In contrast to the previous fully transparent process that H had praised, the board's decision would no longer be open to the public, the media or, staggeringly, even the victim/survivor. Now, only those people whom the bishop and the accused priest agreed upon would be present. That meant a predator priest could exclude their victim from hearing the board's decision. Because it was held in secret, the bishop could vary the decision – for example, a recommendation that a priest be defrocked – without anyone, including the victim, ever knowing.[38]

Michael Elliott thought it was "catastrophic".

> I felt it would be a significantly abusive process for a complainant who may be a victim of sexual abuse to have to seek the consent of their abuser to be present to hear the findings and recommendations of the case ...

The bishop may not then follow the recommendation, but no-one would know, and I think that was the intent.[39]

John Cleary was implacably opposed to the reforms. As diocesan business manager, he was supposed to sign off on the new Ordinance as administrator. He refused.[40] Farran got around Cleary's refusal by making Assistant Bishop Stuart the administrator briefly, to sign off on the reformed Ordinance. Stuart saw his duty to be one of clerical obedience to his bishop's wishes. However, he also wrote to Farran, telling him that he agreed with the board's recommendation to defrock Lawrence.

When Colin Elliott, president of the Professional Standards Board, saw the new Ordinance, he was outraged and immediately resigned. In his resignation email to the diocesan council, he was savage about "The cruel indifference of compelling a victim to seek permission of his/her alleged tormentor to attend the delivery of the judgment", which "warrants the strongest condemnation". Colin Elliott told me the reforms were "crazy":

Here we are, we've got the best Ordinance of all time. We're gaining the confidence of people. We're showing our openness, our transparency ... They want to say that you can't do that anymore. You've got to go cap in hand to the bishop and secretly give him your determination ... it's imposing more harm than anything, on the victim.

Elliott had been profoundly shaken by listening to victims' stories at the board hearings. "Oh Anne, there were many, many nights I went home and just cried," he told me:

The victims were just the objects of an act of self-gratification ... acts usually performed in a situation of loving care and respect. But when performed in this way, it's ... a process of de-personalised, objectifying of the victim, [who] doesn't come away from that act with a sense of gratification, endearment, love, but a burning hatred for what happened. And that has to affect the personality. The personness of that human being [is violated]. That's a terrible affliction and it leaves them – upset, empty of their normal personhood and humanity.

Elliott saw the original 2005 Ordinance as "good church law" which offered "restorative justice" and "hopefully assists victims to understand they are no longer mere objects". Despite his resignation, the 2012 reforms to the Ordinance went ahead.

At the end of 2012, after Farran had been struggling with an aggressive opposition group for three difficult years, he finally retired. Throughout his troubled time in Newcastle, he had kept on worshipping at the cathedral. "I wasn't going to let them beat me. And in a sense like – you know … smiling assassins – I thought I would face them like that."

That's a nice image, of the smiling assassins. But there's a problem. The assassins were not all smiling. Some were issuing death threats.

CHAPTER SIXTEEN

UNLEASH THE DOGS OF WAR

"ONE DAY AN old woman came up to me and spat on me," Steve told me. The woman had said to him, "You're nothing but a troublemaker." Being spat on, however, was the least of Steve's worries. He arrived home one day to find a bullet on his front step. Then there were the threatening phone calls, late at night: "If you keep doing what you are doing, you are putting your grandkids at risk!" These threats continued for years.

Steve reported them to police. He told Michael Elliott, who supported him and kept records. Steve had to move twice when he realised his harassers knew where he lived. "Threats, I'd get weekend after weekend, people ringing up, threatening me, threatening my kids, threatening my grandkids." Over the course of one night in 2011, he received almost fifty abusive and threatening text messages in quick succession, another arriving every few minutes. They accused Steve, a child sexual abuse survivor, of being a paedophile.

8.11 p.m. Paedophile lose my number

8.22 p.m. Leave my number alone u parasite rock spider we'll find you.

8.24 p.m. You've been warned

8.39 p.m. Lose the number sico you were given or how u obtain it obviously through the wrong sources you re a paedophile.

8.55 p.m. msg my daughters number again paedophile

9.06 p.m. go away rockspider

9.09 p.m. we will see who you are be careful

9.16 p.m. how brave are you now Mr paedophile

9.26 p.m. Mr brave where do you live Mr Steve

9.39 p.m. where do you live paedophile stop your rockspider antics

9.40 p.m. my son wishes to know where you live dog

9.42 p.m. where do you gutless Steve

9.51 p.m. what's the number of your premises paedophile. Gutless. man
up u piece 'o' snake shit. You will come undone for your paedophilia
sick cunt …

It continued all through the night, on and on.

2.09 a.m. Tell me how much UR into children

2.15 a.m. U FUCK'N THEIV'N CUNT …

And on they went, finally finishing the next morning.

9.30 a.m. WE KNOW NOW WHO AND WHAT YOU ARE

The police traced the number to the brother of a woman who was a
senior lay person in the church. Steve told me: "He was known to police;
he was a thug. But nothing ever came of it. The cops weren't that keen on
it all then. The cops sort of saw it all as, um, pie in the sky sort of stuff."

Once, late at night, Steve received a phone call from a private number;
the caller, who sounded like an older male, told him: "Back off or your family's gonna get it." The same night, someone broke into Steve's car, which
was parked outside his house, and rifled through his possessions.

Steve told me he thought the intimidation had started way back in May
2001, when, the day after the committal hearing, he was walking through
a park in Port Macquarie.

I got hit in the back of the head with a cricket bat and knocked out …
At that point I didn't connect it to them … the police made a report and
they said, "You must have been robbed", and I said, "Nothing's gone."

When Michael Elliott started to pursue other sexual offenders in the
diocese, and when Rushton was outed and Lawrence was suspended,

the threats and intimidation ramped up enormously. They were especially directed at Steve, Michael Elliott, John Cleary, Colin Elliott and the bishop who replaced Farran, Greg Thompson, as well as diocesan staff.

If you thought you were dealing with a Christian community, the death threats and intimidation, the vandalism of cars and homes, seem completely shocking. But if you reframed and realised that hidden within the church was a paedophile ring – then it became unsurprising. You were dealing with a criminal network, desperate to cover up and evade detection, but also desperate to continue the activities to which they were addicted.

On 6 January 2013, Steve was talking on his mobile phone outside his unit in Adamstown when he saw one of Lawrence's cronies, a church warden at the cathedral, lurking in his yard. The man was one of the group who had met with Phillip Aspinall to persuade him to get rid of Farran. Steve was so stunned to see him brazenly walking through his yard towards the road that he didn't challenge him. The next day, Steve was driving on the freeway from Newcastle to Sydney, doing 110 kilometres per hour. The steering felt strange. He stopped and found that all the screws on his back wheels had been loosened – the wheels were about to fall off. Had he not noticed, the likelihood of a serious accident, even a fatality, was high.

Ten days later, both Steve's and Michael Elliott's cars were vandalised, their windows damaged and large screws driven through their tyres. Elliott reported the damage to the Newcastle police, noting that Steve "has recently been a vocal critic of [the man Steve had seen in his yard] and others … in the context of [the man] and others' ongoing support of known sex abusers within the church."

In April 2013, the driver's seat window of Michael Elliott's car was smashed in and a hex screw driven into a tyre. He sent pictures to the police. Intruders removed the fly screens from his children's windows. It sent a clear, menacing message: they knew where his children slept. His beloved dog disappeared and was never found. Elliott was devastated by the loss. Steve admired Elliott's steadfastness in the face of the threats and thought the police "didn't understand the connection" between the threats and what was happening in the diocese. "They thought, oh, this person over here has had his tyres slashed, and this person had a bullet on his step … but they didn't see it as an orchestrated sinister campaign … clearly to shut us up."

Elliott wrote of his experience:

> In 2014 I had a security system and cameras and an alarm system at my
> place of residence due to concerns for my personal safety and that of
> my family. In 2012/13 I moved residence five times within a twelve-month
> period due to concerns for my safety. These safety concerns are directly
> related to the matters Mr Smith is involved in.[1]

Elliott filed no fewer than twelve police reports during this period,
dealing with all the threatening phone calls and texts, including death
threats, as well as forty incidents of vandalism to cars. He also applied to
Optus on Steve's behalf for a silent number to stop the abuse.

By 2013, Steve was in a relationship with Rachael, who was precious
to Steve and made a huge difference to his life. One day, while driving,
Rachael realised she was being followed. Frightened, she rang Steve on her
mobile phone. He calmly instructed her how to lose the person following
her. The next day, however, she found her car brakes did not work. Steve's
son, Kieran, was a motor mechanic and had just serviced the car. He knew
there had been nothing wrong with the brakes. Now, Kieran found the
brakes had been tampered with.

For Steve, all the threats and abuse "kicked a lot of doors open. I'm ten
years old again. These people are in control." But he kept going.

On 2 July 2014, Steve entered the fray in the comments section of an
online article in the *Newcastle Herald*. An indirect threat to shoot him and
his family was published. A "Sam Ryan" wrote:

> What a waste of taxpayers money this witch hunt is … there is not real
> hard physical evidence that any sexual abuse actually took place … during
> this witch hunt royal commission into churches …

Steve shot back in the comments section:

> You cannot be serious! There is overwhelming evidence that abuse has
> occurred and was occurring in epidemic proportions. Your idiotic com-
> ment is an insult to all those who have lived with this horror all of their
> lives and who have finally found the courage to speak up. You should be
> deeply ashamed of yourself.

"Rodney Dean" replied:

Steven Smith I have no feeling for these made up stories and … I do not
give a stuff about your feelings or these lying children who are now adults.
I do not want my money funding liars witch hunt inquiries and there is no
hard overwhelming evidence not a strand of DNA. If I was being accused
I would put a bullet into the accuses [sic] head and there [sic] children
including anyone who believe that crap.

When John Cleary was preparing to give evidence in the Supreme
Court in the Lawrence case, he was woken in the early hours by a threatening phone call. A male caller told him: "Cleary, you're fucked. Your days
are numbered, cunt!" Suspicious vehicles seemed to be watching his home.
Police traced the call to a phone on Queensland's Sunshine Coast. "I've
never really known who did it," Cleary told me, "but I'm convinced it was
an associate of Lawrence. The timing of that was immaculate, because I was
ready to be cross-examined by those guys. And that shook me around."
Cleary's children were then six and eight years old. They still remember
their Newcastle "holiday", as their parents cleverly explained it, when they
were taken into police protection in an apartment in the Newcastle CBD.

Colin Elliott told me he also had screws put through his vehicle's tyres
during this period:

I've never told anybody, but at that time, the yard [of the house] where
I lived was an open yard and quite remote from Newcastle. They never
bloody knew where I lived. [But] … one morning I got up and I've got a
flat tyre. Round about the same time, I had three flat tyres. All on the one
day, all with the same style roofing nail that John and Michael had been
subject to, the same puncturing of tyres.

Michael Elliott said "those responsible were linked to and supporters
of a number of abusers within the church. I have no doubt they are linked
to my work within the Diocese."

Intimidation through indirect threats also occurred. On the afternoon of 16 May 2011, Michael Elliott arrived for a meeting of the diocesan
council. He reached the lift at the same time as Chris Bird, the rector at
Adamstown, who was a Lawrence acolyte and then Australian head of the

secretive Society of the Holy Cross (SSC), which George Parker belonged to. Lawrence and Goyette were now parishioners at Adamstown, and Bird had refused Michael Elliott's request that he implement the standard safety protocols for defrocked ministers, which prevented Lawrence giving a service or having access to children. Now, Bird refused to get into the lift with Elliott. He told the receptionist, "I can't get in the lift with him, or I'll be up on assault charges", and said that he would ram Elliott's head through the wall.

Bird also threatened a diocesan office worker, Debbie Torok, on 2 August 2013, when he saw that she was working on Professional Standards matters. "What are you doing getting involved in all that?" he said to her. "I know where your kids go to school and where you live." Torok recalled: "Somewhat taken aback, I didn't respond … He was deadly serious in his demeanour and tone. At the time I had two daughters attending St Philip's Christian College, Waratah." She was "rattled" by the incident.

Ostracism was another technique used in this virulent, aggressively pro-respondent culture. After the Lawrence judgement, parishioners at the cathedral directed their hostility at members of the Professional Standards Board such as Professor Trevor Waring, the psychologist and university chancellor. When Waring attended the cathedral, which was his parish church, Lawrence's supporters turned their backs on him. On another occasion, Waring was washing dishes at the cathedral after a function, when Chris McNaughton sidled up to him and told him to wash his hands because he had blood on them. Some of this group also berated Bishop Farran and Assistant Bishop Stuart to their faces after services.

After John McNaughton's letter describing the Professional Standards Board hearing as a "Kangaroo Court" was published in the *Newcastle Herald*, Colin Elliott's wife, Jenny, "came home in tears" after attending the Cessnock church. The parishioners had turned on her as the wife of the president of the board that had defrocked Lawrence. Colin Elliott became distressed at this point in my interview with him. His wife's experience was a turning point for him. "I decided then: 'Who do they think they are, to get away with this?'" He read up on the *Defamation Act* and served both the *Newcastle Herald* and John McNaughton with a Notice of Intention.

I was bloody serious. I did get advice and so did Michael. I went around to John McNaughton's home and … left it there. I negotiated a settlement with the *Newcastle Herald*, details of which are off the record. And I got an apology, or what was called an apology, from John McNaughton that I refused to accept … I haven't heard of him writing any more letters about that subject to the *Newcastle Herald* since.[2]

Colin Elliott had the highest praise for Michael Elliott and John Cleary.

I got on wonderfully well with Michael. I thought he was a very compassionate, understanding bloke who … wore his heart on his sleeve and he really cared for the victims. I'm sure that we wouldn't have got anywhere with the Lawrence case with H had it not been for Michael's brilliance… he had a gift of being able to be decisive but fair, and he had a great understanding of the needs of victims, and he had a lot of them. I haven't heard of anyone complain about the way he handled anyone … None of those complainants who came forward did so because they wanted compensation. They did so because they had been injured, they had been hurt and they didn't want that church worker to be a church worker anymore.

The things that happened to Michael Elliott and John Cleary during that era, they were dreadful … And they still got up and had to go to work, you know. But for Elliott and John Cleary, I don't think any of this would have ever come out. Those two were the reason I did as much as I did.[3]

Assistant Bishop Peter Stuart said that he had never in any previous parish come across a group like the supporters of Graeme Lawrence, who were the most "difficult, intractable and hurtful" people he had ever met.[4] A Christian parish it may have been, but virtue was elsewhere.

Meanwhile, despite the death threats and attempts at intimidation, Steve was resolute. He wasn't about to go away and hide. He read everything, turned up at board hearings, wrote letters to the newspaper, attempted to persuade Joanne McCarthy about the seriousness of child sexual abuse in the Anglican Church, and took on the trolls in social media and the comments section of the *Newcastle Herald*. "It just kept getting bigger, and bigger and bigger," he recalled. Without realising, he was becoming a leader in the survivor fraternity. In this capacity, he turned up to all the trials of child sexual abusers. Including Jim Brown's.

CHAPTER SEVENTEEN

I THOUGHT THEY ENJOYED IT

WHEN THE ROYAL Commission into Institutional Responses to Child Sexual Abuse began holding hearings in 2013, a constant presence outside were members of the Care Leavers Australasia Network (CLAN), waving placards: "You're never too old to be charged with child sexual abuse." Commissioner McClellan described out-of-home-care institutions as "dangerous hotspots" for child sexual abuse.[1] In the private sessions of the commission, they represented 43 per cent of victims, by far the largest category.

The story of Jim Brown concerns one of their number, Philip D'Ammond, and the St Alban's Boys' Home orphanage. D'Ammond is an Indigenous man who was adopted by a white doctor, Phyllis D'Ammond, in 1962. She was abusive and belted him with a dog lead, leaving welts. He had a stutter, and she would lock him in the toilet until he could say a whole sentence without stuttering. When he was nine years old, in 1971, she sent him to St Alban's. He felt rejected but relieved to get away from her. Phil was returned to her after nine months, but by the time he was thirteen, in 1975, she was dying, and he was placed in St Alban's permanently.

It was hard, having no one, no family. When the school holidays arrived, he faced the bleak prospect of being the only boy left in the home.

Mrs Barry, the matron, introduced him to Jim Brown, a tall, heavy man of about twenty-five. He was a lay youth worker in the church, and one of Peter Rushton's lovers. Brown and Rushton were both on the board of St Alban's. Brown used to regularly take the 6.30 a.m. chapel service at St Alban's, despite not being a priest. He was involved as a youth worker with the Anglican churches at Kurri Kurri and Weston, outlying hamlets in the poor coal-mining area, just over an hour west of Newcastle.

Now, miracle of miracles, Brown was willing to take Phil home with him for the holidays. His gaze slid over the boy appraisingly, and Brown commented that Phil had "the best skin he'd ever seen", making Phil uneasy.[2] Brown promised Phil he'd get to ride dirt bikes and race hot-rods, and that he could be in the pits at the raceway, with the pit crew. "He had me hook, line and sinker."[3] It sounded like a holiday you might read about in *The Boy's Own Annual*. Phil agreed, desperate not to be the only child left at the home. He told me he was excited by what Brown promised. "Yeah, like the speedway, and I already had a thing for motor bikes, dirt bikes … I thought, like, I'm in heaven. I thought all my Christmases had come at once, that first meeting, until we actually got to his place."[4]

What Phil didn't know, however, was that Brown was a serial paedophile. Along with Rushton, he preyed on the boys at St Alban's. Within twenty minutes of them arriving at Brown's house, Brown gave Phil alcohol. By bedtime Phil was really drunk. It was a small flat, in half a house, and had only one bedroom with one bed.

> We got into bed, and I'm right on the edge of the bed, with me back to him, and then whoof, over comes the big arm, because he's a big man … he said, "There's no need to sleep over there, come here." He cuddled me from behind. And I could feel his erection. I pissed meself, I wet meself, got out of bed and tried to hide in the bathroom, with a door with no lock. I was terrified. *Terrified*.[5]

During the day they would do normal things like go shopping or work on Jimmy's hot-rod. At night, Brown got Phil to watch pornography with him, plied him with alcohol, LSD and marijuana, and then the sexual assaults started: masturbation, oral sex, attempts at anal sex. Brown said, "It's fine, Michael and me do this all the time." It is likely this meant Michael Cooper, an Anglican priest Phil met at Brown's, one of the Cessnock Anglo-Catholic crew, who died in 2007 but was publicly exposed by the church in 2015 as a serial predator who "enticed children with alcohol and drugs and sexually abused them." He also watched hardcore pornography with them.[6] On one occasion Cooper also molested Phil. Sometimes another boy would be there, and once D'Ammond saw Brown having anal sex with him. There were always boys with Brown.

D'Ammond spoke of a terrible loneliness. That made it hard to report the abuse. Apart from Brown, he had no one. Brown took him on a two-week holiday and sexually abused him throughout. An essential part of the cruelty was that Phil's abuser was also "Jimmy", the man who gave him treats and who loved it when Phil called him "my old man". In 1977, Brown became D'Ammond's guardian. To report him meant losing the only person he'd had a close relationship with; "I didn't want to be in the world on my own, and this was a dilemma about reporting him."

D'Ammond met Rushton during this period. Rushton gave chapel services at St Alban's. At first Phil thought he was a fat, jovial man, but he soon realised Rushton was an abuser too. Rushton clearly knew what Brown was doing and would grope Phil. Phil thought Rushton was the ringleader, infiltrating St Alban's, almost as if he were training Brown. When Rushton left to go to Wallsend, Michael Cooper took over at St Alban's.

D'Ammond recalled 1975 and 1976 as:

> the bad years. I did not tell anyone, and I had no one to tell ... I did not think I could tell anyone about Jimmy's abuse ... I did not think I would be believed by the matron at St Alban's. I thought I just had to comply with Jim's behaviour to survive.[7]

After the abuse, Phil's life spiralled out of control. The drug habit started by Brown, dropping acid and smoking hash, escalated to heroin addiction, to mask the pain and forget what had been done to him. Phil did twenty-five stints in rehabilitation, his first when he was sixteen. He also went to jail six times, totalling eighteen years, for offences including breaking and entering, armed robbery, multiple common assaults, and malicious wounding with intent to cause grievous bodily harm. Phil said, "I was harbouring a lot of pent-up anger towards Jimmy, and I misdirected it at others. I have now received counselling for anger management and the trauma of sexual abuse."[8]

In jail, Phil met Yvette, and when he was released after a ten-year stretch in prison they began seeing each other. "I got married in Kurri and I was actually living a normal life for the first time. Yvette's family seemed to take to me." Phil felt he was turning his life around. It was an arduous task, however, and he was full of self-doubt.

> I did prove myself, because I got a job on the council, it was one of those government jobs where it was only for six months, and then I went back and did another one, where I actually learnt how to concrete ... Within three months I had my own crew, they gave me a truck to drive. Anyway, I was a boss man. The family really could see the good in me.[9]

However, Brown was always lurking in Kurri and did everything he could to undermine Phil's fragile sense of self. He asked what Yvette's parents thought of their daughter marrying a criminal.

> Brown had a knack of catching me out by myself. I might be up at the paper shop, or getting fuel or whatever, but whenever I was on my own, Brown was saying to me stuff like, "It's got me fucked why you got married. What have you got to offer her?"

The worst comment, for Phil, was when Yvette was pregnant with their daughter, and Brown asked, "What colour balaclava are you going to get the baby?" The harassment had an effect. "It ended up splitting us up. The balaclava [comment] was the end of my marriage." Phil was struggling against feelings of worthlessness.

> I was trying so hard to prove myself that I wasn't a hopeless junkie or addict, that I could go to work, hold a job down and raise a family, which I was well on the way to doing. But I'd take one step forward, I'd come across Brown, and take ten steps back. I was always wondering if the family were just being nice to me. That's all I did, question myself ... my head was well and truly done in after my marriage fell apart. I started using again, and then my sights turned on Brown.

In 1996 and 1997, Phil complained to police about Brown's sexual abuse when he was a kid.[10] As noted earlier, Paul Rosser defended Brown so aggressively and savaged Phil so brutally that he fled from the witness stand. The trial collapsed.

The next twelve years were bleak. Phil's life spiralled out of control. There was drug addiction, crime and anger. He told me he wanted to reopen the case against Brown, but:

> I knew that I couldn't win, because I needed more evidence than just me ... But if I could have got one other victim, or two or three, or as it turned out, twenty in the end ... I needed at least one other statement which would show that I wasn't telling any lies ... we are talking about a serial paedophile here.

By 2010, Phil's wish had come true. Many more victims of Brown had come forward. I have read all the sickening police reports of his multiple crimes. The evidence was overwhelming. In 2011, Brown pleaded guilty to twenty-seven charges of child sexual abuse relating to nineteen male victims, including masturbation and oral and anal rape. The victims told of Brown's manipulative grooming methods, by which he presented himself as the "cool guy", inviting boys over and enticing them with spas, videos, cars and hot-rods. He would lower their parents' guard by promising wholesome, supervised churchy fun. In reality, Brown was using pornography to lower the boys' inhibitions, giving them alcohol and drugs, and then abusing them. His modus operandi often involved a spa at his house, where Brown would get a child drunk or high before molesting the almost comatose boy, sucking their penis or masturbating them. He also molested children when they were asleep or in a drunken stupor. He would say to his victims, "What would your parents think of you if they knew what you were doing?" As if the child were to blame. They were shamed into silence.

Brown was prolific, addicted, unstoppable.

Sometimes a boy would escape the web Brown had woven. Others became ensnared, and the sexual assaults would escalate over time. In their statements to police, his victims spoke of the agony and the blood when they were anally raped. Sometimes they were emotionally confused when, as they got older, Brown discarded them and moved on to other, younger boys. Most of his victims were aged between ten and fourteen when the abuse occurred, but in one instance he abused a boy as young as eight. His victims told of their shame and humiliation, and the destruction of their lives.

By 2010, Michael Elliott was investigating Brown, and there is a revealing file note from 13 September of that year about a conversation they had. Brown told Elliott that Rushton had groomed him and drawn him in to a culture where sexual abuse of boys was accepted as normal. When George Parker abused Steve, Steve was aware of the sexual abuse of boys at Woodlands and St Alban's. He remembers being parked outside these homes while Parker and other priests went in. "There's no question in my mind that the likes of Rushton, Parker, Cooper, Father James Brown and Jim Brown treated that place as a shopping centre." (Father James Brown was a priest and another prolific abuser.) Paul Gray, Phil D'Ammond and CKG, a key witness in the royal commission, were all victims at St Alban's.

Brown pleaded guilty to all the charges. Steve went along to his sentencing. "Jim Brown would have to be the grub of grubs," he told me. Steve arrived at the Maitland courthouse with Michael Elliott, who was wearing an Anglican Church badge. Steve saw the look on the survivors' faces when they saw that badge.

> They were going to lynch Michael Elliott. There were some rough and tough guys there, ex-crims, and bikies and some big mean-looking blokes, like busted-up blokes, and Michael's got his badge on that says "Anglican Church of Australia".
>
> I said, Mick, lose the freakin' badge. For a start ... And I went round all these blokes one by one. They knew who I was. I said, "Listen, this bloke, Mick Elliott, is a good bloke. He's here to help you blokes." We all ended up going for lunch. So, you know, it was all cool, eventually.[11]

During the trial, Rosser claimed Brown was "delusional and did not see himself as a paedophile and just thought that he was gay".[12] None of the victims bought that. The prosecutor was on the mark when he said of Brown, "he had no insight, empathy or understanding in relation to his actions".[13] Many of Brown's victims had not been believed by the church for a long time, which, as it had done for Steve, caused them further suffering.

Steve related a dramatic moment when the judge sentenced Brown and allowed him the opportunity to speak.[14]

This is a classic guy who never really understood the wrong of what he'd done. As an explanation of what he had done, Brown said from the dock: "I thought they enjoyed it …" You felt the air rush out of the room … there were twenty victims of Brown sitting in the courthouse … If the blokes could have got to him, they would have killed him.[15]

One of the victims, Ray, said afterwards, "You've got people who have committed suicide." He expressed his anger with church officials for ignoring his complaints in 1985.[16]

Brown was sentenced to ten years in prison. The victims were outraged. The sentence was doubled on appeal, in 2012, to twenty years, twelve without parole. Judge John North in his judgement said that "Brown had a tried and tested modus operandi when it came to procuring young boys for his sexual gratification."[17]

Phil D'Ammond was thrilled by the increase in Brown's sentence and spoke to the press. "Finally, someone listened to us – that it's not alright to go raping children."[18]

The legacy of Brown's abuse was lifelong. Phil now lives alone in a Redfern housing-commission flat. He told me he hardly has contact with anyone, only going out for his methadone.

Steve said to me, quietly, "Horrendous man, Brown."

CHAPTER EIGHTEEN
GASLIGHTING THE BISHOP

AFTER BISHOP FARRAN retired, in February 2013 he was replaced by Greg Thompson, a former Newcastle boy. He was a popular choice and won many votes at the synod. Given what happened next, it seems likely some mistakenly hoped that Thompson would return the diocese to its old ways.

Previously, Thompson was bishop of the Northern Territory. Rod Bower joked that this made him ready for anything. "I remember him telling the story, he's doing this baptism somewhere in the back of Kakadu, and some old lady said, 'Don't worry, the crocodiles never eat the bishop!'"

Thompson's experience evading crocodiles was likely to be useful, given the "nest of alligators" waiting for him in Newcastle. In 2014, at the annual General Synod, held that year in Adelaide, Thompson climbed into a taxi with Keith Allen, who immediately told Thompson that "he had more [child sexual abuse] files than I did".

Thompson thought this "self-revealing" disclosure by Allen was key to understanding the culture at Newcastle. He told me:

> That's about entitlement ... You've got away with this for the last forty years ... he's protected. And him telling me means that I'm becoming compromised, because [now] I knew it. So that's part of what I'd call the grooming culture around bishops. They get told stuff, and then if they don't act on it, they're ... party to it.

If Allen was expecting Thompson to be a bishop like Shevill, Holland or Herft, however, he was mistaken. Thompson would never cover up abuse. Why not? Thompson had been abused himself.

Thompson told me there was an unconscious element in his decision to return to Newcastle as bishop. It was time for a reckoning. The furore in Newcastle over child sexual abuse opened all the doors he had closed on his own abuse.

About six months into his time as bishop, Thompson encountered Detective Sergeant Jeff Little (now Detective Inspector), whom he described as "a real character", and whom we will meet later in this book. Little had several investigations underway into child sexual abuse in the Anglican Church and when the royal commission requested it, he gathered information for their inquiry. He did an enormous amount of work for Case Study 42. At first, Thompson thought Little was suspicious of him, thanks to the church's history of cover-ups. Little laid it on the line for him: "Bishop, there are wolves among the sheep and the shepherds, and you've got to work out where you stand."

This stayed with Thompson, and he kept quoting it to people. Little's penetrating question – whose side are you on? – was a call to truthfulness. You could be part of the problem or part of the solution. Over time, Thompson convinced police that he was not part of the protectorate. He spent about six hours at Newcastle police station, telling his story.

*

Born in 1956 to a poor family in the coal-mining area of Muswellbrook, Thompson was one of eight children. They lived in a modest fibro bungalow. Thompson told me: "I grew up in a family where we were objects ... we were there for the parents, not them for us." Thompson's paternal grandfather was a train driver. Thompson's maternal grandfather was a vaudeville comedian in a travelling carnival troupe and a "trickster" who frequently didn't pay his debts. His mother was an attractive snake charmer who appeared on the cover of a 1940 edition of *Pix* magazine.

His mother married at eighteen. By the time she was thirty, she had eight children. She had no emotional capacity for the arduous task of caring for so many kids in poverty. The Thompsons were isolated and had no support from extended family.

Thompson's mother mistreated her children. She:

> clearly had a mental health condition … undiagnosed … So, it was an hor-
> rendous environment … Food was used to manipulate. Sometimes we
> wouldn't have enough food … She was the centre, and the children were
> there to please her and to fight over her.[1]

Thompson's father had violent rages, directed at the children, which
culminated in beatings.

> Dad was very bright and worked on the railways and resented it. And was
> away a lot. But then he would just be a storm, so when it was unleashed,
> watch out … I didn't see anything towards Mum. But the children …!

To make some extra money, the family took in boarders, who slept in
Greg Thompson's bedroom. One of the boarders sexually abused Greg.
His parents' reaction was instructive: "They didn't want to pursue the
matter. I was terribly upset, and they didn't ask me why I was upset. But
they told [the boarder] to go away the next day." In that era, the waters of
silence closed over the heads of the abused. Greg's parents never spoke
of it again.

Domestic violence was common in the world Greg grew up in. Child sexual abuse was part of a culture in which children were treated harshly. "The
private family environment, where the man is in charge of his home and
belts his wife and knocks his kids around," was considered normal. "Physical abuse of children was endemic. Child abuse was endemic." Despairing,
Thompson used to sit on a hill near Muswellbrook and think about this
bleak life. "There has to be something better than this," he told himself.

He found it by turning to the Anglican Church. His family was not religious and his parents were ambivalent about his embrace of Anglicanism.
But for Thompson, the church became "a safe harbour … I was the only
one to go to university, I was the only person to pursue a vocation with the
church … it was my choice to be different to my family."

Over time, Thompson reached a fatalistic acceptance of his childhood.

> I liken it to where they chop down a tree and you can see the rings, the
> years of fire and drought. I think our lives have all those rings in it …

I don't feel hate for my parents … They survived and they had nothing …
And even the abuse as a child, it's not in the forefront of my mind …
I'd left it behind thirty, forty years ago.

The sexual abuse Thompson experienced at the hands of senior Anglican clergy, however, was different. When he turned to the church as a way
out of his troubled family, he thought he had found a community that took
virtue, compassion and charity seriously – a community in which people
lived their lives in the sight of God.

A photo of Thompson as a teenager shows an attractive young man
with unruly curls. In 1975, when he was nineteen, he met Newcastle bishop
Ian Shevill and canon Eric Barker. Impressed by the intelligent, earnest
young man, they took him up as a protégé. He was flattered by their interest. They invited him to go with them to see an R-rated movie, *Drum*,
ostensibly about slavery but depicting sex scenes with themes of domina-
tion and race, including white men raping black women and black men.
Thompson sat wide-eyed, startled that these pious churchmen would
want to see such a film.

He was even more stunned when both priests suddenly plunged their
hands into his groin at the same moment. He sat frozen, utterly shocked.
Later that evening, Canon Barker pinned Thompson against a wall and
tried to have sex with him. When Thompson refused and pushed him off,
Barker told the teenager that he would have no future in the church unless
he had a sexual relationship with him.

So *that* was how it worked in Newcastle!

Thompson's experience throws important light on why the Parkinson
report into child sexual abuse in the Anglican Church in Australia found
that more perpetrators trained at St John's College at Morpeth in the
Newcastle diocese than anywhere else. Some trainees went there under a
system of sexual patronage. Shevill wanted Thompson to train there. There
was a cluster of child sexual abusers who went through Morpeth, including
Peter Rushton, George Parker, Graeme Lawrence and Stephen Hatley Gray.
When Shevill, Rushton and Lawrence attained power in the diocese, they in
turn sent their favourites to Morpeth, establishing the next generation of
abusers, such as James Brown and Ian Barrack. When Thompson realised
this about Morpeth, he refused to go. Instead, he left Newcastle altogether
and eventually trained at Ridley College at Melbourne University.

*

If those who appointed Thompson as bishop thought they would be getting one of Shevill's protégés, they had completely miscalculated. There was no one more psychologically prepared than Thompson to finish the work of exposing child sexual abuse in the Newcastle Anglicans. Thompson identified the habits of mind at the centre of the denialism about child sexual abuse that he saw in his parents and in the church.

> They know, and they don't know. They don't want to know because the implications of their world changes. Their relationships, the Fathers had baptised their children, all those photos ... are no longer romanticised ... It changes the world to know. And that's eating of the fruit of the knowledge of good and evil. It changes your perceptions.

For many in the church, it was easier to preserve good memories and dismiss survivors as liars. If the abuse was grudgingly admitted, it was minimised. Describing his experience, Thompson told me: "I was confronted with disbelief or indifference." Some people accepted that "it did happen, [but said] it wasn't that bad. 'People get over these things. Why can't they all move on?'"

But as a survivor, Thompson knew sexual abuse of children and young people did happen, and that it was "that bad". He understood that survivors couldn't just "move on". He knew that the code of silence meant apologies were rare, and he understood the reluctance of survivors to come forward. It had taken him forty years to do so.

Thompson had first-hand knowledge of the culture of sexual predation; he was a galvanising new force. Rod Bower observed: "St Ignatius says, where the bishop is, the church is." As bishop, Thompson "personified the institution" but he was also a survivor. This combination gave him a moral authority that would dramatically shift attitudes.

After arriving in Newcastle as bishop, Thompson went on a six-month "listening tour" of the diocese, meeting with thousands of people, trying to understand their grievances and to discover "what kind of leadership they wanted from me".

Child sexual abuse wasn't mentioned much. Only on a couple of occasions did people refer to it, he recalled.

"What about the [child sexual abuse] victims?" One evening, I saw people tell that person, "Let's all move on." ... I had the strong impression that people couldn't talk about the sex abuse that has taken place in the diocese ... There were quite a large number of people with a narrative that clergy had been unfairly treated, and I left with the feeling, those evenings and days, that there was little empathy for victims ... it was suggested to me that the discipline of clergy [such as Lawrence] had been far too harsh ...[2]

At Thompson's consecration ceremony as bishop, a former bishop of another diocese, George Browning, bowled up to him and told him, "You must go and meet with Graeme Lawrence and Greg Goyette and care for them. He's been treated unfairly." Browning also warned Thompson that Lawrence was "quite active still ... and had a lot of influence".

He certainly did. Thompson was repeatedly told that he should "consider undoing the discipline that Bishop Farran had done ... in the cathedral particularly." He was told that Farran had been "a bit of a steamroller. He seemed to ride roughshod." The defrocking of Lawrence was attributed to Farran's "belligerence" or to "his inability to work with Lawrence – [as if] it was simply personal differences."

Thompson was also frequently told that Farran's disciplining of Lawrence was homophobic, and that Lawrence had been punished for having "gay" sex. Thompson disagreed. Lawrence had abused the boy, H, when he was still an underage teenager. It wasn't a "relationship", it was sexual abuse. Thompson's own experiences gave him empathy for H and the others. He thought this false narrative about homophobia was "used to subvert the discipline of these clergy ... It's quite clear to me that there was a predatory culture ... in relationship to children."[3] Adult sexual orientation didn't come into it.

Thompson was right. Research shows that outside the church, paedophilia is more often heterosexual than same-sex. As a progressive Anglican, Thompson supported women priests, gay clergy and gay marriage. "There is no homophobic feeling in my life ... My response would be [the same] to heterosexual people if this became known to me – and I think Bishop Farran rightly identified this as predatory behaviour."[4] Thompson himself was deluged with angry letters and emails from Lawrence supporters, accusing him of treating Lawrence unfairly: "How dare you do what you're doing. You're selling [out] ... you're homophobic ...

They're quite clever at trying to paint themselves as the victim and the martyr."[5]

As bishop, Thompson frequently received intelligence about past and present abusers. Michael Elliott briefed him, and survivors came forward. He learned, for example, from "a former warden ... that Graeme Lawrence had men's parties with young boys". Thompson told me a certain member of the laity also "knew of it, and I think he may have had an interest in boys". People turned a blind eye, either because they were directly involved with it or because they were mates with those who were, or simply wanted to protect the church's reputation. Through conversations with parishioners, survivors, Michael Elliott and others, Thompson came to understand how this predatory culture had come about. People had been "compromised" by their relationships with Lawrence:

> I think that was the power of Lawrence. He knew a lot about everyone. How do you vote against Lawrence when he knows your frailties, your vulnerability? It was quite clear that if he didn't like you, you became on the outer, and if he liked you, on the inner. So, there was this polarising of people, and that's a groomer's strategy.

When Michael Elliott alerted Thompson to the yellow envelopes containing the records of child sexual abuse complaints, Thompson asked him for a report on them. He was the first bishop to carefully examine them. He was astonished to find nothing in the files about Lawrence, despite the existence of a number of credible complaints of child sexual abuse before the 2009 case that led to Lawrence's defrocking.

Thompson thought one reason why there was so much hostility to Lawrence being disciplined was that some men feared that if Lawrence were outed, they could be too.

> There's quite a lot of now older men, who were groomed. I had a man tell me about a priest who he didn't believe did anything wrong, but [his] son would go with him to the cathedral choir and sing, and then come home very late at night. He didn't question it ... this was a man in his eighties, he didn't question that his son could have been offended against, by this priest, who'd gone to jail [for child sex offences].[6]

*

When Joanne McCarthy first interviewed the new bishop, she didn't know he had been abused as a child. However, Thompson "just started choking up ... we stopped the interview because it was about supporting him". McCarthy told Thompson she thought it was "fantastic" that someone with "a survivor's point of view" was in the role: "The diocese ... needs a bishop like you."[7] From the start, unlike Farran, Thompson received sympathetic coverage from McCarthy and the *Newcastle Herald*, both as an abuse victim and for his efforts to transform the diocese.

Thompson was at first uncertain about disclosing his abuse publicly, but McCarthy, an experienced journalist, gave him good advice: he should get on the front foot. "You have to," she said, "because otherwise you're going to be completely vulnerable. It will come out anyhow, but in the wrong way."

The public revelation that the new bishop was a survivor himself was explosive. No Anglican bishop had ever before disclosed that they were a victim of sexual abuse. There was nationwide interest, and it focused attention on child sexual abuse in the Anglican Church in a way it had not been since the Hollingworth affair. For survivors such as Steve, it meant the highest church official in Newcastle was one of them, a person they could trust and identify with.

On 17 June 2015, Thompson marked 500 days in office by apologising publicly to survivors of child sexual abuse. It was a watershed moment in Newcastle.

> I'm devastated by the accounts of abuse. If you are a victim or a survivor
> of abuse, I want to encourage you to come forward. I want to assure you
> that when you do share your story the Church will believe you and you will
> be supported in that process. I know that as a diocese in the past we failed
> some victims and survivors of sexual abuse ... We fostered a culture that
> intimidated them and kept them silent.[8]

In October 2015, Thompson made a groundbreaking move at the synod, the annual gathering of Newcastle clergy and laity. He invited two Anglican priests who had been sexually abused, Reverends Les Forester and Bob Peattie, to address the meeting. The audience was spellbound.

Forester told them that during the abuse, "I was absolutely terrified ... my whole body shaking, and I can recall thinking, 'if this doesn't end ... I'm going to die.'" Peattie described his abuse as "pure evil", resulting in "continuous suicidal thoughts". Forester spoke of the need for cultural change: "It's been part of church culture to be silent and [to] be silent about the silence." Thompson commended their "extraordinary courage" in speaking publicly.

However, support for survivors, while growing, was definitely not universal. The *Newcastle Herald* reported that some senior cathedral parishioners didn't attend the 2015 synod. When Thompson refused to reinstate Lawrence and instead apologised to survivors, the criticism and undermining grew ever stronger.

Thompson thought it was "the symptom of a dysfunctional environment where a small group can hold the diocese captive". Lawrence's supporters raised questions, "not only about my own abuse, but [about] these two other survivors ... What was the point? Why were we focusing on the past? 'Let's all move on, Bishop. There is no good digging up the past.'" There was a view that "this has brought shame on the church, it's brought shame on people they revered", and now Thompson had "brought it into the church".

At the same synod, the objectionable section 77 of the 2012 Ordinance, which allowed an accused priest to determine who could attend the board's judgement, was at last overturned.

*

The intractability of the opposition, especially among worshippers at the cathedral, presented first Bishop Farran and then Bishop Thompson with a choice: appeasement or war.

Farran's regime was an important transitional one. It did make great strides – but he also tried to appease the opposition. That meant he could not completely dismantle the grey network which had protected abusing clergy. When Thompson was elected bishop, many of this group were still in powerful positions.

From the very beginning of Thompson's term, he was aware of the overlap between the powerful elite of Newcastle and the Anglican laity. At his installation ceremony, in the front row of the cathedral were powerful figures from the Liberal and Labor parties, the lord mayor, city councillors, lawyers and businesspeople – quite a few of whom, Thompson told me, eventually "ended up before ICAC [the Independent Commission Against Corruption]".

> St Paul talks about wrestling, not with flesh and blood, [but] with powers and principalities ... that's what we were doing, the power base of our diocese was connected with the power base of the city. The powers and principalities, they're oppressive and they harm.

Thompson noticed the same names appearing over and over on key committees, people who were hostile to professional standards. With the same personnel, Thompson thought, how could anything really change? Farran told me he thought it was harder for Thompson, because he was a more sensitive person with an abuse history. However, it was Thompson, a survivor, who jettisoned the appeasement strategy, declared war and started dismantling the grey network.

The first to go was Keith Allen. Although Allen had bragged to Thompson in 2014 about having more files on child sexual abuse than the bishop, despite repeated requests he had failed to produce them. This was serious. The diocese had been subpoenaed by the royal commission, meaning it was required by law to forward all relevant files and was at risk of significant penalties if it didn't.

In March 2015, Thompson again asked Allen for the files. Thompson particularly wanted to know how sexual misconduct had been handled before the 2005 Ordinance, and about the "yellow envelopes committee" that had advised Bishop Herft. Soon after, at a meeting with Thompson and Cleary, Allen told them that "all the files in his possession [had] now been destroyed", as they were more than ten years old. At a later meeting, however, Allen admitted that he had given George Parker the file pertaining to his case.[9]

During this period, from 2013 to 2015, John Cleary's habit of making file notes immediately or soon after a meeting proved invaluable. Cleary took few notes during meetings, and was usually quiet, holding his cards close to his chest, which encouraged Allen to blurt out revelations in an unguarded way. According to Cleary's file note of one meeting, Allen said he didn't trust Michael Elliott and wouldn't "work with or speak to him". "Elliott is just a bounty hunter and the sooner we get rid of him the better," Allen said. Cleary recorded that Allen was "proud of" a motion that Paul Rosser moved, and Allen seconded, to have Michael Elliott sacked.[10] Discussing previous bishops, Allen said Holland "was a nice man but a ditherer"[11] who, like former bishops Roger Herft and James Housden (1958–1972) and assistant bishop Geoffrey Parker (1974–1982) "swept away matters" and "did nothing" on child sexual abuse.[12] He noted that "Herft had only ever reported one matter to police."[13]

Allen told Cleary that Bishop Appleby had been a "good operator". Cleary reported in his file note that "I read 'good operator' to mean Appleby was good at covering up matters."[14] Allen also said, according to Cleary, that:

> Father James Brown had an association with Peter Rushton and inferred that they were part of an organised paedophilia network that was largely centred around the Cessnock area.[15]

Allen pointed out that the Panel of Triers, a disciplinary committee on which the paedophiles Rushton and Lawrence both sat, had not been called in forty years. Lawrence, meanwhile, "was of the greatest concern to him … and had the most to be concerned about personally with the Royal Commission". Allen bragged that he had "saved three priests from a fate worse than death" and made no apologies for this, because he had "protected his bishop and the diocese" by doing so.[16] Allen told the meeting that "he and Rosser did a good job for George Parker" and that "Steve Smith was mad", to which Cleary replied that he knew of no "diagnosis" to support such a claim.[17]

At one meeting, Allen advised Cleary and Bishop Thompson that the best way to avoid cross-examination at the royal commission was to indicate that they had "no files or notes" and that they would have to rely on their memories. They could then simply declare, if asked questions, that they "couldn't recall". Allen said he was "Alf Holland's legal adviser" and that he had "told him that if the Royal Commission come asking any questions, he is to say he doesn't remember anything".[18]

Thompson and Cleary listened, quietly appalled. Thompson told me: "I came away feeling this is such serious, unhealthy, criminal practice." They reported it to the police. Thompson was also critical of Allen's conflict of interest as a senior office holder in the church who also acted as a criminal lawyer for clergy, including George Parker, with whom he had a "close association". But Thompson had realised that bishops did not have the power to remove a problematic member of the laity such as Allen from a church position. Thus in 2015 the synod passed the Responsible Persons Ordinance, which for the first time gave the bishop power to deal with misbehaving laity. Under that Ordinance, Allen's refusal to forward the files and his long-standing and open hostility to Michael Elliott and professional standards allowed Thompson to ask Allen to stand down immediately from all positions.[19] When Thompson challenged the power of the existing network, "That's when they got stuck into me, that's when things started to heat up."

The perceptive Detective Little thought the opposition forces had made a mistake. "They mistook Bishop Thompson's kindness for weakness." Thompson knew he had to stop the network protecting predator clergy, "mates looking after mates".

> What's particularly distinctive about the story of abuse in this diocese is the habituated protection of perpetrators and the undermining of survivors as they came forward. You could call it like a religious *Sopranos*: people who pretended to be religious behaved appallingly. And organised crime against survivors.[20]

Thompson observed a frequent disconnect in the diocese from the brutal reality of child sexual abuse, and an impulse to maintain a falsely positive image of the church.

> It was living in a bizarre world. The Mothers' Union, which is big in the diocese, had Lady Day [celebrating the annunciation to the Blessed Virgin Mary], which is lovely ... [But] no one's under sixty, they bring their banners, and they're like sailing ships, marching down the aisle ... I'm thinking, we're dealing with bloody shit. And you people are just rehearsing what you do every year. There's a kind of disconnect with reality. The institution wants to portray a certain image, but the reality is different.[21]

*

For the old guard, Thompson's revelation that he was a survivor was as if he'd soiled himself in public. They turned their backs on him when he was in the cathedral and openly berated him. He felt unwelcome in his own cathedral. Thompson had "on multiple occasions ... felt unsafe in the cathedral". So did Assistant Bishop Stuart, who told me:

> My anxieties were often raised whenever I was in and around the cathedral. Oh yes ... my primary experience was being verbally berated and berated in writing ... being attacked ... you'd line up to say farewell to people at the church door and ... you'd steel yourself for what might be said to you.[22]

Like Steve, Colin Elliott, John Cleary and Michael Elliott, Thompson faced threats, ostracism and vandalism.

> Most of the trauma of Newcastle was daily living. The sense of threat. I had a really high level of sense of threat. Personal threat, physical threat and emotional threat, reputational threat. Because I think that's what they were counting on. I would back off, because of the risk to my reputation.

Worst of all was the gaslighting – the attempts to cast Thompson as mentally ill. He refused to live at the grand Bishopscourt, instead staying in a modern house at Merewether surf beach. Bishopscourt, bequeathed to the diocese in perpetuity by a wealthy parishioner, symbolised the power and grandeur of the Anglican Church, and its upkeep cost $70,000 annually. All over Australia, such grand bishops' "palaces" were being replaced. As business manager, in 2015 John Cleary oversaw the sale of Bishopscourt for $5 million. He told me, "It's just not a good look for a bishop to live in a castle." Anglicans in Sydney, Grafton and North Queensland also "did exactly what we did". Palatial residences for bishops, Cleary said, were "so yesterday".

> I think it's best practice [to sell them], because the church can't really ... have seven bedrooms at Bishopscourt on two acres in the middle of the city ... and then say, "We're not sure if we've got enough money for redress [for survivors]."

Despite extensive consultation over the Bishopscourt sale, it caused incredible anger among the opposition group, as if Thompson were personally thumbing his nose at tradition.

The sale wasn't just seen as wrong, but as evidence Thompson was mentally unbalanced. A group signing themselves the "Senior Professionals of Newcastle" sent an angry, 1500-word letter to the Episcopal Standards Commission, to the archbishop of Sydney, Glenn Davies, to the primate of the Anglican Church and to the royal commission. They claimed Thompson was mentally ill, perhaps as a result of his childhood abuse, and that he hadn't informed the diocese of this alleged mental illness. They demanded his former dioceses be contacted about his illness. They bewailed that "the name of the late Bishop Shevill, a man highly respected during the years of his episcopate, should be besmirched in this fashion". They complained that at the time of the alleged abuse Thompson was nineteen, so had been "a consenting adult". He may have "misinterpreted" Shevill's "behaviour" or "statements". (What exactly was ambiguous or consensual about hands plunging uninvited into your groin, they didn't explain.) They cast doubt on the abuse having ever occurred, yet condemned Thompson for taking "no action at the time, thus potentially exposing younger members" of the church to an abusive priest. They also claimed to be "personally aware of a number of cases in which a claim of sexual abuse has been falsely made, for reasons of malice or personal enmity".

The "Senior Professionals of Newcastle" explained that they had also written to the primate that the Episcopal Standards Board might "require a medical, psychiatric or psychological examination [of Thompson] ... in view of the apparent complex history of health problems, possibly beginning over 40 years ago when he alleges, he was the subject of abuse". They also complained that Thompson didn't go to the cathedral enough, without acknowledging their hostile behaviour when he did.

The signers of the letter included staunch Lawrence supporters: Simon Adam, Stephen Booker, Robert and Jocelyn Caddies, Pamela Dowdell, Suzanne Evans, Gregory Hansen, John and Margaret McNaughton, Lyn Scanlon, William Scott, David and Mary Stewart, Laurie Tabart and Virginia Wheeler.

Thompson was badly shaken when he read it.

What triggers me is the indifference, the disbelief, the arrogance of people that diminish survivors, and turn away from them: that triggers deep
anger … If they could do it to a bishop, they could do it to people who
wanted to speak about crimes against children.[23]

He felt humiliated but also angry that the signers had knelt and received
communion from him, while behind his back they were organising this
awful letter.

Thompson took long walks along Merewether Beach, nursing his
bruised soul as he trudged along the sand, listening to the surf pounding,
watching the waves churn up everything in their path.

CHAPTER NINETEEN
THE HEART
OF DARKNESS

IF PAEDOPHILES ARE capable of telling themselves that the child "enjoys it", as Jim Brown did, they are capable of anything. Some of the clergy and laity who were hostile to Michael Elliott's work had no idea of the horrors passing across his desk. Elliott encountered more fully than anyone the heart of darkness that was the paedophile network in the Newcastle Anglican Church. Take his shocking discovery of the Dungeon.

In May 2010, Elliott had learned that a Cessnock man, David Walker, who worked at the Cessnock Gaol, was a paedophile who regularly held "men's and boys' parties" at his house, attended by "large numbers of Newcastle clergy". Walker would film the parties and hid a huge number of video tapes in the walls of his home. His house, a large one in rural Cessnock, had secret passages and a hidden dungeon containing BDSM (bondage, discipline and sado-masochism) equipment such as handcuffs, racks and whips. Walker had hidden cameras set up around the house to film the sexual acts. He was the prime suspect in the murder of a teenage boy. In a file note, Elliott explained: "Police were closing in on Walker when he committed suicide by shooting himself in the paddock of his property."

Elliott also noted that "Walker has written into his will that his good friend Father X [an Anglican priest] was to destroy a number of videos." Police later found that Father X had burnt the videos at Walker's house prior to their arrival. Elliott visited the house but found it had been stripped. There were places where something – likely the BDSM equipment – had clearly been ripped from the walls.

Elliott observed:

> There appears to be links to Walker and the known clergy paedophile crew
> Father Peter Rushton (deceased) Father James Brown (deceased) Father
> Ray Nelson, (deceased) and others. The ring also used to have some affil-
> iation with the St Albans boys home (for wards of the state …).

*

Meanwhile, Michael Elliott never gave up investigating Steve's case. Steve was raped by Parker in a parked Jaguar in the garage at the West Wallsend Rectory on many occasions. He still hates Jaguars. Parker told him the car had been left there "by a friend". Who? There can't have been too many Jaguars in Newcastle at that time.

That's what Michael Elliott thought, too. In April 2014, he contacted Detective Benson at the Newcastle police to tell him about a possible link between George Parker and a notorious paedophile, Ashleigh Jarrold, a dentist from the inner Newcastle suburb of Hamilton. Jarrold had been convicted of sexually abusing children and jailed in 2007 for five years, which in 2009 was extended on appeal to seven years and five months.[1] Jarrold drove a Jaguar and had gone overseas around the time the car was stored in Parker's garage, between 1972 and 1975. Elliott had read a police statement from a victim of Jarrold, which mentioned the paedophile turning up to his house in 1978 in such a car.

Jarrold also held men's and boys' parties. He was one of the worst of the worst – and part of a very active paedophile ring in Newcastle. Jarrold's network included the Catholic priest Father Peter Brock, who was the brother of the editor of the *Newcastle Herald*, Roger Brock. (There is no suggestion Roger Brock was involved.) According to evidence presented in court, Father Brock would sit naked on the couch and masturbate, while a teenage boy would be plied with alcohol and then abused by Jarrold and other men. The police prosecutor, Sergeant David Wild, described these occasions as a "paedophilic smorgasbord".[2]

Father Brock also abused twin brothers John and Paul Parmeter. The abuse of the boys, who were from a devout Catholic family, began in 1968, when they were nine years old. Brock, who was awarded the Order of Australia for his services to music education, gave the Parmeter boys music lessons. According to John Parmeter, Brock befriended his mother and became his father's drinking buddy.[3] The "music lessons" were part of grooming; "hugs" became increasingly sexual, and eventually led to games of strip poker, in which the priest ended up naked and committed ever more serious sex crimes against the boys. John said it seemed impossible to tell his devout parents, who believed in Brock: "I could never tell anyone that this happened." Parmeter felt "powerless to combat the secret crimes of the priest".[4]

The abuse escalated, with Brock taking John to a Newcastle house, where Brock watched as the boy was plied with alcohol and sexually assaulted by several men. Brock and Jarrold were always present, but other men were also involved. On the first visit, after John had been assaulted, he heard someone say, "It's someone else's turn now." There was no sex between adults on those occasions, only sexual acts done to the child.

In 2008, John Parmeter had a private meeting with Brock on a park bench and confronted him with the damage he had done. Brock later wrote to him, acknowledging having caused harm but taking care not to mention how.

> I acknowledge that my actions have caused you pain and distress, no matter how unwittingly or unintentionally on my part. I am ashamed and sorry for that and offer this sincere apology. I hope this letter can help you on your journey.

After the Parmeter brothers went to the police, Brock was charged with multiple offences in October 2008. The psychological damage caused by Brock's abuse, however, was such that between hearings John felt too fragile to continue. The DPP dropped the twenty-two charges.[5] After an internal investigation by the Catholic Church, the bishop of Maitland-Newcastle, Michael Malone, expressed publicly his "considerable joy" that Father Brock would return to his ministry, giving the false impression that Brock had been found innocent.

The link between the Catholic and the Anglican abusers was that Ashleigh Jarrold also preyed on the two sons of a caretaker at the Anglican cathedral, who appears to have been complicit in the abuse.[6] In the 1970s, there were sessions watching pornography at the man's cottage. On several occasions, Jarrold went off to find an underage boy to bring back. The boy would be drugged or plied with alcohol and sexually assaulted.

For Jarrold, the cruelty was the point. He was compulsive. His lawyer, John Woodward, also appeared for Graeme Lawrence. While on bail, Jarrold groomed, online, a "boy" whom he thought to be fifteen years old but who was actually an undercover detective. Jarrold sent him child pornography and told him about other boys he had abused. He arranged to take the boy to a hotel to have sex. Surveillance showed Jarrold masturbating while talking online to the boy.

Jarrold also produced and disseminated child pornography. When detectives searched his home, they found an appalling cache of recordings and several thousand images, of which 129 featured children, including degrading and sadistic acts. In correspondence between 2003 and 2008, Jarrold discussed child sexual abuse, rape and defecation. He wrote of the pleasure he had hearing children screaming in pain as they were tortured and raped. And he said he would "have to kill them so they wouldn't go to police".[7]

Given Jarrold was a paedophile who drove a Jaguar, and Steve reported a Jaguar in the garage where he was abused, was there a link between Jarrold and George Parker? Steve always believed the car belonged to Jarrold. Jaguar advertisements from the 1970s show muted colours of grey-browns and brown-greys. Steve remembered the car as grey, but it was registered as brown. Was it Jarrold's? We will never know.

*

What was clear was that rather than individual paedophiles operating in isolation, some of the Newcastle abusers were part of an organised network. Michael Elliott had been tipped off by a church worker that the Cessnock area had a "dark" history in terms of sexual abuse, and it likely wasn't only the Dungeon he was referring to. He learned that Fathers Ogle, Brown (the priest, not Jim Brown the lay worker) and Rushton were involved, and that "many" video recordings had been made of their offences. Elliott followed it up.

The best evidence we have of this network of abuse is from a witness referred to as CKG by the royal commission, but whom I will call simply G (neither pseudonym has any relation to his real initials). G arrived at St Alban's in January 1968, when he was about ten years old. "I remember feeling very lonely and isolated," he said. At St Alban's, he was often "fostered out" on weekends. Once, he and another boy were sent by the matron, Mrs Barry, to stay at the pretty little coastal town of Woy Woy on the NSW Central Coast. When they got there, there was only a priest and an older woman, possibly the priest's mother. G remembered being given a cup of cocoa, and:

> the man saying to the woman, "Don't worry, it won't hurt him. It's only a sleeping pill. He won't know anything." I later woke up in bed with the man. I was feeling dopey and leaking sperm from my rear. My mouth was sticky and gluey. The man took me to the beach and told me to wash in the surf.

When G was about thirteen, Peter Rushton took him to another priest's house in Cessnock. G was given port wine and cigarettes and felt "a spinning in my head … The next thing I remember waking up very sore leaking from my rear. I believe that I was drugged and anally raped. I cannot recall the priest's name." Another time:

> I was sent to the Bellbird rectory by either Mr or Mrs Barry to mow lawns, clean cars or clean up … Once we were alone … Father Ogle asked me if I wanted a drink. It was an alcoholic drink and made [me] feel like I was spinning. I blacked out and when I awoke I was very sore in my backside. Father Ogle put me in his car, gave me a dollar note, and drove me back to St Alban's. He threatened me, "Do not say anything to anyone or you'll be in big trouble."

On another occasion he was unwell and in the sick bay at St Alban's when Father James Brown came and fondled him. G resisted and Brown threatened him: "Don't tell anybody anything about … today." G alleged that the warden and Father Rushton both watched while he was naked showering and made him bend over and wash his toes.

When G was fourteen or fifteen, Father Walter Ogle took him to a house at Nulkaba, near Cessnock.[8] "There were another two men in the house. All three men tried to fondle me, but I resisted, I started swinging around and I said, 'You're not going to get me … I don't want to do it.'" They put him in a white straitjacket to restrain him, and then "continued to fondle me". Back at St Alban's, G tried to tell the matron, who sent him to "the rockpile", where as punishment he shovelled dirt and rocks to prepare soil for the garden and oval.

Around the same time, he was picked up by Ogle and taken to a priest's house near Wallsend.

> I recall being in a house with five men. One of the men was Father Ogle. I cannot remember the names of the other men. The men started complimenting me on my body. They said to me, "Would you like to be in the movies? Would you like to be on TV?" They told me to take my shirt off, which I did. They started feeling me up and commented on how muscly I was. After this, all of the men left the room and were clearly elsewhere in the house. One returned. This man started fondling my genitals. I elbowed him in the nose. The man's nose bled and he called to the others for help. I grabbed my shirt and ran for the door. As I was trying to get out, the other men pulled on my shirt but I got out and hid in some hedges nearby. I recall the men searching for me for hours.

Although G was a ward of the state, he knew where his father lived. He walked there and told him what had happened. "My father said, 'We can't do nothing son. They [the Anglican Church] are too big.'" G went to the police station in Cardiff, "against my father's wishes". He tried to tell the police officer that some men "were trying to get me". The police officer would not listen. He told G, "We can't do anything about it." The boy returned to his father, who took him back to St Alban's.

The former residents of St Alban's Boys' Home are divided as to whether abuse was facilitated by the caretakers or whether they had been well looked after. Some deny any abuse occurred at all and speak very highly of the Barrys and the care they provided. There was some suggestion that earlier caretakers before the Barrys had a similar name, "Farrie" and could have been confused with "Barry". Others, such as Paul Gray and G, remember being sexually abused and allege that Mr Barry facilitated it. In his sworn statement to the royal commission, G said he disclosed to Mrs Barry that he had been sexually abused several times.

> I was usually punished for doing so. (For example, by being made to write essays about Jesus, or being beaten by Mr Barry, or being sent to The

Rockpile.) ... I did not tell Mr Barry about my abuse, because I believe that he knew what was happening and was supporting the abuse.

G also thought that other boys knew of the abuse and would call out "Ompa, Ompa" while making thrusting movements suggestive of anal sex. One possibility is, of course, that some boys were abused but not all, hence their different memories.

G left St Alban's just before his sixteenth birthday. He never got over the abuse. "I suffer mentally and physically every day," he told the royal commission. The sexual abuse left him with problems with trust and sexual intimacy, and with how he related to his children. He also reported long-term physical effects, such as bowel problems. He was abused from 1968 to 1972, from the age of ten to fourteen. G's testimony clearly suggested an Anglican paedophile ring, with priests working together to facilitate one another's abuse, secure in the knowledge they were unlikely to suffer any consequences.[9]

*

When people learned I was writing this book, they frequently assumed that child sexual abuse only occurred in the Catholic Church and that it was a result of the expectation that Catholic priests be celibate. Child sexual abuse has consistently been framed as a consequence of sexual repression and frustration. The anger over child sexual abuse in the Catholic Church has been particularly potent because the Catholic Church imposes such strict controls over sexuality – celibacy for priests, chastity before marriage, no divorce, no same-sex relationships – yet some Catholic priests have sexually abused children. The sheer hypocrisy!

If we see child sexual abuse as a consequence of these strictures, one understandable response is to assume that adopting more liberal attitudes to sex, educating ignorant clerics and abolishing celibacy will solve the problem. Joanne McCarthy, who was raised in the Catholic Church, said to me that "churches just get really hung up about sex. And I think if they didn't, a lot of this shit would go away. If they read a little more science and a little less bloody theology ..."

Celibacy, unless it is voluntary, seems to me to be a cruel and unnecessary imposition on human beings, who need deep and close attachments and sexual intimacy. But if it were abolished, would child sexual abuse really "go away"? No. Anglican priests have not been required to be celibate for centuries. Some of the worst abusers were in heterosexual marriages – such as Robert Ellmore, who horribly abused the young daughters of the principal of Morpeth College, Lance Johnston, when they were six and eight years old. Ellmore was a serial paedophile and had been convicted of a sex crime in 1957, but he changed his name and found no impediment to becoming a priest. He gained access to the Johnston girls in the 1970s by babysitting them. The damage he inflicted on those children was immense and lifelong. Ellmore was convicted for these crimes in 1998. He was jailed for eleven years in 2002 for more child sex offences committed in the Newcastle, Bathurst and Sydney dioceses over forty-four years. In his case, heterosexual marriage was clearly no impediment to paedophile behaviour.

The false idea that sexual frustration causes child sexual abuse is caught in the bizarre but revealing remarks of Philip Gerber, director of professional standards for Sydney and Newcastle Anglicans until 2007. After Ellmore's conviction, a mother of a victim said, "[Gerber] told me he had met [Ellmore's] wife, that she was a good sort, not bad looking, not ugly or overweight," as if any of these characteristics would explain child abuse. The mother retorted that Ellmore's wife was "not eight" – that is, Ellmore was aroused by little girls.[10] Mr Gerber has since formally apologised to the victim's mother for his comments.

During research for this book, as people came to trust me, I learned about the existence of a seedy sexual subculture of predation in Newcastle. The official world of public prudery, the professed adherence to "faithfulness in service", was obeyed by many clergy. But it also existed alongside brazen flouting of those codes of conduct. Those inside "the family" were promoted and installed, usually by Graeme Lawrence, into positions of power. Anyone likely to disapprove of or expose their sexual activities was sidelined.

The group around Lawrence and Rushton had a libertarian sexual ethos. Their activities had nothing to do with sexual repression or celibacy. Some in the group – such as Lawrence and Goyette, and Brown and Rushton – were in long-term relationships, but they also had other adult sexual partners, and they also abused underage boys. A confidential file note by Michael Elliott from August 2010 records a priest who told him that he was:

currently supporting a male adult who alleges he was historically forcibly raped by Graeme Lawrence when he was a child at a party involving
other clergy.[11]

Such "men's and boys' parties" were part of the culture of sexual entitlement, even to children, and at the heart of it was the abuse of power.

Following the sexual liberation movement of the 1960s and 1970s,
there was a widespread acceptance that sex was good, pleasurable and
could be enjoyed freely by consenting adults, having been repressed for
centuries by the church. The issue was no longer whether sexual activity
had taken place outside of holy matrimony, but whether it was consenting,
or if an abuse of power had taken place. Most of us today would agree with
all that. But then some, including the Newcastle Anglican abusers, took
sexual liberation one disastrous step further. If sex was good and repression bad, and if children were sexual beings, why shouldn't they enjoy sex
too, with adults? Therefore, the logic went, it was not morally wrong to
initiate a young teen into what they claimed was a sexual "relationship"
but was actually abuse. A child can never "consent".

During the 1970s and 1980s, some paedophiles – the North American
Man/Boy Love Association, for example – argued for sexual liberation to
extend to sexual relationships between adults and children. Even without explicitly endorsing such a movement, the Anglican paedophiles in
Newcastle had a similar sexual ideology. They told themselves that they
were doing nothing wrong. Sex with children was okay, and was even a
good experience for the children. Such beliefs enabled the sexual abuse
of children and were evident in the abuse of H by Duncan and Lawrence;
initiating a boy into sex was doing him a favour.

At the heart of this attitude was male entitlement. I agree with Joanne
McCarthy when she told me:

This whole thing is about gender ... boys' clubs, blokes getting away with
what they've always done ... These patriarchal structures ... this is the end
point, this is what happens when you get that sense of entitlement and that
no one can stop you ... This is how bad you can go ... We've reached the end
point of letting men get away with whatever they want ... even children.[12]

CHAPTER TWENTY

THE GOOD COPPER

SINCE 2001, STEVE had been looking for a "good copper", someone who was serious about child sexual abuse, to reopen his case against George Parker. In 2013, he finally found one.

In 2012, Steve had seen Detective Chief Inspector Peter Fox speak at the Newcastle Leagues Club and again on *Lateline* on ABC TV. Fox claimed that the Catholic Church in the Hunter Valley had engaged in a cover-up of child sexual abuse by priests, and that the Newcastle police had failed to investigate these crimes, essentially making them complicit in the coverup. These sensational allegations would have reminded many viewers of two previous exposés of corruption: the 1995–1997 Wood Royal Commission into NSW police corruption, including police links to organised paedophile networks; and, in Victoria, the blocking of an investigation by Detective Denis Ryan into child sexual abuse by a "Catholic mafia" operating in the Victorian police force in the 1970s. (Ryan was eventually vindicated during the royal commission, as part of Case Study 28 on the Ballarat Catholic diocese. The former and serving Victorian police commissioners, Mick Miller and Graham Ashton, apologised for the shocking way Ryan had been treated.)

After Fox's explosive claims, a special commission of inquiry was called by the NSW premier, Barry O'Farrell, to commence early in 2013. Steve went along, hoping he might have found the right police officer to take up his case. However, Steve was surprised to find himself unimpressed by Fox in the witness box. Fox had presented himself as the hero of child sexual abuse policing, but under questioning by the special commission his claims were shown to be exaggerated, or sometimes even false. His claim that the Catholic Church in the Hunter Valley had engaged in a cover-up of child sexual abuse was found to be true. However, his allegations against the police, and his account of his own role in the police investigation, did not stand up to scrutiny.

On *Lateline*, Fox had said he had been "ordered to stand down" from a Newcastle police investigation into child sexual abuse in the Catholic Church called Strike Force Lantle. In fact, he had never been involved in the investigation to begin with. He had instead been stationed at Port Stephens, a smaller police station forty minutes north of Newcastle. A task-force like Strike Force Lantle needed the resources of the larger Newcastle CBD office, as only a large station could spare an officer to investigate historical crimes. Moreover, Fox was a detective chief inspector, which would normally be too high a rank to be placed in charge of such an investigation; the officer in charge would usually be a detective sergeant, who would do the investigative work with the help of a constable and report back to a detective inspector or higher.

Fox was also leaking to Joanne McCarthy all the time, which senior police were unhappy about. He even gave McCarthy the confidential police statement of a victim, "AJ", without permission. When AJ saw her statement quoted in the *Newcastle Herald*, she was devastated. Fox claimed on *Lateline* that he had a special relationship with AJ, who was alleged to have said, "I only want to speak to Peter Fox". He gave the impression that only he had the trust of this survivor and perhaps of others too, and that he had therefore been the best person to lead Strike Force Lantle. However, AJ gave evidence at the special commission that none of Fox's claims about her were true. When I spoke to her, she confirmed that she never said she would speak only to Fox. In fact, he had approached her out of the blue, after getting her name from Joanne McCarthy. AJ also gave evidence before the inquiry that on *Lateline* Fox had, without warning her and without her permission, shared confidential details of her case with hundreds of thousands of viewers. She felt used.

A month before Fox made his *Lateline* claims, Detective Jeff Little, the actual chief investigating officer on Strike Force Lantle, had completed the investigation and sent a mammoth 3000-page brief of evidence to the DPP. The investigation, therefore, was in extremely good shape. Little's brief became the basis on which Catholic Archbishop Philip Wilson was convicted in 2018 for failing to report allegations of child sexual abuse against a priest in 1976. (Wilson was later acquitted on appeal.)

Strike Force Lantle had undoubtedly taken a while to get going. Three officers started work on it, then each went on sick leave. However, as the special commission concluded, as policing is a very stressful occupation, successive officers going on sick leave could be attributed to bad luck rather than a conspiracy. In fact, at the time, Fox was himself on sick leave. Fox also claimed that one of the officers did not have the necessary experience to run Strike Force Lantle. This was also untrue. When cross-examined, he admitted his assertion was based only on the police "rumour mill".[1]

The exaggerations continued. One of the briefs of evidence Fox claimed to have prepared turned out not to exist at all. A computer disk which he claimed to have sent to the NSW Ombudsman was nowhere to be found in their files. Fox claimed a policeman had warned him about a "Catholic mafia" within the police force – but that former officer, under oath, denied ever having said it. Meanwhile Fox, despite not being assigned to the inquiry into Catholic priest Denis McAlinden, a notorious abuser of little girls, was found to have accessed the records of the investigation and changed them to list himself as the officer in charge.

Steve was listening to it all, ears pricked. The special commission found in its final report, released on 30 May 2014, as follows:

> The commission finds no credible evidence to support the notion that there are senior police in Northern Region Command of the New South Wales Police Force, including Newcastle City Local Area Command, who were prepared to take steps to try to ensure that alleged child abuse offences involving Catholic church officials were not investigated or not properly investigated ...
>
> The commission considers that by at least 2010 Fox had lost the objectivity required of an investigating officer ... he no longer possessed the detachment necessary for properly investigating such matters. In short, he had become a zealot ...
>
> Fox's evidence should be approached with caution; Fox gave evidence to the commission that was implausible. Fox was also prone to exaggerate aspects of his evidence ... Fox had engaged in conduct that was inconsistent with the integrity required of a police officer. He provided sensitive information about police investigations (including internal police report and a victim's statement) to a journalist.

Joanne McCarthy, under cross-examination on 25 June 2013, expressed concern that Fox's *Lateline* comments had muddied the waters by confusing the call for a royal commission with internal police conflicts:

> when I saw some of the questions … and I saw Peter Fox saying – you know, his responses to it, I sort of went, "Oh my God, what is this?" … I saw it and just went, "Oh, no, please don't make it an internal police thing at this point."

McCarthy also knew that Fox was thinking of writing a book about his experience. Wayne Roser SC asked her: "Have you seen writings by him which [are] to be included in this particular book?" McCarthy answered: "I had a quick flick through it, and I thought, 'He won't get a publisher for this,' because it just had about 2000 defamation actions in it, so I thought that he was going to be up against it."[2]

Fox did write a book, called *Walking Towards Thunder*, published in 2019. And he was up against it, as McCarthy correctly predicted. Detective Inspector Jeff Little sued for defamation. The book was pulped, and Little received a payout in an out-of-court settlement.

*

After ruling Fox out as his potential "good copper", Steve kept going to the special commission each day, looking for another police officer who might help him reopen his case against Parker. Then Jeff Little took the stand. "I watched Jeff Little give evidence, and he tore skin off … Like, this guy was red-hot, so prepared, so switched on."

Little was a tall, strongly built man with piercing blue eyes and buzzcut hair: he looked every inch a detective. He was watchful, self-contained, reserved, as if holding a lot back. There was something formidable about him. Little avoided the media assiduously, scornful of what he called "glory hunters". Steve liked the way Little was so well prepared and answered questions economically, with a flinty directness. He had a nice turn of phrase. Little told the commission that Fox "had ridden to glory on a saddle of lies".[3]

Detective Chief Inspector Wayne Humphrey, Little's senior officer, explained why he chose him to head Strike Force Lantle. When Little returned to general policing after stints in the Federal Police and on over-seas peacekeeping missions, Humphrey got to know him in the "lonely hours on night work at Port Stephens". He thought Little's "demeanour" and "determination" suited the Lantle investigation into child sexual abuse perfectly. Humphrey described Little as:

> a very interesting fellow. He understands a request is enough to get things done. He is extremely thorough. He has extremely high-level skills in com-puter work and, above all else, he is not a person that will be bullied by any person of any rank, [is] particularly loyal to the command ... Doggedly determined, I think, would be his best description.[4]

The special commission of inquiry had asked Ian Lloyd QC, the emi-nent Crown prosecutor and criminal lawyer, to do an independent review of Little's management of the strike force. Lloyd described Little as a "highly competent investigator", whose management of the taskforce, and the brief he prepared for the DPP, were "outstanding". "In all my years of prosecuting crimes, and we're approaching thirty-seven years now, the report is as good as I've ever seen." Acknowledging that Lit-tle had conducted a complex investigation over sixteen months, Lloyd observed that by the "mountain of evidence he uncovered I would have thought he would be working day and night".[5] The brief was 3000 pages long with a 255-page summary, supporting claims of concealment of child sexual abuse by members of the Maitland-Newcastle Catholic diocese. Lloyd also commented on Little's ability to form a "very fine rapport" with victims.

Steve came to understand over time that Humphrey's description of Little as an unusual person was true. Little was a very strong character. He had to leave home at fourteen and took entire responsibility for himself at that young age. He worked before and after school and on weekends to pay for rent, food, uniforms and accommodation. He cooked for himself and did his own laundry as well as studying, without any family or other support – while still a school kid. He bunked in with some military men for a while. He always kept himself clean and respectable. Since boyhood, he had wanted to be a police officer. When his school friends found out that he looked after himself, paying his own way, they envied what they saw as his freedom. Little envied them for the families they had around them.

The headmaster found out too and was astonished that someone so young had been quietly providing for himself.

Little had come back to general policing after a distinguished career in the Federal Police, doing stints in specialist investigation units and then in overseas human rights and peacekeeping missions, in Timor from early 2000, the Sudan, Jordan and elsewhere between 2002 and 2007. His peacekeeping roles involved complex investigations, managerial roles, instruction, training and management of police forces in developing nations.[6] In 2010, while at Port Stephens station just before he was seconded to Strike Force Lantle, he was awarded the Australian Bravery Medal. After returning to Australia, he decided that his vocation now lay in general community policing. One of his passions was investigating child sexual abuse – pursuing those who, as he put it, "preyed on the vulnerable".

Steve knew this was the person he had been looking for, but he still had to convince Little to take up his case. On the front steps of the courthouse, they finally met. Steve recalled:

> I was on a walking stick at the time because I had osteomyelitis, and I was really sick. Jeff was on a stick because he'd had a knee operation, so we hobbled out the front and I said, "How you going, Jeff?" He said, "Do I know you?"

Steve introduced himself. They began chatting about their walking sticks. Little, for his part, was impressed by Steve, because he showed empathy, asking how the policeman was coping with being under fire at the inquiry. A few days later, Steve said:

> "There's something I want you to have a look at for me." And Jeff said, "Mate, I'm up to my arse." I said, "I know, no pressure, just ..." I told Jeff a real quick little thing about the case. He said, "If I get a chance, mate, I'll have a look."

Steve wasn't hopeful. He didn't think Little would have the time or energy to look at his matter while attending the inquiry every day. But to Steve's surprise, he did. "After about four or five days, he'd come back and he said, 'Mate, I want to see you.' And I said, 'Why?' And he said, 'There's something in this ... This is wrong.'"

Little knew that to reopen the case and get it to committal was going to be an uphill battle. He had to convince the DPP and the police that there had been a miscarriage of justice. And they had to accept that the first investigation and brief had been inadequate. But he was determined.

Steve was thrilled and grateful.

A few months later they set up the taskforce Strike Force Arinya 2, headed by Jeff Little, to look into my case ... So he'd already started looking at my matter, and they'd kept it under wraps. Then one day he said to me, "Can you come in and make a statement?"

It was now 2014, and Steve was ready, with the help of Rachael, Michael Elliott's support and the counselling he'd received, to disclose all the abuse in a police interview, including the penetration and the multiple rapes. It was emotionally exhausting and took a long time. Steve described to me Little's empathy and kind, respectful manner. Sensitivity on the part of police when survivors tell their stories is vital. It is a strange kind of intimacy, the bond that develops between the detective and the survivor as they tell the most humiliating details of sexual abuse.

For a case to succeed, the thoroughness and exactness of a brief of evidence are crucial. This was the second time Steve had experienced a police investigation. The two experiences could not have been more different. Steve was surprised by the energy and zeal Little displayed. "He was dogged, determined ... He was into everyone ... he was like a dog with a bone." Little obtained sixty fresh statements from people who were witnesses in one way or another.

Little organised walk-throughs of all the places of abuse, at Minmi, Edgeworth and Gateshead, while another police officer filmed Steve explaining what had happened and where it had occurred. Little was respectful but forensic, questioning, checking facts, the veracity of Steve's memory, the layout of the rectory, the rooms, vestries and churches where abuse had occurred. Such videos can be shown to the judge and jury to help them to assess the victim's truthfulness.

It was emotionally harrowing for Steve to revisit the places where he had been abused, but Rachael's loving presence, waiting outside, strengthened him.

Detective Little told me that police are not there to find evidence to *confirm* a story. The key is to remain neutral, rather than having a confirmation bias. "I am there as a 'collector of facts', and when a case meets the threshold, I put it before a 'trier of facts' – a judge." If there is a fact that contradicts what the complainant alleges, you put it in. "You are there to find the truth."

With forensic care, Little tested every sentence of Steve's statements. He told me that all of Steve's story was supported by the evidence. Little interviewed people in relation to the case in other states and arranged for a Western Australian detective to interview Steve's ex-wife. He interviewed Steve's stepmother. He interviewed George Parker's parishioners at Edgeworth, West Wallsend and Gateshead. Many still adored the priest and thought "lovely Father George" couldn't possibly have done anything wrong.

Little thought they were "institutionalised", by which he meant so indoctrinated by the church that they believed a priest was beyond reproach. They couldn't bear to admit anything to the contrary. He flew to Queensland and interviewed former altar boys, parishioners and priests. He checked whether Steve and his brother's descriptions of the rectory at Gateshead were accurate. Had the bathroom window been boarded up, as they described? To verify whether that was true, Little interviewed Reverend David Simpson, who lived at the Gateshead rectory before Parker. Simpson confirmed that it was.

Importantly, the former parishioners at Gateshead whom Little interviewed confirmed that there *was* a morning tea after the service on that day. Moreover, Little found that the church Parker went to next was only a few minutes away. So, it would have been possible for him to have morning tea and then drive to the next service.

Little wanted to test whether Steve was right about Parker reaching around and grabbing his brother's groin in the car. He searched used-car advertisements and, when that drew a blank, contacted numerous car-enthusiast groups for the same make and model of Galant station wagon as Parker had owned in the 1970s. He finally found one a few hours from Newcastle in the Sydney suburb of Como. Little obtained the manual and examined it to make sure all the measurements were exactly the same as the model Parker owned. Then he put a constable in the back, placed a book on their lap so as not to violate their personal space, and reached around.

Yes, Parker could have reached a boy's groin from the driver's seat.

Getting the police and DPP to agree to reopen the case was very difficult, because they had to be convinced that the original investigation was inadequate. The new brief of evidence had to be thorough and watertight. Little described the original file as "malnourished". There had been an insufficiency of evidence. This time it was different; Little's brief for the DPP on Steve's case had a 300-page covering report and was 3000 pages long.

However, now he had to hit the pause button. All the campaigning for a royal commission had finally paid off. In 2013, it was announced that the Newcastle Anglicans would be Case Study 42 in the newly established Royal Commission into Institutional Responses to Child Sexual Abuse, meaning the criminal investigation into Parker had to be put on hold. Royal commission statements and evidence might prejudice the case.

Steve was frustrated by the delay, but he was also buoyed by the opportunity the commission would have to investigate child sexual abuse and cover-ups, with its power to subpoena documents and to cross-examine witnesses under oath. And he was extremely grateful to Detective Little for opening his case again. It was a life-transforming experience to have a tough-minded, good copper look at the evidence and then believe him. The symbolism of the place where Steve first met Little affected him deeply.

> All of a sudden, you find a cop that's prepared [to take my case on] … this all came from approaching him on the steps of Newcastle Court, of all places. Where Parker, Lawrence and Rosser had all laughed at me after the trial fell over. The irony wasn't lost on me.[7]

PART FIVE

THE ROYAL COMMISSION AND ITS AFTERMATH

CHAPTER TWENTY-ONE

NO EXPIRY DATE FOR JUSTICE

THE ANGLICAN HEARING of the Royal Commission into Institutional Responses to Child Sexual Abuse began at the new Newcastle Courthouse in August 2016. The royal commission had by then been running for almost four years. By the time it delivered its final report on 15 December 2017, it would be the longest-running and most thorough investigation of its kind anywhere. There was tremendous interest in it worldwide. There had been other inquiries, in the UK, Ireland, Canada and the USA, but none had been so lengthy, comprehensive and remorselessly forensic. The commission examined allegations of child sexual abuse in more than 4000 institutions. There were 6500 private sessions with survivors, 440 days of public hearings, 1200 witnesses, more than 1.2 million documents examined, and seventeen published volumes of findings and research reports.

The royal commission was remarkable in another way. It was both reflective of and a powerful contributor to the ongoing cultural revolution that ushered in a new sensibility about child sexual abuse. The national mood shifted decisively in favour of listening to and believing survivors and respecting their suffering. By the time of the final hearing, many survivors paid tribute to the commission's chair, Justice Peter McClellan. Fair-minded and prodigiously hard-working, McClellan was a plain-speaking man who did not genuflect towards powerful, high-status clergy. Cardinal George Pell copped a grilling, as did Roger Herft and all the other former bishops of Newcastle. McClellan showed acute moral judgement and was quick to pounce on dissembling, self-deception, obfuscation, euphemism and outright lying. He repeatedly presented perpetrators and protectors with their actions in simple, stark terms.

McLellan also showed kindness and empathy to survivors. Leonie Sheedy from the Care Leavers Australasia Network told the *Guardian* in 2015 that McClellan "gets it".[1] Like many people who had spent time in care, she was wary of authority figures and was at first suspicious of him. However, at a CLAN meeting in a garage, he asked everyone to call him Peter, then listened attentively all afternoon to survivors. She was impressed. "He has made us feel at ease, he is gentle, and you can tell he cares." She gave him a cushion with the logo of his beloved Melbourne football team emblazoned on it. At one of the hearings, she realised he was sitting on it. He took it to every hearing.

A great deal of focus was on the Catholics, the largest Christian denomination in Australia, representing 46 per cent of churchgoers in 2014. The Catholic Church had the largest number of abusers, with more than 2000 investigated by the commission, and 4444 allegations of abuse. The Anglican Church, the third-largest denomination, with 11 per cent of all churchgoers in 2014, had more than 1000 child sexual abuse complaints. Between 1980 and 2015, the Catholic Church paid out $280 million to survivors, and the Anglicans just over $34 million. All but one of the Anglican dioceses in Australia had received complaints in the past thirty-five years. One of the very worst was Newcastle.

The commission had come to Newcastle to ask who knew about the abuse, when did they know about it and what had they done?

*

In his opening address to the royal commission in 2013, McLellan said that bearing witness to survivors would be a large part of the commission's role. There is a desperate desire in the hearts of survivors for recognition of what they have been through. For Steve, giving truthful public testimony about the sexual abuse he suffered as a child was part of his healing. He never gave up seeking justice. Telling his story in public took enormous courage. But it was a central life purpose.

I want people to come forward. That's my main aim in life, to get people
who've been abused and haven't spoken up and are struggling to speak
up … Tell someone what happened to you so you're not struggling, you're
not on your own.[2]

However, for Steve, writing his statement and answering lawyers' questions meant reliving it all. It triggered his PTSD symptoms, and his anxiety
levels soared. Unlike in 2001, however, he wasn't alone. He had a good psychologist and doctor. He was now in a stable relationship with Rachael,
who was loving, steady and fiercely protective of him. He had friends and
allies in Michael Elliott and Bishop Thompson. He had a terrific lawyer,
Peter O'Brien, who had worked for many survivors giving evidence to the
royal commission. But reinhabiting the past still meant entering an emotional danger zone.

The royal commission also posed a second challenge for Steve. When
the royal commission investigation into the Newcastle Anglicans was
announced, Detective Little's investigation into George Parker was close to
completion. As well as reinstating the 2001 charges, Little intended to charge
Parker with twenty additional offences, including buggery of a minor. But
the royal commission meant the court case had to be delayed. Parker was
old and ill. Would he die before a second trial? Steve also worried that the
imminent court case might prevent him telling his story at the royal commission. There was a danger that evidence before the commission might
prejudice the forthcoming trial. On the first day of the commission's hearing
in Newcastle, crown prosecutor Ian Temby QC asked for names associated
with the Parker case to be suppressed. Steve recalled, "We were sitting there
on tenterhooks, we didn't know what would happen … we all panicked." To
his immense relief, there was a way around it: Parker was given the pseudonym CKC, while Steve would be called CKA and his brother CKB.

The royal commission had clear terms of reference, which acted like a
filter, meaning it only examined those cases that best showed how institutions responded to child sexual abuse. The Anglican diocese of Newcastle
was Case Study 42, and it was one of the most important cases the commission examined, as Peter McLellan later acknowledged. Detective Little
and Kirsty Raffan, one of the royal commission solicitors, worked tire-
lessly, pulling together all the documentary evidence, mapping offenders
and those who had protected them. They knew who should be subpoenaed

as witnesses and what evidence could be used in cross-examination. Little also used surveillance, such as wiretaps on phones, to map the paedophile network. Raffan described Little as working "hard, fast and well". The same was true of Raffan, who gained Steve's admiration for her 100-hour working weeks. By the time assisting counsel Naomi Sharp SC began, there were few questions she did not already know the answers to.

Everyone at the Anglican Newcastle office was anxious. More than 10,000 documents had been subpoenaed by the commission, sending Assistant Bishop Stuart and the office into a frenzy, searching through the archives. Stuart told me how daunting it was.

> The breadth of the information wanted and the names of particular people they wanted files on, and the period of time it wanted us to cover ... going back, I think it was fifty-five years ... a team of us went out to the archive at the university and scoured file after file.[3]

Thompson believed the diocese could not have prepared for the royal commission without Stuart's work ethic. The archives were disorganised, so it was challenging work. They sent "a huge volume" of archival material to the commission, which then "wanted electronic information ... It was massive ... a very, very demanding time on everyone". As he went through the archives, the enormity of the suffering inflicted on survivors struck Stuart.

> The deepest concern was, I think ... Were we facing a ring? Had there been an organised criminal activity that had gone on here? ... the most sinister form, had we been subjected to the very worst of predatory paedophile behaviour in an organised form?[4]

That was *the* question.

The royal commission sent shivers down the spine of many clergy and laity in the diocese. Everybody was lawyering up, which immediately aroused suspicions about what other people were saying and doing. Farran told me there was a strong sense that each individual was on his or her own.

> It was very hard ... I realised you were by yourself ... if you saw people at the royal commission, they didn't want to talk to you. Two close

colleagues made it clear they didn't want to talk to me. We'd worked together for years … so everybody was … self-protective.

Some had far more to fear than others. As Steve said, "No one ever thought they would be in a witness box, answerable to a royal commission for their conduct."

*

The very first day, Naomi Sharp, the senior lawyer appointed by the commission to act as Counsel Assisting, had the role of presenting and testing evidence and witnesses. Smartly dressed in a black jacket and white blouse, her glasses perched on the end of her nose, Sharp stood in a packed courtroom and gave a riveting opening address. She named Peter Rushton and others, including perpetrators from Morpeth College. She described how they had preyed on St Alban's Boys' Home, and the activities of George Parker (referred to as CKC), Graeme Lawrence and Jim Brown. She calmly outlined in explicit and exact terms what had been done to children: "anal rape", "oral sex", "masturbation", "genital fondling", "sucked his penis", "digital anal penetration".[5]

Speaking matter-of-factly, in a manner that was explicit but not salacious, was one of the very important things the royal commission did. There was no polite fudging, and no vague euphemisms such as "indecently touched". The community needed to know exactly what had happened to these children, and to bear witness to it. On and on it went, with many clergy who attended utterly shocked by what had been going on in their midst. Colvin Ford and his wife, Judy, saw one of Rushton's victims looking anxious. The man "had a little wooden pig that he was playing with, and my heart broke".

Outlining Jim Brown's crimes, Sharp quoted what Brown had told Michael Elliott about feeling "groomed into a culture within the Anglican diocese of Newcastle where sexual abuse of boys was accepted as the norm". That culture was what the royal commission intended to investigate.

The first of the survivors to be interviewed was Paul Gray. Gray had a gentle, sad face and a soft voice. He read his statement with his head bowed and shoulders hunched. He spoke hesitantly, and at times his voice broke, or he exhaled in a sigh. Gray was the survivor I'd first seen on 7.30, talking about how Rushton had abused him when he was an altar boy in Cessnock and at outdoor camps held by the Church of England Boys' Society. Rushton was also his godfather.

When Gray was ten years old, Rushton anally raped him in the bedroom of the rectory. Until he was fourteen, he was raped on a weekly or fortnightly basis by Rushton, often after Rushton had delivered a church service.

> Father Peter would cut my back with a small knife and smear my blood on my back ... that was actually symbolic of the blood of Christ – as he continued to anally rape me. After the sexual intercourse, he would clean my wound with white towels.[6]

On other occasions, Rushton demanded oral sex be performed while he was in church, dressed in his clerical robes. Once, Gray testified, a woman entered the vestry while Gray was performing oral sex on Rushton. She "saw us and left immediately ... she sat in the congregation and stared at me during the church service". This woman did not report the matter to the church or to police. It was Paul Gray she stared at, not Rushton, the abusing priest.

When Gray told of being taken by Rushton to Yondaio Youth Camp, and the boys being chased by the men to the cliffs and then anally raped, he gasped and paused, as tears began to flow. A support person ministered to him, giving him water, sitting close to him. Justice McLellan leant over and gently asked if he wanted a recess or someone else to read his statement.

> Gray: No, I need to read it.
> McClellan: You want to read it.
> Gray: No, I *need* to read it.
> McClellan: Very well.
> Gray: It's important to me.
> McLellan: Yes, I understand.[7]

Paul Gray kept reading, his sobs growing louder. It was a keening, a grief-filled lament over what had happened to him as a boy, flowing out into the world. Sometimes he paused, gathered strength, and then read on.

The worst thing, Gray said, was when Rushton took him to St Alban's. He had begged Rushton, "Don't leave me here." Rushton left him. He was led by three men to "what they called 'the fucking room', where they took turns to rape me." Gray was taken by Rushton to St Alban's repeatedly over the next eighteen months.

> Sometimes two or three men would visit me at the same time on the same day ... [One of the caretakers,] the person I call the gatekeeper, would keep me quiet before and after the abuse by beating me, if I ever made any noise at all ... on one occasion there were between six and eight men present. These men made me and five other boys lay face-down on beds ... each of the men picked a boy and each of the boys were taken into different rooms and abused.

Gray was openly sobbing, but kept on.

"Could I have a drink of water, please? I need five minutes. Could I have five minutes?"

After a short break, Gray told the hushed courtroom how when Rushton's paedophilia became public in 2009 it acted as a trigger and he began suffering flashbacks. "Since then, memories of sexual abuse experiences have continued to flood back to me." Gray suffered a complete breakdown. He was admitted to psychiatric hospitals several times. He has struggled ever since with the aftermath of the trauma. Gray's story has been corroborated by other men abused by Rushton at Yondaio camps, St Alban's and St Luke's at Wallsend. Five men came forward from St Alban's and eight from Wallsend.

When Gray finished his testimony, he was done with his open, brave weeping. He asked the courtroom to "abide" for a moment of silence for all those who "could no longer face the struggle of carrying the scars of their child abuse another day and chose to end their suffering by taking their own lives." McClellan agreed, speaking of "the tragedy" that is child sexual abuse and its long-term effects.

The courtroom fell silent.

*

Steve was to appear on the third day of the Newcastle hearing, on 4 August 2016. Rachael took a photo of him before the proceedings got underway. He looks very serious. He is wearing a suit with two ribbons pinned to his chest. Rachael had sewed them for him. One ribbon was in remembrance of his mother. The other was in remembrance of his friend and fellow altar boy Michael, also abused by Parker, who committed suicide by jumping from the roof of a Sydney motel.

Fundamental to Steve's experience of the royal commission was having Rachael beside him. He had fallen in love with her way back in 1981. She had come to visit her mother, who was suffering from alcoholism, in the psychiatric hospital where Steve was a patient after his first breakdown. They had gone their separate ways, but they'd been good friends since 2007, reconnecting after both their marriages had ended. By 2013, friendship had turned into love. Love can be a kind of alchemy. On my very first visit to interview Steve in 2019, I noticed a sign in his kitchen. It said, "You are loved." Rachael rang several times during the conversation. She was worried about his bad cough (he went to hospital with pneumonia the next day), but also about me interviewing him (for good reason, as the interview might be triggering). Steve told me then about Rachael's "philosophy of love". I was intrigued. After a difficult childhood with a troubled mother, she emerged from it unusually caring and empathetic. She seemed one of those people who are a blessing to those around them, a balm to the soul. "Rachael has this way where she sees the good in everything," Steve told me.

> She can make a positive out of anything, she really can … she's taught me so much about how to react to people, or not to react … She's kept me on the straight and narrow, and she's never left my side.

On the first day of the royal commission, her presence was crucial. Before the commission started, Steve, Rachael and Michael Elliott – accompanied by a burly security guard, because of the threats to Steve and Michael's safety – went for a coffee at a café well away from the courthouse, where a throng of reporters and protesters was milling outside. Steve recalled:

> [The security guard] didn't know who I was, and he just assumed I was there with the church … that's who employed him. We were sitting there having a cup of coffee and he said, "So why have all these victims waited so long to come forward, what's all that about?" Rach nearly fainted; she thought I was going to rip this bloke's head off.

Steve was quite capable of punching him. "If that bloke had said that to me five years before, I'd have thrown him down the stairs … How stupid. But Rach has taught me." Steve had changed a lot. Each event – receiving compensation, forming an alliance with Michael Elliott, working with his psychologist, receiving a public apology from Farran, his case being reopened by Jeff Little, the revelation that Bishop Thompson was a fellow survivor, all those who had believed him – had slowly wrought a transformation in his spirit.

> Rach looked at me and was waiting for the explosion. But I just said, "Well, mate, ever heard of Auschwitz?" He looked at me. "I said it doesn't matter when justice is delivered, as long as it is delivered." He got all confused. I sat and talked with him for about ten minutes and then, [stricken], he got up and walked outside. He realised who I was and what it was all about.

"In that moment I was in awe of Steven," Rachael told me. "How he could bring such understanding, gentleness and strength together at a time of high stress." She recognised how far he had come. Rachael turned to Steve and said:

> Five years ago, you would have put that bloke through the window … I'm so proud of you, that you've sat there and actually explained to this guy about concentration camps and about how justice has to be delivered no matter when it's delivered, it's got to still be delivered. There's no expiry date on justice.[8]

Steve took the witness box under his pseudonym, CKA, and surveyed the court room. He saw plenty of supporters, but enemies too, glowering at him. There was a sea of lawyers. Rachael was in the front row. Taking heart and confidence from her presence, he decided to just keep looking at her.

Steve read his statement. He detailed the grooming, the first assault to the last … and the horrifying extent of it over the period 1971 to 1975. Fondling, groping, masturbation, digital rape, oral and anal rape … The courtroom was shocked and silent. Steve was only overcome when he read the description of his mother's funeral in 1977 – how Parker had given the eulogy, how Steve had to walk behind his abuser while holding up his mother's coffin, and how he had almost dropped it. He asked for tissues. McLellan asked if he wanted a break. Steve said no. He fought on.

Steve told the commission that he had lost his faith, and that:

> I have found the process of dealing with the church as abusive as the sexual abuse itself. I was made to feel that the offences against me were worthless, because I was a boy abused by a priest who was protected by the church. I was also left with the impression that my life was worth nothing to the church.

Naomi Sharp now asked him some clarifying questions. She asked about the 1984 meeting with Appleby, about the death threats he and his family had received, and the day he had found the rear wheel nuts of his car loosened.

Next Steve faced cross-examination by lawyers working for the perpetrators and their protectors. He looked across at Rachael, who was watching intensely. "She was sitting forward on her chair ready to spring. Whoa, I thought, settle down, Rach ..."

A lawyer representing Bishop Appleby, Peter Skinner, was first. He told Steve that Appleby "doesn't, with no disrespect to you, doesn't recall you at all, and certainly does not remember meeting with you in the way that you have described in 1984." Skinner asked if Steve had a memory lapse.

Steve was firm. No.

Then John Booth, representing Paul Rosser, interrogated Steve about his previous uncertainty about the date of the sexual assault at Gateshead, implying Steve had memory problems. Steve pointed out that he had never claimed to be certain about the date, and that he had quickly corrected the year before Parker's 2001 trial began, when evidence emerged to confirm it.

Steve's lawyer, Peter O'Brien, with an unruly black curl over his forehead, was not as smoothly coiffed as the silvertail lawyers for the bishops and Archbishop Herft, but he was sharp and to the point. When Booth mentioned the register, O'Brien leapt to his feet and pointed out that there were questions about the register's authenticity, to be examined at a later point. McLellan agreed, and Booth had to rephrase his question.

In all this, Steve refused to budge, standing up to the cross-examinations extremely well. He even showed his sense of humour. When he left the witness box, his relief was immense.

By the end of the third day, a portrait was already starting to emerge of devastating and extreme child sexual abuse, of paedophiles given free rein, their activities covered up by a pro-perpetrator network in the Anglican Church of Newcastle.

At the end of each day, Ian Kirkwood and Joanne McCarthy of the *Newcastle Herald* filmed a pithy wrap-up of the day's proceedings. As the hearing went on, they looked more and more shell-shocked.

CHAPTER TWENTY-TWO

IF ONLY I'D BEEN TOLD

IN HIS BOOK *States of Denial: Knowing about Atrocities and Suffering*, the sociologist Stanley Cohen describes different kinds of denial that allow perpetrators and their protectors to evade truthful recognition of wrongdoing. The first form, "literal denial", is very direct, a simple denial of fact: "It did not happen" or "They are lying" or "I didn't know – if only I'd been told." Such denials were seen often in the Newcastle Anglican hearing.

Documentary evidence before the commission showed there were many red flags about Rushton. Bishop Holland received six warnings about Rushton's offending in just two years, 1979 and 1980. Five people who had gone to Holland about Rushton's sexual abuse of an assistant priest's son gave written statements to the commission. A sixth person, Pamela Wilson, who also knew about the abuse of the boy, gave oral evidence to the commission.[1] Instead of immediately reporting Rushton to the police and disciplining him, Holland had done nothing and then promoted Rushton to archdeacon of Maitland in 1983. The father of the abused boy was marginalised; he left the diocese and eventually the priesthood. He never recovered.

Holland, now in his nineties, gave evidence by video link, with his head bowed, age spots visible on his balding scalp. Despite his age, he was perfectly lucid. Holland seemed a wily, rigid and complacent man, one of those people who see only what they want to see. After hearing the testimony of Paul Gray and Phil D'Ammond,[2] it was painful to hear Holland praising Rushton as a popular priest, busy, well organised and well respected. He was not aware of any allegations about Rushton. Holland said he had "no recollection" of ever being told of any child sexual abuse during his time at Newcastle. Had he been told, Holland claimed, he would have acted decisively, bringing the parties together. This showed how confused he was, since child sexual abuse is never a conciliation matter but a crime to be reported to police. Despite the evidence of multiple witnesses, Holland denied ever being told about Rushton's abuse of the priest's son.

Holland was also alerted to another prolific abuser, Jim Brown. A parishioner, Suzan Aslin, gave evidence that in 1979 she warned Professor David Frost, her academic teacher, a friend of Holland and a synod member, about Brown. She told Professor Frost that Brown had groomed her fifteen-year-old son and made sexual advances towards him, kissing him in front of her and saying, "I will have you!" She also wanted Frost to tell Holland that she had discovered Rushton and Brown were planning a "sex tour" of Europe. In Frost's statement to the commission, he explained that when he told Holland what Aslin had disclosed, Holland looked "stiff and white-faced ... [and] asked me to leave the matter entirely with him".[3] According to Aslin's evidence, Holland rang her sometime later and pronounced himself "appalled" by what she'd divulged. However, Holland did nothing.

At the commission, Holland claimed he had "no recollection" of meeting or talking to David Frost or Suzan Aslin.

"Is it your testimony," Naomi Sharp asked in dulcet tones, that it was "a figment of Ms Aslin's imagination? Bishop Holland, are you telling me the truth in answer to my questions?"

"Yes, I am," he replied.

Justice McClellan intervened, asking bluntly, "You were CEO of the diocese and licensed [Rushton] to do his criminal activities. Do you acknowledge any responsibility?"

"No."

McClellan: "Do you accept any responsibility in having failed to exercise your management responsibilities effectively?"

Holland: "I don't acknowledge responsibility, because I didn't know any allegations had been made against Rushton."

Holland admitted he had no formal structure to deal with child sexual abuse. He justified his decision to allow Rushton and Brown to foster orphan boys, because he "assumed they were ... doing an act of mercy, to look after homeless boys." "I trusted the priests to do their work because of the promises that they made to God." He told the commission he now accepted that Rushton's prolific abuse did happen, but "only because I've watched some of the media and the media says that these things happened".

The royal commission made a number of damning findings against Holland in its final report into Case Study 42. Regarding the veracity of his testimony, the commission concluded: "His evidence should not be accepted." It found that Holland's failure to act when he was told that Rushton had abused the assistant priest's young son in 1980 represented a lost opportunity to prevent Rushton from perpetrating further abuse. "Bishop Holland failed to take any action to report, risk manage or discipline Rushton, who the diocese has now acknowledged to be a prolific offender." Ignoring Suzan Aslin's warning about Jim Brown in 1979 meant that Brown also continued to abuse children. Brown was eventually convicted, in 2012, of sexually abusing twenty children. As the royal commission pointed out:

> Thirteen of those children were abused after 1979. Bishop Holland's failure to act at the time in relation to Brown was another tragic lost opportunity to prevent further abuse by Brown.[4]

Holland's assistant bishop, Richard Appleby, gave evidence that he too was a "decisive" chap, if only he had been told. He maintained that he had no recollection of any child sexual abuse in the Newcastle diocese during his time there. At this point in the hearing, I concluded that a capacity for selective amnesia must have been a prerequisite for high office in the church at this time. According to Appleby:

> The thing that I probably regret more than anything else is that I was not told back in those years of this abusive behaviour, in that had I been told I would have been in a position to do something about it and I would have acted decisively, but I was not aware of it in those years.[5]

But as Sharp pointed out, several people said they *did* tell Appleby about the abuse. One of them was Steve, whose testimony was that on 13 August 1984 he told Appleby he was sexually abused by Parker and warned him about Rushton and other perpetrators. Rushton's abuse was an open secret among altar boys. Appleby assured Steve he would follow it up, but did nothing.

The royal commission came to the scathing conclusion that Holland and Appleby:

> When able to ignore disclosures of allegations of sexual abuse, chose to do so … When they were unable to ignore allegations … [they] responded in a manner to protect the reputation of the diocese in preference to the proper investigation of the allegations or the taking of any steps to prevent further abuse … By their acts and omissions, [they] enabled alleged or convicted perpetrators to continue working with access to children and without alerting other members of the clergy to the disclosed allegations.

*

Perpetrators need protectors. It was not only the higher echelons of the clergy who played a central role. Many laity also offered protection. They engaged in what Cohen calls "interpretive denial", which doesn't dispute the facts but redescribes and reinterprets them so that they are normalised, minimised or rendered seemingly harmless.

The commission heard that at 5.15 a.m. on 12 February 1990, Appleby received an urgent phone call from Holland. There was a commotion at the Wyong rectory, south of Newcastle. Holland wanted Appleby to demand the resignation of the priest, Stephen Hatley Gray. Appleby hotfooted it to Wyong. He demanded that Gray resign on the spot. Gray agreed.

Later that day, Gray was arrested for raping a fourteen-year-old boy between midnight and 4 a.m. A witness, a friend of the victim, alleged in his police statement that Gray had plied them with alcohol, and that he had then seen Gray anally raping the victim. The boy was begging, "It hurts, Father Stephen, please stop," but Gray continued to rape the boy, who kept pleading with him to stop. Gray then let the victim go. He collapsed onto the floor, saying, "I feel sick." At Gosford Hospital he was provided with a rape kit.[6]

What happened next is instructive about the role of the laity in the cover-ups in Newcastle. Among the exhibits considered by the commission were John Cleary's explosive file notes, handwritten records of meetings between 2013 and 2015 with Keith Allen. Sharp described them as Allen's "moments of candour" about child sexual abuse by the clergy and how it was handled.

There were startling revelations in a file note from 5 March 2013, when Allen unexpectedly turned up at Cleary's office and spilled the beans about Stephen Hatley Gray. Allen told Cleary about all the other times Gray was known to have committed child sexual abuse, like the time he had raped an underage boy on a rectory table full of lamingtons. Cleary's note said that "Mr Allen thought it was amusing to bring some lamingtons along to a meeting" about the matter. Or the many occasions Gray met under-age boys under the Wyong railway bridge, plied them with cigarettes and alcohol, and "things went on" which "to this day the police don't know about". According to Cleary's note, Allen mentioned five other clergy who knew of Gray's behaviour, including Holland and Appleby, and said that Reverend Keith Clark of The Entrance parish also "appeared to be familiar with the story". Clark suggested that because of Gray's activities, it would be best to "move him on".[7] At another meeting with Cleary, on 11 February 2015, Allen mentioned other cases of abuse by clergy about which nothing was done, including the "hanky panky" group at Wallsend (Rushton's parish) and the priests, including Reverend James Brown, known as "Shevill's boys". Cleary took this to mean that these priests had been sexually abused by Shevill in the past and were now offenders themselves.[8]

In interpretative denial, minimising, neutralising, euphemistic language removes any imperative to act. Cleary's file notes showed Allen persistently using phrases usually associated with "boys-will-be-boys" locker-room banter about adult sex. The sexual abuse of children was reframed as "hanky panky", rather than a serious crime. Priests abused as boys by Shevill, now abusers themselves, did not represent an intergenerational pattern of abuse but were merely "Shevill's boys". Rather than admit another priest was a paedophile, Allen described him as simply "a worry" because he had "too many little boys around him". Rather than acknowledge the existence of a paedophile ring working together to commit child rape, Allen talked about a harmless-sounding "boys' crew" in the Cessnock area.

The redescriptions at the heart of interpretive denial allow the refusal of empathy. The moral horror of what has happened to the victims is not registered. A grotesquely discordant emotional response becomes possible. Thus it was considered funny that a priest anally raped a boy on a table of lamingtons – so funny that Allen brought lamingtons to the meeting, as a joke. The royal commission's final report said: "His humour was disturbing and demonstrated a callous disregard for the child victim and a complete lack of insight into the gravity of child sexual assault." This sightlessness makes it unsurprising that covering up the abuse was seen as fine, as when Allen described Appleby as a "good operator", which Cleary understood to mean "good at covering up matters".

The protectors did more than just reinterpret events to protect the church, however. In a sensational day of evidence before the commission, Keith Allen admitted that he had falsified the date of Stephen Hatley Gray's resignation. Describing the exchange, Joanne McCarthy told me Allen was "carpeted" by Justice McClennan:

> It was the only time I've seen McClellan actually angry. Super controlled, but angry. Allen tried to not answer, and McClellan just lifted himself up and leant forward and he basically bullied him into answering. It was like a super senior representative of their profession basically pulling him up, and it was a real professional thing. It was saying, this is not the way we act. And you are not going to get away with that lawyer's response. And he just, he got the response out of him. It was extraordinary to see.

Under fierce questioning from McLellan, Allen admitted that he had "ripped up" Stephen Hartley Gray's original resignation letter and told him to write another one, dated 11 February, the day before the crime for which he was forced to resign. If Gray had resigned as priest of Wyong before the rape occurred, he was technically still "in good standing" with his bishop and, as McClellan pointed out, could "go somewhere else" – that is, go to another parish and maintain his income and licence as a priest. Defended in court by Allen, Gray got off with a three-year good behaviour bond and a $100 fine: as Sharp said, a "very generous" result for raping an underage boy. The falsified resignation letter enabled Gray to be employed as a youth worker in the Willochra diocese in South Australia, and then as a parish priest in western Victoria, where Roger Dyer met him.

> McClellan: But the document on its face is false and will allow a false representation to be made, wouldn't it?
> Allen: Yes.

> McClellan: You were party to the circumstances in which the false docu-
> ment was created, weren't you?
> Allen: Yes, I certainly destroyed the first resignation.
> McClellan: ... It looks like a fraud, doesn't it? ... It is a false representa-
> tion as to his status?
> Allen: It could be described as that, sir.

As Allen, a lawyer, admitted to falsifying a document, a ripple of shock ran
through the courtroom.

Another gasp was heard when Sharp read out a pre-sentencing report
by Reverend David Williams, a former parole officer, which all but exoner-
ated Gray. Williams cited the favourable views of Bishop Holland and the
bishop of Ballarat at the time, John Hazelwood: "Both Bishops are aware
of [Gray's] great gifts, and they do not regard this offence as necessarily an
indelible impediment to his rehabilitation to work as a priest in the future."

Williams' report adopted a distancing, minimising, normalising tone.

> Stephen Gray's involvement in this offence appears to be of the nature
> of an isolated aberration and contrary to his moral standards of conduct.
> Alcohol appears to have been a significant ingredient ... combined with
> the state of relaxation induced by a leisurely night off ... his normal con-
> trol of his sexual behaviour was reduced.[9]

So, a drink and a leisurely night off turned his mind to child rape?

*

Asked about the diocese's handling of abuse allegations, Allen told the
commission that when the committee examining complaints in the yellow
envelopes met, the perpetrator, parish and victim were never identified.
He said that the registrar, Peter Mitchell, would have to rifle through all
the yellow envelopes to find whichever case was under discussion, as there
was no identifying information on the outside. McLellan asked in disbelief:

> how would the registrar know which one to look at unless there was at
> least some identifying information on the outside? ... Mr Allen, what you
> are saying doesn't sound believable.

Allen's evidence was contradicted when Sharp dramatically produced a yellow envelope which did have a name, a parish, a date and a victim on the outside, as well as a record of who had accessed the file and when. She said to Allen that his claim was "absolute nonsense".

Allen continued to stonewall, denying any knowledge of the names of perpetrators accused of child sexual abuse. To admit such knowledge would make him and the other committee members, including Bishop Herft, liable for concealing serious indictable crimes, since they did not report them to police. As a solicitor, Allen was clearly aware of this.

One of John Cleary's explosive file notes recorded Allen predicting that the yellow envelopes would cause trouble at the commission.

> [T]he biggest concern ... was Bishop Roger Herft. [Allen] indicated that Herft will be in trouble ... because of Herft's handling of the ... Envelopes through Herft's ... envelope advisory/review committee. Mr Allen was also a member of this committee, alongside Mr Helman, Diocesan solicitor Robert Caddies, Keith Allen, Dean Graeme Lawrence, and the Registrar Peter Mitchell and Richard Appleby.

Allen had advised Cleary and Thompson that this committee "self-determined" whether or not to take action on a complaint. Cleary understood this "to mean that the panel itself, rather than the law, determined whether the church should report matters to the police ... this was done to minimise the matters." Allen acknowledged he felt "uneasy about" the management of the envelopes and "in hindsight" it was "wrong".[10]

The commission now interrogated Allen about the management of the envelopes holding the church's sexual abuse secrets. Allen admitted he had been worried about Herft because "The issues didn't seem to go anywhere, or anything happen much." McLellan forced another admission, about Allen's meeting with Cleary and Thompson in early 2015, at which Allen had appraised the performance of previous bishops.

"Bishop Holland's standard approach was the 'do-nothing approach'. That was your opinion, wasn't it?"

Sharp further grilled Allen about the same meeting, including Allen's assertion that Herft's administration was marked by:

a culture of: (a) Not reporting child sexual abuse matters to the police. (b) Claims exposure risk was the only concern (c) Discipling the priest was never on the radar in discussion. (d) [or] ... Herft would say "it was my domain to discipline clergy and not theirs." (e) Herft only ever reported one matter to the police. That being the matter of Peter Mitchell defrauding the Diocese.[11]

McLellan peered over the bench again and demanded of Allen: "Now tell me, '(a) Not reporting child sexual abuse matters to the police.' For you to say that you must have known there were matters he had not reported to the police: correct?"

> Allen: Yes ...
>
> McLellan ... you are recorded as advising that there was a "culture of not reporting". Now for there to be a "culture of not reporting" there has got to be multiple occasions ... you became aware of these matters through your work on the advisory committee to the bishop; is that not correct?
>
> Allen: Yes.
>
> McLellan: And you didn't report them to police either, did you?
>
> Allen: I didn't have the envelopes or access to their contents.
>
> McLellan: But you knew about the allegations?

Allen replied forlornly, with less and less conviction, "I didn't know a name ..."

"Isn't it pretty obvious you would go to the police? This doesn't sound like a very effective advice mechanism, does it? It's a bit like boxing in the dark ..."

Allen replied lamely, "That is what happened, in my memory ..."

McClellan was once again incredulous. He asked, "You were prepared to participate in this over a number of years, were you? ... allegations of sexual abuse that came before this ad hoc committee ... I take it [on] multiple occasions, would that be right?"

> Allen: It was probably correct, sir ...
>
> McLellan: Did you ever tell the bishop, in relation to these allegations of sexual impropriety, that the only proper course was to go to the police?

Allen: I don't think so, sir, but I don't think anybody did.

McClellan: Do you think they should have?

Allen: Hindsight, yes.

Then Sharp went in for the jugular. "Were you aware during your tenure on this brown envelope committee that it was a criminal offence if people had reasonable grounds to suspect child sexual abuse and did not report it to police?"

"We were all aware of it. There were three lawyers." (Committee members Allen, Caddies and Helman were all lawyers.)

That was why Allen continuously maintained that there had not been names on the envelopes, despite unmistakable evidence to the contrary. By not reporting the complaints of abuse to the police, he was breaking the law.

McLellan then tried another line of attack.

McLellan: Mr Allen, you have now told me on a number of occasions that you don't have any records and, as a consequence, you don't have any clear recollection of a number of matters – correct?

Allen: Yes.

McLellan: Mr Cleary records you ... advising him that the best approach for the commission is to indicate ... "you have no files or notes" and that you "can only rely on your memory ... this will prevent cross-examination by lawyers." Were you following this advice when you answered my questions?

After some to and fro, Allen was asked again, "Are you following your own advice?"

"I suppose I am, yes."

After Allen's three days in the witness box, McClellan put it to him that "what you sought to defend was, do you accept now, indefensible?"

Allen: Probably indefensible.

McClellan: That was because it was a do-nothing and a cover-up and protect the church approach, wasn't it?

Allen: That was a factor, sir.

McClellan: And you were part of that practice, weren't you?

Allen submitted. "Yes."

*

Archbishop Roger Herft walked into the royal commission with a big future. He walked out a ruined man. It took three gruelling days in the witness box. Herft's amnesia was remarkable; so many times, he said, "I don't recall" or "I can't recollect" or "I have no memory." However, during a tough but respectful cross-examination, he was broken. There were no American TV courtroom histrionics. Just Sharp, McLellan and Steve's lawyer, Peter O'Brien, presenting Herft, time and again, with unmistakable evidence of all his opportunities to do something about Rushton, Lawrence and Parker. But he had done nothing.

There was the time in 1998 when removalists discovered child pornography among Rushton's possessions and complained to the diocese. The royal commissioners were astonished to learn that Herft and a committee tried to establish whether it was adult or child porn by despatching Rushton's lawyer and close friend Greg Hansen to ask him. Unsurprisingly, Rushton denied it was child porn and threatened the diocese with legal action. Herft accepted Rushton's word, because, like Bishop Holland, he "had a very high view" of priests; "those who were ordained were of a very high moral and spiritual integrity".[12] Herft suggested that Rushton "consider a thirty-day retreat in early 1999 ... with a spiritual director ... in reflecting on the deeper issues and shadows that enabled and encouraged the particular situation". Rushton's consideration of his "deeper issues and shadows" lasted all of one night. His paedophile activities continued unchecked.

"I was deeply fooled," Herft told the commission. Herft did nothing further to investigate Rushton, despite credible complaints in 2002 and 2003, including one allegation that Rushton "had his own group of boys". The commission concluded in its final report that Herft accepted advice given in 1998 by Paul Rosser "to avoid receiving disclosures of child sexual abuse in order to avoid putting himself in a situation where he was obliged to report the alleged conduct to the police." Effectively, this meant "that Bishop Herft should remain wilfully blind to allegations of child sexual abuse".

Herft explained that sexual misconduct was dealt with based on the:

Matthewian Gospel principle, which was if a brother or sister in the church, or in the community, had something against another, that they would try to engage, firstly, with the person they had the difficulty with.

In practical terms, this "Matthewian Gospel" meant Steve, as a child of ten years old, would have to engage with Parker to stop the sexual abuse. Herft admitted this mediation "absolutely" would not work with child sexual abuse and said there was a "feeling" it should be reported to police. Then Sharp pointed to case after case in which allegations of child sexual abuse had not been reported to police. McLellan intervened again.

> McLellan: But don't you think you needed to know immediately there was
>   an allegation that one of your priests had committed a crime?
> Herft: Yes.
> McLellan: I take it you didn't put in place any steps to ensure that happened?

No, Herft admitted.

> McLellan: Is it right that at least during the first half of your tenure as
>   bishop there was really no framework at all for dealing with allega-
>   tions of child sexual assault?"

Herft agreed that it was a hopeless framework.

> McClellan: Even though there was the 1998 report into paedophilia by the
>   diocese of Tasmania, and the Wood Royal Commission?
> Herft: Yes.

One code-of-conduct document from Herft's time as bishop was read out at the commission. It outlined that "certain sexual behaviour with children constitutes a criminal offence". At the word "certain", a collective shudder of horror went around the courtroom.

At the end of three tough days, Herft asked to address the court before he left the witness box. He apologised to survivors.

> I have let them down and let them down badly, let down the survivors
> in ways that remorse itself is a very poor emotion to even express. But I

want to thank the commission for holding me personally accountable, holding the Church personally accountable ... I hope that the Church ... will be one which has not only woken up, Your Honour, but become more and more transparent and accountable to the lost and the least, the most vulnerable, and as CKA's [Steven Smith's] lawyer reminded me, certainly, that there is a special and particular eternal reference in terms of our care for children ...[13]

Then Herft left the witness box.

On the last morning of his evidence, Herft approached Steve in the foyer. Steve had watched all Herft's testimony and had seen the moment when he was broken. Steve thought that Herft knew it too. His brilliant career was over, but so too was his self-deception. Steve felt Herft recognised, in a way that Holland and Appleby hadn't, the terrible damage that he had done.

Despite the harm Herft had done him, when Steve saw the archbishop was broken, he felt compassion and pity. Through the crowded foyer, Herft moved towards him. When Herft saw Steve, his mouth wobbled. He was about to weep. Watching, the whole room crackled with tension. The court sheriffs, fearing an altercation, began descending.

Instead, when Steve saw the crumbling archbishop, he stepped forward and placed his hand gently on Herft's arm.

"I'm sorry," Herft said, his face falling apart.

Steve replied, "It's alright mate, I forgive you. It's about compassion."

He forgave him because he felt Herft not only apologised, but was truly sorry. Steve still held to the values of forgiveness he had learned in childhood.

Then Steve said, "It's on you now." He meant that Herft must face with courage what was coming: the disgrace and the loss of his reputation. To be forever known as a bishop who knew about child sexual abuse and did nothing.

Reverend Paul Robertson witnessed the moment and was so moved by Steve's generosity and kindness that he wrote a letter to the *Newcastle Herald* and to Michael Elliott about this moment of forgiveness.

Here was an act of grace, meeting mute distress. Sensing a spirit of forgiveness, a step towards healing, it was for me a profound moment ...

This incident seemed to bring a feeling of hope for me, in what has been too often, a dark time. Even if it stays with us only, it will remain a lasting memory. Unforgettable.[14]

Michael Elliott was amused. He wrote to Steve, "So now you're Jesus!" Steve just laughed.

In her final report, Naomi Sharp was savage about Herft. "His response was weak, ineffectual and showed no regard for the need to protect children from the risk that they would be preyed upon. It was a failure of leadership." In the aftermath of the royal commission, Herft resigned as archbishop of Perth. He was not prosecuted by the DPP for the crime of not reporting child sexual abuse. However, the Episcopal Standards Commission, the senior Anglican body for disciplining bishops, defrocked him, and he was deposed from holy orders in December 2021.

CHAPTER TWENTY-THREE

THE SENIOR PROFESSIONALS OF NEWCASTLE

AT THE END of Keith Allen's three momentous days in the witness box, lawyers dragged their wheeled suitcases stuffed full of documents out of the courthouse and headed for a drink together. A few demonstrators packed up their placards. Reporters hovered, interviewing someone. Reeling after all I had heard that day, I swung my backpack on and decided to walk along the riverfront back to my hotel.

The mighty Hunter River to my left looked a kilometre wide. Great container ships pulled by tugboats were gliding out to sea. Ferries, sailboats, kayaks and motorboats scurried about. Walking past one of the swish new riverfront restaurants, I saw a cherubic boy of about ten, his head flung back, with the careless insouciance of youth. But as his family entered the restaurant, he suddenly looked self-conscious, as though he was unsure what to do next. He looked so young and vulnerable. It was unbearable to realise he was the same age as Steve and Paul Gray and so many others when they were raped. I flinched and turned away.

Before leaving the hearing that day, the last thing I'd typed on my iPad was a question, in all capital letters: WHY??? As I walked, I reflected on why Allen and others from the powerful laity had been so eager to protect the clergy at any cost. The desires of the paedophiles were heinous but simple. The cover-ups by the church hierarchy were dreadful, but you could see the logic: the protection of reputation, avoidance of scandal, fear of losing their income, houses and careers should they turn whistle-blower. But the laity – what did men such as Keith Allen get out of it?

The sun was dipping now, flashes of light alternating with dusk, buildings starkly illuminated or disappearing into shadow. Suddenly there was a burst of brilliant sunlight, and I saw high on the hill above me the spires of the Anglican cathedral lit up by the last rays of afternoon sun. Towering above every building below, its imposing bulk dwarfed everything else.

I walked up to the cathedral. It is open to anyone. That afternoon, there was a solitary worshipper and me. Outside, a sign advertised concerts of choral music. Inside, the building was grand in the extreme, thick stone pillars down each side, huge, beautiful stained-glass windows, and an ornately carved wooden pulpit. I could imagine the tall figure of Dean Graeme Lawrence sweeping along in his white lace and gold brocade robes, and how, amid this grandeur, a congregation might feel close to God. How elevated an ordinary worshipper might feel by associating with high-ranking clergy, becoming a leading member of the laity, and acting as a protector. A humdrum life escaped, the mark of distinction upon them.

The power and the glory.

Then I got it. So much of this terrible story was about status and the pursuit of social significance.

*

Next to take the stand was Robert Caddies, with two more extraordinary days of testimony revealing the culture and mindset of the influential laity. Caddies was a close friend of Graeme Lawrence and a former president of the Newcastle Club. As well as having been a legal adviser to the diocese during the Herft period and a member of CASM, Caddies admitted he had contributed to Lawrence's legal fund.

He was a small, nondescript man wearing spectacles, a grey jacket and a spotted tie. His mild appearance belied the ferocity of his letters and complaints, in which he had attacked Lawrence's successor as dean, James Rigney, as well as bishops Farran and Thompson, trying to get rid of them all.

Caddies had co-authored the letter from the self-described "Senior Professionals of Newcastle" to the royal commission attacking Thompson. When this letter came up on the screen, there was an audible gasp from the courtroom. Joanne McCarthy told me:

> I was flabbergasted when I saw that letter ... it was breathtaking ... how far down the track had they all gone ... making excuses for these offenders, still believing it up to that point ... it was easier to demonise Greg Thompson in the way that they did ... the littleness of them really struck me.[1]

There was a fiery exchange when McClellan laid it on the line:

> McClellan: You have led coordinated opposition to [Bishop Thompson], haven't you? ... [The dispute is over] the bishop's desire to ensure that the sexual abuse matters are properly and thoroughly dealt with, isn't it? ... You were wanting the royal commission to investigate the bishop, is that what it amounted to?
>
> Caddies: No, not to investigate, but to address certain questions ...
>
> McClellan: ... at the end of the third paragraph you say you are gravely concerned ... that Bishop Thompson apparently took no action in relation to his own abuse?
>
> Caddies: Yes.
>
> McLellan: Do you see in that second paragraph you express concern about Bishop Thompson having made an "unsubstantiated" claim about another priest?
>
> Caddies: Yes.[2]

Caddies tried to retract: it wasn't a complaint, he said, but an innocent inquiry; they were just "asking", "suggesting" and being helpful. "We felt these matters might assist the commission."

McClellan was having none of it. He put to Caddies that there was a "little bloc in the cathedral that seeks to undermine Bishop Thompson", and that this faction was the source of the complaint.

When Caddies prevaricated, giving a long-winded reply, McClellan asked again: "This group of 'quite senior professionals' are working together to undermine Bishop Thompson ...?"

McClellan asked several times if Caddies was "doubting the credibility of Bishop Thompson's statement ... Were you seeking to say to the commission that because it has taken so long [for Thompson to report his experience of sexual abuse], the bishop's credibility should be looked at?"

"No, no, not at all."

"Not at all?" McLellan asked with disbelief.

"I don't believe so."

As McLellan pulled apart the letter and its assumptions, Caddies finally admitted it.

"Yes, I suppose that is, Your Honour."

Ian Kirkwood and Joanne McCarthy's daily wrap-up for the *Newcastle Herald* led with the angry exchanges between McClellan and Caddies. Whatever reaction the "Senior Professionals of Newcastle" had expected from the commission, this was not it. Bishop Thompson told the newspaper:

> It was a gift to be publicly validated ... Although it was only twenty minutes of evidence, it was a message to those who had sent the letter. They weren't going to walk away without knowing how it had been received.[3]

After the royal commission was so critical of the cathedral bloc's "coordinated opposition" to Bishop Thompson, he directed Assistant Bishop Peter Stuart to sack the entire Christchurch Cathedral parish council. Senior Anglicans were stood down from leadership positions in liturgy. He did so in consultation with the Newcastle Anglican diocesan council.[4]

*

The hearing adjourned until November. When it recommenced, Bishop Holland came under fire for claiming he had never been told that Peter Rushton sexually abused the priest's son. However, the priest's wife and four other parishioners all provided statements confirming they had met with Holland about it. Sharp used the damning words: "those representing Bishop Holland were advised his credit was in issue", meaning his truthfulness was called into question.

The commission also recalled Bishop Appleby and demanded that he explain himself. Appleby had claimed in his oral evidence that he had "no recollection" of the 1984 meeting at which Steve told him about Parker's abuse. He had checked his diary "with great care" and there was "absolutely no entry showing Smith came to see him". The commission subsequently subpoenaed his diaries, which showed that Steve was right: Appleby had met with him in 1984. Appleby apologised profusely and claimed to be "hugely embarrassed" by having missed it "among the thousands of entries".

After the vainglorious bishops, Caddies also returned to the witness box. Why, as a committee member of CASM, did he apparently form an opinion that the diocese did not have a serious problem with child sexual abuse? Why did CASM's framework emphasise "conciliation", when this was clearly an utterly inappropriate approach to cases of child abuse? McLellan asked him: "What were you trying to achieve by the conciliation of a criminal offence?"

Caddies said that any offences involving children would be handled by the bishop. He claimed to be unaware of any complaints involving children going to Jean Sanders. But Sanders told the commission there had been about thirty such complaints. How did a member of the committee she chaired not know that?[5]

Sharp directed Caddies to the "Senior Professionals" letter, which claimed: "We are *personally aware* of a number of cases in which a claim of sexual abuse has been falsely made." Caddies explained that he had read about "many cases of so-called recovered memories ... people who have subsequently been shown not to have actually had those [experiences] and they have been under hypnosis." Sharp asked if he was aware of any cases of such "false recovered memories" in Newcastle. "I'm not aware, no." But as Sharp pointed out, the letter writers had claimed to be "personally aware" of false claims. This was "a fair criticism", Caddies conceded. Retorted Sharp: "you have said something here that is not true, in your complaint about the most senior member of the diocese?"[6] A flustered Caddies said no, yes, no ... Sharp asked if the letter writers' concern about "false recovered memories" was really about the allegations against Graeme Lawrence? Caddies denied it.

McLellan now put it to Caddies that the unhappiness in the diocese centred on Lawrence, "the sexual behaviour of some of the church people over time and the way the problem has been addressed by the church". "The bishop has tried to deal with it, face up to the problem," McLellan suggested, "and there has been resistance?" Caddies answered piously that no signatory to the letter would approve of "inappropriate sexual behaviour" and that they all supported Bishop Thompson's leadership in "creating a healthy future".

Sharp was sceptical, even incredulous. "Are you just making this up as you go along, Mr Caddies?" Caddies got huffy at this point and told her he was a solicitor of some forty-five years' standing and an officer of the Supreme Court of New South Wales. "All I ever wanted for Dean Lawrence and for other people," he told the court, "is for a – for due process."

Sharp took to this with a scalpel. She got Caddies to agree that Lawrence and the others had been given fair notice of the case against them, that they had the opportunity to participate in the board hearing but declined, and that they had been able to have legal representation. She pointed out that Lawrence had challenged the process in the Supreme Court and lost.

Eventually, Caddies admitted that due process had not been violated, and that Lawrence had done himself no favours by refusing to attend the hearing. Sharp asked Caddies whether he "was happy with the outcome ... do you think it was right?" He answered: "*If one believed the facts as alleged, probably, yes.*" It turned out Caddies had not attended the 2010 hearing, either. He now admitted that when he had seen Lawrence's teenage victim H give evidence at the royal commission, he thought him an "impressive witness".[7]

The demolition of Caddies at the commission was a pivotal moment. It had exposed the nonsense behind the false claims and entitled pretensions of the senior laity and challenged the "groupthink" behind their blind faith in Lawrence.

But then, Caddies spoke of his gratitude for the care Lawrence had given him and his family when his mother died.

> This man had been our priest for twenty-four years ... I can just speak of my own mother's death ... he was there from 7 a.m. in the morning until she died after midday. And he sat with us, he blessed her, he prayed with us, we held hands, and we said the Lord's Prayer ... It was this wonderful pastoral care that I can never forget.[8]

Now, at last, we get to the heart of the matter: the depth of attachment to Lawrence. We confront the extraordinary contradiction in human behaviour – the powerful perpetrators of Newcastle also frequently gave excellent pastoral care to people at their most vulnerable. Caddies didn't just admire Lawrence. He loved him.

*

There was great anticipation when the object of Caddies' affections, Graeme Lawrence, finally took the stand. He was sullen, arrogant, contemptuous, lofty and at times angry. It was an extraordinary performance. Lawrence stonewalled for two days, denying any sexual abuse of H as an underage teen. He gave the impression of a man used to brazenly lying.

Sharp remorselessly went through all the sexually explicit cards that Lawrence and Goyette had sent to H. When Lawrence explained that the line "thank heaven for little boys" was a play on a song performed by Maurice Chevalier, McClellan bluntly observed that "There's a picture showing a penis on the card", and asked sceptically, "the song has nothing to do with naked penises, does it?"

"No, it does not."

Sharp went through the rest of what she called the "smutty" cards, and Lawrence maintained they were all innocent fun. Sharp asked bluntly: "Are you lying?"

"I'm not lying," Lawrence said primly, "and it's rude of you to say so."

Lawrence admitted he knew that Andrew Duncan was sexually abusing H when he was fifteen yet did not report it to police. He told Sharp, "I was more concerned about [Duncan's] alcoholism."

> Sharp: More concerned about his alcoholism than a sexual relationship he
>   was pursuing with a fifteen-year-old boy – is that right?
> Lawrence: That's correct.
> Sharp: Did you report his alcoholism … to your superiors?
> Lawrence: Yes.
> Sharp: But you didn't report your suspicion that he was having sex with
>   an under-aged boy …?

He did not. Lawrence told the commission he "couldn't remember" why he didn't tell his bishop. The reason, we now know, was that he started sexually abusing H himself.

Lawrence was caught out lying many times. Rod Bower, watching the live stream, was stunned to hear Lawrence deny laughing at Steve on the courtroom steps at Parker's 2001 trial. He named Bower as the person laughing instead. Bower told me it was payback:

seeking to implicate me is classic Lawrence ... I had said something in my statement to the royal commission that he didn't like, about the dinner at the deanery [when Lawrence made a sexual advance], and he tried to character assassinate me. That was classic Lawrence. That's how he worked ... All the time. That's why you didn't oppose Lawrence.[9]

Fortunately, Bower could quickly produce evidence, from his diary and car log, that he had not been in Newcastle for Parker's trial.

Lawrence also lied in claiming he only knew of one priest accused of child sexual abuse during his time in Newcastle: George Parker. Reminded of Stephen Hatley Gray, Lawrence admitted he did, after all, know of two cases. He'd "quite forgotten" Gray's "behaviour". Sharp pounced on the word "behaviour" to describe the rape of a fifteen-year-old.[10]

Sharp pointed out that Lawrence also knew of yet another abuser, Allan Kitchingman, who was convicted of sexually abusing a boy at the North Coast Children's Home. Lawrence claimed he couldn't remember. Sharp quickly showed that he'd given a glowing character reference in court for Kitchingman, which had helped convince Judge Ralph Coolahan to let him off very lightly. Lawrence declared flatly, "I did not give any oral evidence in the court. I was never present in the court." Sharp immediately produced the court transcript, in which Judge Coolahan said, "Dean Lawrence spoke very highly of the offender and his work, both within and without the church." Lawrence claimed this "totally mystifies me ... I have no recollection whatever of doing that".

McLellan asked sceptically if he'd given evidence in court on any other occasions. Lawrence answered no. "But you don't remember the one occasion on which you did?"

The commission made a number of adverse findings against Lawrence. In relation to Steve, it found that Lawrence had engaged in "deliberate obstruction" in the lead-up to the 2001 court case by not informing police or the DPP of George Parker's whereabouts. Steve's lawyer, Peter O'Brien, summed up Lawrence and his destructive role in the diocese: "Mr Lawrence, others say you are a paedophile; you were the fox guarding the hen house."

CHAPTER TWENTY-FOUR
THE TRIAL OF LAWRENCE FOR RAPE

BEN GIGGINS, A Newcastle courier driver, was watching Lawrence give evidence with his wife, Jane. Ben and his mother Jenny had been involved in the Waratah Anglican Church since his childhood. In the 1990s, Ben was a member of an Anglican youth band with an improbable name, "Ovine Aviation". He was the roadie and did the sound and light. The band played at church services, including at the cathedral.

Jane noticed Ben was unusually quiet, watching Lawrence intently. Later that night, she asked Ben, "Nothing ever happened to you back in the day?" Ben "just fobbed it off". But he lay awake in bed that night, unable to sleep.

Ben knew that Rob and Bronwyn Wall, friends from his childhood, had given evidence to the commission that in 1995 they told Bishop Herft about two boys who said Lawrence had sexually abused them at Anglican camps. Herft did nothing and threatened them with defamation. Recently, Rob Wall had stopped Ben while he was doing a delivery, saying, "Now's the time. If you know anyone who has been sexually assaulted, now is the time to come forward." Ben had replied that "people move on, they get older, they have families ... they might not want to dig it all up."

Now, Ben lay in bed, thinking of what Wall had said.

The next day, he rang his wife from his delivery truck and said, "Pull over."

"You know when I told you nothing happened?" he said. "Actually, it did."

"Yeah, I know. I knew."

"Wives," Ben told me in an interview, "can tell when you are lying."

Ben now told her he had been sexually assaulted by Graeme Lawrence.

What had happened was this. When Ben was about fifteen years old, in 1991, he and his mother, Jenny, had attended a youth service at the cathedral. After putting equipment into a storeroom, he suddenly encountered Lawrence, who suggested a walk to look at photographs of famous clergy hanging on the walls and the celebrated "Book of Gold". This was a commemorative book with a splendid gilt cover made from melted-down wedding rings donated by Newcastle families after their loved ones had died in World War I.

Lawrence then invited Ben to the deanery after the service.

> "Some youth are going to come back to my place, would you like to come back, a bit of an after party, so to speak, meet other youth?" …
> I thought, "Yeah, that's a good idea", and just went back to normal, back to the service.

Ben asked his mum, who was sitting in the cathedral, and she agreed. The dean was an important person so it was quite an honour, and she assumed other kids would be present.

Following the service, Lawrence took Ben along the short path from the cathedral to the deanery. As they entered the house, Giggins became nervous. It was completely empty; no one else was there. Lawrence led him through the house and into a small room. On the walls were pictures of naked young boys. Giggins froze. When Lawrence asked him if he liked the pictures, Ben said no. Then, in a sudden, swift movement, Lawrence grabbed Ben's shoulders and said, "Relax, it will be okay," as he pulled the boy's T-shirt over his head so that he couldn't see and pinned his arms. Lawrence then forced Ben onto his hands and knees, pulled Ben's pants down and again told him to relax. Shaking and scared, Ben heard Lawrence's belt being unbuckled and trousers falling to the ground. Lawrence's clothes smelled of incense.

Lawrence then played with Ben's penis and testicles for about ten to fifteen seconds. He kept saying "relax" and "do you like that?" Ben started to cry and said, "No, I don't like it. Stop." Then he felt the tip of Lawrence's penis at his anus. Lawrence pushed down on Ben's back, then held on to his shoulders and armpits and penetrated him. Ben felt pain and crept forward to try to get away, but Lawrence also moved forward and pushed in harder, penetrating him four times. Then there was "one forceful one". At this point Ben was able to move forward enough to get up and pull his T-shirt down and his pants up. He rushed out the door.

As Ben ran, Lawrence called out after him: "Don't bother telling anyone. You're just a boy and I'm the dean. No one will believe you." Ben told no one, not even his mother, who was patiently waiting for him in the cathedral. He told her he wanted to go home. She later described him as "angry", "agitated" and "snappy" on the drive home. Once there, Ben showered immediately and saw "blood in his underpants and in the water at the bottom of the shower". No matter how much he washed himself he still felt dirty. He was in pain and cried himself to sleep. The next day at school, he was still very sore.

Ben stayed in the Anglican Church but kept close to others and away from the dean. On one occasion, Lawrence reminded him: "Don't bother telling anyone, you know who I am." Years later, Ben was at a railway station with his mother when he saw Lawrence. According to Jenny, Ben suddenly went pale and froze.

From 1991 to 2016, he said nothing, even though the rape affected him profoundly. It was only after the royal commission hearing ended that he finally told his family and friends about it.

His mother was devastated. Jane was shocked too, but that Ben was a sexual assault victim explained a lot about his sometimes puzzling behaviour. In 2013 and 2014, when Bishop Thompson was being threatened by the opposition gang, the "parish recovery" process meant putting sympathetic people around him at the cathedral. Ben was one of them. Going back to the cathedral meant confronting unresolved trauma, triggering anxiety and anger. "It was after that I went off the rails and built some pretty big walls, and just closed off," he told me. Jane was caring for their toddler son and also became anxious and depressed. Their marriage suffered.

Ben was wary of going through Professional Standards, "ringing the institution where the abuse has come from … It was, you know, are they investigating their own?" Instead, he rang a solicitor, Niesha Shepherd. She got a royal commission lawyer to come up from Sydney to take his statement. About six to eight months later, in 2017, "the police got in touch with me and asked me to come in and do a statement".

Ben found telling people was "a weight off the shoulders. But then there was a daunting prospect of … are people going to believe me?" Ben had lived for so many years with Lawrence's taunt, "You're just a boy and I'm the dean. No one will believe you." He lived with the knowledge that his powerful perpetrator was the second-highest-ranked Anglican in the diocese, with a great aura surrounding him.

Attending the police station was intimidating, but the investigating detectives, Jeff Little and Chris Browne, were kind, empathetic and attentive. "They invested so much time and energy … they believed me." Little interviewed everyone Ben had known in 1991 who might have observed something, including the builder who repaired the deanery after the earthquake, who provided crucial details that proved pivotal in the case against Lawrence.

On 14 November 2017, Lawrence was arrested and charged. Detective Little rang Steve and told him the news. He knew what a destructive role Lawrence had played in Steve's life. Little told him: "As he opened the door and saw me standing there, the colour drained out of his face."

*

On the very first day of Lawrence's trial for the rape of Ben Giggins, Steve was inadvertently involved in a controversy. Giselle Wakatama, a local ABC journalist, interviewed him as a survivor of Anglican Church sex abuse. When the news item ran on various ABC outlets, it mentioned the royal commission and described Lawrence as a man who "wielded a great deal of power throughout the city" as part of a "gang of three".

The next day in court, Lawrence's defence team objected that this brief news item might prejudice the jury. A person can only be tried for the crime for which they are being indicted and trial evidence cannot include other elements that might influence the jury, such as media coverage of Lawrence at the royal commission.

After due consideration, judge Timothy Gartelmann decided the bulletin did have the potential to give rise to a miscarriage of justice. The jury was discharged. Justice Gartelmann considered the matter carefully and decided on a judge-only trial.

I was covering the Lawrence trial for *The Monthly*. Steve was extremely upset that he might have accidentally damaged the case that Little had worked so hard on. I could see how vulnerable Steve still was to being disbelieved. I wondered if Little would be angry. Instead, he kindly patted Steve on the shoulder and said, "Don't worry about it, mate, could've happened to anyone." He asked me to take Steve outside for a cup of tea, to "settle him down". Later, Little asked me quietly, "Is he okay?" I nodded. Given the trial might have fallen over at that point, I was impressed by the detective's restraint.

I was intrigued by the Anglicans who turned up to support Lawrence. On several occasions I sat next to Robert Caddies. There were some rather weird people supporting the disgraced former dean. A woman wearing a silk blouse and a large hat and carrying a picnic basket, as if she had just arrived from a vicar's garden tea party, glared daggers at Steve. A pale man dressed in flowing garments, with long white hair and a staff, looked to have just stepped off the hills of Nazareth herding goats. The former president of the Mothers' Union, Pam Dowdell, another signatory to the "Senior Professionals" letter, brought her knitting basket. She sat there knitting furiously, nodding whenever Lawrence said anything. At one point, when he gave a particularly hyperbolic answer, she called out loudly, "Good boy!"

As soon as the trial began, however, I doubted their hopes that Lawrence would be found innocent would be realised.

The prosecutor, Craig Leggat SC, was a small and wiry man who reminded me of a Dickensian thespian. He wore a peculiarly ragged barrister's wig with a sprout, a curly, wispy end to it, and wore red tartan socks. He arrived at court each day with an enormous purple suitcase. Sometimes, in the quieter moments before the session began, he appeared to be dozing off. But then he woke up and was brilliantly on point, revealing he had listened carefully to everything. He proved a clever and sharp interlocutor.

Leggat outlined the case in slow and measured tones, like a kindly teacher. He patiently explained that the two charges were sexual assault and aggravated sexual assault, meaning rape or sexual intercourse without consent, while knowing that Ben was not consenting and that he was under sixteen years old. Consent, Leggat told the court, meant a conscious and voluntary agreement.

While complainants can remain anonymous, Ben Giggins had courageously allowed his name to be used. Leggat kept repeating his first name, and also frequently deployed "Jenny" and "mum", preferring the intimate terms to the cooler word "mother".

Quietly, after pausing for emphasis, Leggat outlined the crime in great detail. He described how Ben's mum trustingly agreed that her son could go to Dean Lawrence's house to "meet other youth". How there was no one there. The room with pictures of naked boys. How terrified Ben was. Lawrence suddenly flipping Ben's T-shirt above his head, trapping him. Forcing him onto his hands and knees. Asking him if he liked it, as he raped him … the pain. Ben's escape and Lawrence telling him no one would believe him. The blood afterwards, Ben's shame and the feeling of being dirty no matter how much he washed.

In court, Lawrence was smartly dressed, usually wearing a check shirt, open at the neck. Sometimes he had a camel sweater casually draped over his shoulders. He looked nonchalant, or bored, peering over his spectacles as if above it all. When Leggat finished, Lawrence leant back on his chair, eyes hooded.

Mr Winch, the barrister for the defence, had a manner as crisp as a wilted lettuce and frequently looked as if he might cry. The defence's case was so poor it would have made any good lawyer weep. It relied, as Lawrence had at the royal commission, on blanket denial. He had never met Ben Giggins. He had never invited him to the deanery. He had never indecently or sexually assaulted him. There were no pictures of naked boys in his home. He was not even living at the deanery when the assaults occurred, due to damage from the 1989 earthquake.

The next day, Ben gave evidence "in camera" – with no audience or media present. At "walk throughs" of the cathedral and deanery, as I later learned, he showed the judge and the defence and prosecution teams where he had walked with Lawrence. Ben was worried that the building had been renovated and would be quite different, but it wasn't. Gartelmann noted in his judgement that Ben unconsciously gestured with his body and hands, showing he knew where everything was. He had clearly been to the deanery before. He walked through the house and led them to the small room where he was raped.

Gartelmann found Lawrence guilty, and central to that verdict was Gartelmann's assessment of the relative credibility of Lawrence and Giggins. He described Giggins' evidence as having "the clear ring of truth". Giggins, he said, was "calm, shy and quiet", and despite obvious embarrassment over such an intimate crime, gave answers with a "high degree of credibility", with "detail" and "subconscious physical movements" indicating "genuine" recollections of a traumatic assault. He did not seek to advance his own interests and acknowledged where he could not remember.

In contrast, Gartelmann did not find Lawrence credible. He was "defiant" and "became particularly combative when tested". Lawrence "demonstrated an intent not to concede matters against his own interests at the expense of truthfulness". His evidence had "inconsistencies". He denied ever having met Giggins, but another member of Ben's youth band, Dominic Eve, remembered Lawrence once greeting Giggins using his full name, "Benjamin", rather than Ben, which he thought was a "bit strange". The incident stayed in his mind. In a police interview, Lawrence denied that youth bands ever played at the cathedral, but it was clear from the cathedral register that they had. During cross-examination, Judge Gartelmann said, "It was evident that the accused knew ... that it was incorrect but sought to justify it as he perceived an interest in maintaining it was correct."

My own observation, watching Lawrence over the weeks of the trial, was of an extraordinarily arrogant man, as if through sheer force of personality he could compel those listening to comply with his denials. Lying seemed second nature. Lawrence constantly looked at the judge, as if appealing to him as a peer: we are the high-status men above these lowly people. He resorted to name-dropping. On the question of the pictures of naked boys in what he called "the ironing room", he said scornfully: "I could hardly have had the governor and governor-general or the premier of the state or John Howard with those etchings on the wall."

Prosecutor Leggat asked Lawrence what relevance John Howard, who became prime minister in 1996, could possibly have to an allegation of rape in 1991? Lawrence said: "Merely to affirm and confirm I had no such materials on the wall." Leggat replied sharply: "You were prepared to make a self-serving statement."

Lawrence's penchant for self-aggrandisement was frequently on display. He used the word "great" many times. As Leggat went through all the occasions when the band might have played at the cathedral, Lawrence met his suggestions with withering scorn. "I can assure you I would have been deluged with complaints" if a humble youth band had played, rather than the "great religious music" in the "great English tradition for a great occasion". He spoke of "the great canticles" and "the great

English composers like Purcell and Stanford ... the great masters of music like Bach and Haydn". Even Sea Sunday, dedicated to sailors, featured "great naval hymns". On and on he went in his rich, baritone voice, glasses perched on the end of his nose, his mouth turned down in a disapproving fold as he insisted that the decidedly not-great youth band would never have played on any of these "great" occasions in the cathedral.

Prosecutor Leggat didn't miss a beat: did Lawrence meet Giggins "after the less-great services"?

The defence's central argument was that the December 1989 Newcastle earthquake had so damaged the deanery that Lawrence was not living there at the time of the offences. Lawrence described the damage as "fairly catastrophic. A movement of walls, falling masonry, general destruction." Indicating large gaps in walls, he flung his arms open about a metre in a dramatic flourish. Lawrence claimed he and his partner were forced to move out straight away, taking all their furniture with them, while the deanery was repaired. Under cross-examination, however, he admitted that a removalist's receipt showed they actually hadn't moved out until 30 April 1991. As Judge Gartelmann noted in his summing up, it was hard to imagine they had lived in a building as damaged as Lawrence described for a year and a half.

A witness called for the crown, Brett Tilse, a builder who had done the repairs to the deanery, contradicted Lawrence, describing the damage as "just bits and pieces throughout the building". Tilse thought about 50 per cent of Lawrence's furniture and personal effects were left in the building during the repairs. This was another "significant fact", because Giggins remembered a chair and a wardrobe in the room where the assault took place. A plan of the repairs showed that the room was not on the list of those needing work. Even if Lawrence wasn't living there at the time, an unoccupied deanery, Judge Gartelmann noted, "would have provided a convenient opportunity for sexual offences to be committed without risk of detection".

Gartelmann found Lawrence's key witness, his long-time partner Greg Goyette, unreliable, with evidence of collusion between them. Goyette, a rotund man in a maroon jumper and tie, was a music teacher. He kept folding and unfolding his arms uneasily.

In a moving statement to the court, Ben told a familiar story of the aftermath of the assault. It had shattered his confidence and his trust and capsized not only his emotional life and his schooling but also his long-held ambition to become a policeman. He had resorted to drinking and left school before completing year twelve.

Lawrence was found guilty. The lord mayor of Newcastle, Nuatali Nelmes, immediately stripped Lawrence of his 1997 Citizen of the Year and Freeman of the City awards. Steve called for Lawrence's Medal of the Order of Australia – granted when he was an active sexual offender – to be revoked. (This proved a slow process, with Steve writing many letters to the Honours Secretariat about it.)

Detective Little couldn't resist saying to the media outside, "No longer should we say Graeme Lawrence OAM, when in fact the reality is he is now Graeme Lawrence CP, convicted paedophile." He praised the honour and strength Ben Giggins had shown. "The price that Ben has paid and the social injustices that go with being offended by such a man in a powerful position as Dean Graeme Lawrence was in cannot be ignored."

Ben told the *Newcastle Herald*:

[This case] shows people in powerful positions can't hide behind their positions ... If there is anyone else out there, come forward, don't be scared if someone has told you that you won't be believed.[1]

Ben expressed his gratitude to detectives Little and Browne. "The police have been unbelievable; they helped every step of the way," he said. Steve chimed in about Jeff Little: "He is one of the unsung heroes in this town. He has worked so hard to look out for people like myself and Ben and others and he really needs to be recognised for that."

Bishop Stuart, who had replaced Greg Thompson in 2018, told reporters, "Ben is an amazingly courageous man. He has spoken with bravery and openness to bring his concerns before the courts in order that ... his offences [be] properly treated. I have had an opportunity to express the regret of the Anglican Church to Ben and I do so publicly again."

It was a vivid contrast with Team Church at George Parker's trial in 2001.

Lawrence was sentenced on 27 September 2019 to eight years' jail with four and half to be completed before parole. The sentencing was the only time in the whole trial he really seemed interested. His disgrace was complete.

*

Well, almost complete. There were two more allegations of sexual abuse and assault against Lawrence.[2] The first concerned a woman, Lyn Rudkin, who took out a civil case of compensation against Lawrence, the Anglican diocese of the Riverina and the Education Department of New South Wales. Civil cases, as pointed out earlier, differ from criminal ones; the required standard of proof is "on the balance of probabilities" rather than "beyond all reasonable doubt". Rudkin's claim was accepted, and she received a payout of some $600,000.

Rudkin alleged that when she was about eleven years old and a student in Lawrence's scripture class in around 1968, he anally raped her. Lyn had already suffered horrific abuse from two other men by the time she reached late primary school. When she expressed doubts about Christianity to Lawrence, according to Rudkin he saw it as an intolerable form of defiance. Angry, he asked her to wait after class. She alleged that after the other students left, he took her into a different room, grabbed her, flipped her around, pressed her against a desk and brutally raped her. Rudkin had a violent father and feared to tell anyone. She alleged that thereafter Lawrence repeatedly assaulted her after scripture lessons. She never recovered from the multiple occasions of sexual abuse, suffering severe anxiety, depression, suicide attempts and multiple stays in psychiatric hospitals. Courageously, she kept going, however, and went on to raise two sons. She had been supported in a remarkable way by her husband, Richard Rudkin, who was her full-time carer. Written evidence showed that she had disclosed the attacks by Lawrence long before his defrocking or any media reports about him.

Although Lawrence's other victims were male, there were precedents for predominantly same-sex predators assaulting girls as well. The royal commission accepted the veracity of a complaint against Bishop Shevill for the rape of a thirteen-year-old girl at a North Queensland school where he taught in the 1950s. The diocese of North Queensland would later pay the complainant $20,000. There was evidence that Catholic priest Gerald Ridsdale, a prolific abuser of boys, also abused girls. In one tragic case, Ridsdale abused both a brother and sister after their father died.

*

New and shocking allegations about Lawrence were again in the news on 18 August 2022, when *Newcastle Herald* journalist Ian Kirkwood reported the Professional Standards Board determination against Reverend Chris Bird.[3] One of the allegations concerned Steve. The story ran with a photo of Steve outside Christ Church Cathedral, with the caption "VIN-DICATED AGAIN: Anglican abuse survivor Stephen Smith, physically assaulted by Reverend Bird at a synod in 2016". The inquiry found Bird had been responsible for bullying, intimidation and even physical assault over decades.

We met Bird earlier in this book, when he threatened both the Professional Standards Director, Michael Elliott, and a church worker, Debbie Torok. Bird, the rector at St Stephen's in Adamstown, was, like George Parker, a member of the Society of the Holy Cross (Societas Sanctae Crucis, or SSC). A long-time friend and acolyte of Lawrence, he believed that the 2012 defrocking of Lawrence was wrong. Michael Elliott had great difficulty getting Bird to comply with the safety protocols required after Lawrence was defrocked. A former priest cannot officiate over any service, yet there were photos of Lawrence at St Stephen's doing a scriptural reading at the pulpit.[4]

Steve told the board he'd been invited to hear Bishop Thompson's apology to victim-survivors at the 2016 synod. He was standing at the back of the gathering when he noticed Bird staring at him in an aggressive, intimidatory way. Then Bird walked up to Steve and:

> deliberately, forcefully drove his elbow into the side of my stomach. He used enough force to cause me to bend forward and quickly pull my arm across my body to protect myself from him … I was unnerved, thrown … He stood there for a few minutes and then walked back to his seat. He glared at me.

Steve was completely shocked. Joanne McCarthy came up to him and asked, "What was *that* about?"[5]

The main case against Bird, however, concerned Graeme Lawrence and Witness A, a young man of twenty-three. In mid-2018, Witness A, a devout member of Bird's congregation, had been considering entering the priesthood. He looked up to Bird, describing him as a charismatic and influential role model. Bird introduced him to Lawrence, who was out on bail as he awaited trial for the rape of Ben Giggins. Lawrence was:

friendly and warm towards [Witness A], complimenting him on his appearance, his clothes and the work that he performed within the Parish. Witness A rejected a number of Mr Lawrence's invitations to his home for a drink.

The young man first learned of the criminal charges against Lawrence at the end of 2017, but told the board that Bird "took every opportunity to minimise or negate Mr Lawrence's part in crimes with which he was charged". Bird also "pressured him to meet with Lawrence". Witness A finally agreed, and in mid-2018 met up with Lawrence at the Kotara food court. The young man described Lawrence's behaviour as "flirtatious with crude sexualisation of their conversation ... Lawrence showed no interest in discussing religion".

When Witness A wanted to return to the parish to do secretarial work, Lawrence insisted on driving him. He alleged that in the car, Lawrence sexually assaulted him.

> From the moment I got in the passenger seat of his car, it felt like he couldn't keep his hands off me. As he drove the car he continually reached across to the passenger seat where I was sitting and grabbed my right hand with his left hand and put it forcefully on his thigh and penis. He only let it go to use his left hand to grab my penis. This continued the whole way to Adamstown. He drove into Olney Road and parked the car just near Saint Stephen's.

Lawrence then told the young man that he liked having sex with young boys and thrust an iPhone in front of his face; on it were graphic recordings of child sexual abuse.

> He was talking sexy as in filthy talk about young boys what he liked to do to them and why he liked having sex with boys. For example, he said, "I like how their arses are nice and tight." "Boys are so fresh and youthful." "Come on this is what friends do with one another, we can keep it to ourselves and not tell anyone." He accessed child pornography on his telephone and watched it. He put it in front of my face so that I had to watch it. I saw young boys with other young boys and old men having sex, oral, penetrative anal sex, the lot. I had never been exposed to child

pornography before, so I felt frozen and sick. I found it repulsive, and I was scared stiff.

The young man could see that Lawrence was aroused.

> I could see and feel Graeme's penis became erect. Graeme remained fully clothed throughout the entire ordeal … Graeme tried on several occasions whilst we were parked to remove my pants at the front to expose my penis, but I managed to prevent that from happening by fighting against it. I was constantly saying, "No stop this; please stop I feel sick and scared I need to go." I constantly felt like I was pushing him away. At one stage towards the end of the ordeal he had managed to partially climb on top of me … [and] he forcefully stuck his tongue in my mouth and kissed me hard and passionately as he did this, he was masturbating himself with his right hand … I can recall looking down toward his penis and seeing a wet spot on the outside of his beige coloured pants. I can recall thinking that he must have ejaculated in his pants.

Badly shaken, Witness A managed to get out of the car and "walked frantically to St Stephen's". Shortly after he arrived, Reverend Bird came in and Witness A told him in detail about the sexual assault. Bird allegedly said, "I'm sorry this happened to you" but showed no surprise or indignation. He "appeared to accept too easily the distressing circumstances that he described".

According to the summary of the judgement by Margaret Sidis, president of the Professional Standards Board, the young man subsequently left St Stephen's congregation because Bird's attitude:

> changed from the day upon which he disclosed the assault. [Bird] was no longer approachable and open, he was cold towards him and kept his distance and avoided him … [which] caused him to feel that he was at fault.[6]

According to other witness evidence before the board, Bird minimised and normalised Lawrence's assault. Another clergyman reported that Bird told him "Graeme showed [Witness A] some gay pornography at a café". "I can recall [Bird's] wife said something like 'Graeme was probably pushing the boundaries to see if Witness A was interested'," the clergyman recalled. Child pornography was thus rewritten as harmless adult gay pornography, and sexually assaulting Witness A was rewritten as "pushing the boundaries". This minimisation, and Bird's cold reaction to Witness A after the assault, tell us a great deal about the indulgent and enabling culture towards sexual misconduct that had existed in Newcastle. In Bishop Herft's time, Chris Bird had an important governance role on the Board of Investigation during the 1990s, along with Peter Rushton, Graeme Lawrence, Keith Allen and Peter Mitchell. His wife, Merri Bird, had been a contact person for CASM, responsible for receiving child sexual abuse complaints. The fact that Witness A's shocking experience could still occur in 2018 showed that the group around Lawrence was still not entirely defeated.

Judge Margaret Sidis gave Bird six months to show why he should not be defrocked. He could not do so, and in 2023 Bishop Stuart deposed Bird from holy orders. Steve listened to Stuart's passionate and angry address after the board judgement. "Peter was on fire," Steve told me, describing the normally mild-mannered bishop ripping into the culture that had damaged the Newcastle Anglican Church for so long. In a statement, Stuart said that, as bishop, he was "absolutely confounded" that a priest could conduct themselves in this manner" and apologised to those "who have been wronged by Father Bird", thanking them for their courage. "You should never have experienced such harm and distress."

Bishop Stuart said Bird showed no contrition.

Father Bird rails against the professional standards process and further diminishes the people he has hurt. He shows no insight into the adverse impact his conduct has had ... He chose to ignore the opportunity to make amends and demonstrate behaviour consistent with the heart of his vocation. Sadly, I anticipate that those who supported Graeme Lawrence and Father Bird will not recognise that ... both were prepared to set up a church in which people could be harmed and the harm go unchallenged.

CHAPTER TWENTY-FIVE
POWERFUL PERPETRATORS

WHAT DO PETER Rushton and Graeme Lawrence have in common with Sir Jimmy Savile, the British DJ and TV star; Jimmy Williams, a top US horse-riding instructor who trained Olympians; Larry Nassar, team physician to the US national gymnastics team; Grant Davies, owner of a famous Australian dance company; Peter Ball, the bishop of Gloucester in the UK; Wollongong mayors Frank Arkell and Tony Bevan; and so many others?

They were *powerful perpetrators*. The term comes from a seminal 2020 article in the *Journal of Sexual Aggression*, "Powerful Perpetrators, Hidden in Plain Sight: An International Analysis of Organisational Child Sexual Abuse Cases".[1] The authors examined seventeen cases in Australia, the UK and the USA and found that such predators trade on their popularity, power and high status to gain access to victims. Their reputation and position in a hierarchy creates a "halo effect" that enables them to seem "beyond reproach" and to hide in plain sight.

Strangely, although powerful perpetrators are an obvious category of offender, there has been "rarely any mention" of them in the research literature, the authors found. Yet many youth service organisations – schools, scouts, sports clubs, musical academies and churches – include powerful people "with the potential to abuse their authority". The "sheer number" of these youth organisations poses a danger, because the public is often unaware of the powerful perpetrator phenomenon, and safety protocols "generally do not address the potential for this type of child sexual abuse".

"No one will believe you," said Lawrence to Ben Giggins, and George Parker to Steve. That is the halo effect at work. Powerful perpetrators gain a reputation that is "beyond reproach" by presenting themselves as caring, "good" people. When they tell their victims "no one will believe you", they are usually correct. Their carefully curated image means they are trusted enough to gain access to children, and then to escape detection and punishment.

The authors of the study found that even when suspected of misconduct, powerful perpetrators were often so important to their organisations that they could evade consequences. Fear of reputational damage to the institution was too great. These perpetrators were often charismatic, even celebrities, and were "accorded a level of reverence or adoration within the organisation".[2] To borrow a banking term, they were "too big to fail".

The authors might have been describing Graeme Lawrence or Peter Rushton when they wrote:

> one archetype of such offenders [is a] ... charismatic, articulate, well networked, 'caring professional' who is usually a part of the leadership of the institution ... these are people who often have the latitude to be "above the law" ... While these powerful individuals may be some of an organisation's greatest assets, they may also present one of its most significant risks. Cases of child sexual abuse by powerful offenders have accounted for large numbers of victims.

Even offenders who did not have the status to be "powerful perpetrators" used similar grooming techniques to "create the illusion that they were a good person, beyond reproach" in order to evade detection.[3]

*

When a powerful perpetrator uses the halo effect to gain access to children, they are taking advantage of the human tendency to use cognitive frames and schemas to organise our perceptions of the world. It is a kind of shortcut. No one looks up a complex research study to assess the relative risk before attending a church or sending a kid to school. Instead, we work with cognitive frames such as the "helpful person", which unfortunately can mislead us into trusting a seemingly caring person. For the powerful perpetrators in the Anglican Church, the cognitive frame was that of the caring pastor.

Think of Parker, constantly visiting Steve's unhappy mother and listening to her troubles, and Lawrence, whose supporters idealised him and wouldn't hear a word against him. The most important strategy of powerful perpetrators is to groom people around the child. They train people not to look, or to see something other than what is really there. The current bishop of Newcastle, Peter Stuart, who lived through the backlash after Lawrence's defrocking, observed perceptively:

> All of the material on grooming that I've read, indicates a groomer not only grooms an individual for abuse, but family, the community, the setting around all of that ... the predatory person who's set out to do it is actually laying the foundations that [will allow them to] both undertake the criminal activity and not get caught. And to do that, people need not to see what's in front of them. They actually need to see something else.

So how do these powerful perpetrators get people to see "something else"?

In Carla van Dam's striking study of 300 offenders, *Identifying Child Molesters: Preventing Child Sexual Abuse by Recognizing the Patterns of the Offenders*,[4] she writes of molesters who are "too good to be true".

> Like a heroin addict continuously looking for the next "fix", child molesters are constantly "on task" ... keenly attuned to every relevant social nuance, which gives them an uncanny knack for anticipating the needs of adults responsible for children. Many of the molesters reported this exceptional helpfulness ... the elaborate strategies they use to successfully endear themselves to adults ... to ensure unimpeded access to children fits an identifiable pattern.

Van Dam points out that people often struggle to understand how they had an offender in their midst without realising. People "erroneously assume such a person would automatically not be likeable". Yet the offenders she interviewed noted how much people liked them and how people were drawn in by their determined helpfulness. One told her, "I get access to children because I am so likeable and I can read people and know what they want to hear."

She quotes an expert, Gavin de Becker:

"He was so nice" is a comment I often hear describing the man who, moments or months after his niceness, victimized them. We must learn and teach our children niceness does not equal goodness. Niceness is a decision, a strategy of social interaction. People seeking to control others almost always present an image of a nice person at the beginning.[5]

The number one grooming strategy, van Dam points out, was creating the image of a benignly helpful person. There was no better way to groom a child, their family, and community than by using the altruistic mask of a priest. Our cognitive framing tells us – erroneously – that a nice guy is not a child molester.

[Yet] over 95 per cent of child molesters typically are known, loved and trusted individuals who are already firmly entrenched in their communities. It is this insider status that molesters go to such trouble to establish and maintain because that is what allows them to be regarded as trustworthy and "above reproach."

The paedophiles in her study consistently noted how deliberately they would groom the adult community around the targeted child.

"I would obviously have met his family several times ... would have charmed the hell out of his parent(s) and they would be pleased with the way their son responded to me and so obviously liked me. I am clean cut, very intelligent and personable and the parents would feel I was a good influence on the boy."

Having befriended the child's family, there seemed nothing unusual in the perpetrator's dropping around and spending a lot of time with the child. This "grooming" of adults is a well-organised, long-term activity, informed by considerable thought and planning. Some molesters confirmed that they would spend anywhere from two to three years getting established in a new community before molesting any children. A key strategy was helpfulness: "I'll see somebody ... and give them a hand ... it'll give them a false image. I'll give them a hand and then turn around and groom and molest their daughter. And that's the way I am."

They might disarm parents by advising them to put a "lock on a bathroom" or by commenting on the horrors of child sexual abuse, to make themselves seem safe. They deliberately choose families in which the parents are unhappy, stressed or single, then offer handyman or babysitting help to gain trust and access.

Van Dam found that molesters used techniques such as image management and name recognition.

> "You portray yourself as a church leader or music teacher, or whatever it takes to make that family think you're okay ... And you just trick the family into believing that you are the most trustworthy person in the world. Every one of my victims, their families just totally offered ... and they trusted me wholeheartedly with their children."[6]

So the paedophile trains people to look and see something quite false. He is happy to help out at camp. Happy to be a father figure to the children of an overburdened woman with an absent partner. Happy to be an attentive, caring priest, listening to the confidences of a lonely mother. Happy to be a kind neighbour who babysits the kids ... All while seeming to ask for nothing in return.

One molester warned van Dam, "Someone that's overly friendly, that goes out of his way and doesn't ask for the same thing back, that's a clue." Another said that once you have people groomed, you can do anything. They won't believe what others tell them. In fact, once people have been taken in – Lawrence's supporters come to mind – they will usually refuse to admit that their judgement was completely wrong, even when presented with evidence. The paedophile's strategy is to make people feel obligated. Then, if the abuser is outed, van Dam shows, there is a familiar pattern. The molester goes on the offensive, making defamation threats, and there is frequently a savage community backlash – against the victim.

Sir Jimmy Savile, the BBC TV and radio star, also seemed "caring" and raised £40 million for charity, while abusing up to 450 victims, some as young as eight years old. There were many complaints about Savile's behaviour. One witness told the Independent Review into the BBC's

Culture and Practices that during Savile's years at the BBC managers viewed talent as more important than values. When a junior employee complained to her supervisor in the late 1980s that Savile had sexually assaulted her, she was told, "keep your mouth shut, he is a VIP".

Another example was the charismatic English bishop Peter Ball, who abused teenagers and young men. His congregation supported him long after allegations were made, sending two hundred letters of support proclaiming his innocence to police. Although he had received a police caution for an act of gross indecency against a sixteen-year-old in 1993, Ball was allowed to work in churches until 2010. In 2015, he was finally convicted of sexual offences against seventeen teenagers and young men and jailed for thirty-two months.

Like Savile, Ball cultivated high-status backers, who naively believed him.[7] The then Prince of Wales was Ball's staunch advocate and wrote to him in 1995, saying he believed Ball had been wrongly accused, despite the police caution. "I wish I could do more. I feel so desperately strongly about the monstrous wrongs that have been done to you and the way you have been treated." He even organised for the Duchy of Cornwall to provide a house in Somerset where Ball and his identical twin, Michael, also a bishop, could stay. The future king later regretfully acknowledged, in a six-page statement to the Independent Inquiry into Child Sexual Abuse (IICSA) in the Church of England, that "he had been deceived over a long period of time 'about the true nature' of Ball's activities."[8]

The family of one of Ball's victims, who committed suicide in 2012, complained the victim had been portrayed as a liar and a "mischief-maker" by Ball's friends in high places. Ball finally admitted to "misusing his position in authority to manipulate and prevail upon others for his own sexual gratification".[9] The lawyer William Chapman, representing survivors, told the IICSA: "The story of Peter Ball is the story of the establishment at work in modern times ... how [it] minimised the nature of Peter Ball's misdeeds ... and silenced and harassed those who tried to complain."

The halo effect meant that like Bishop Ball, Graeme Lawrence was also, for a long time, invulnerable. He made sure he was seen to be caring, making many parishioners devoted supporters. He assiduously networked at the Newcastle Club. He entertained powerful people at the deanery and continually name-dropped. He seemed to be everywhere after the 1989 earthquake and made sure this work was extensively covered by the local newspaper. Even the *Newcastle Herald*, famous for campaigning against child sexual abuse, at first supported him. Everyone had been groomed to look at Lawrence and see something else.

The halo effect concealed Lawrence's dark side, and it created what some psychologists call "flying monkeys" – his unquestioning and vociferous supporters. In *The Wizard of Oz*, the Wicked Witch of the West uses flying monkeys to do her dirty work. Narcissists like Lawrence develop dominating relationships with their acolytes, who become minions willing to do their leader's bidding. It was not Lawrence who shredded the evidence against him. It was not Lawrence who made death threats and put a bullet on Steve's step. It was not Lawrence who wrote vicious letters to the Episcopal Standards Commission and the royal commission, discrediting Farran and Thompson. It was all done by Lawrence's supporters, his flying monkeys.

Lawrence was not alone in using charismatic authority to gain access to children. Most of the abusing priests, including Peter Rushton, George Parker, Michael Cooper, James Brown, Robert Elmore and lay worker Jim Brown, were popular and charismatic to varying degrees. Steve described how Parker groomed his parishioners to see a caring pastor and not to believe any boy who accused him. Detective Jeff Little interviewed parishioners who refused to believe that "lovely Father George" could have sexually abused children.

Bishop Stuart told me: "What we know of some of the Anglican offenders is that their care [and] other aspects of their ministry, at times were just exemplary. Amazing. And some people were helped by them." Stuart described this as a "disjunction". However, the latest research on powerful perpetrators suggests this may not be a strange contradiction, but a standard grooming technique, part of the disguise, and one that we must be alert to.

*

When Jesus was asked what he meant by "Love your neighbour", he told the parable of the Good Samaritan. It is a story about moral choice, about seeing and not seeing. A badly beaten Jew lies wounded on the road to Jericho. Two people look away and walk past. The Samaritan stops, looks and cares for the wounded man.

Despite it being a Christian community, in Newcastle there was widespread behaviour which was the very opposite of that of the Good Samaritan's. The survivors are equivalent to the person lying beaten on the side of the road. So many clergy and lay people, including those at the highest levels whose responsibility it was to look after the "least and the lost", averted their eyes and ignored the injured. The clergy did so out of self-interest – to keep jobs and houses, to keep in favour with the bishop, to keep a bit of power and prestige by protecting and covering up. Some laity were so focused on gaining social significance, on clawing their way up the church hierarchy, that they forgot the radical egalitarianism at the heart of the teaching of Jesus. They forgot especially what Jesus told his disciples about children.

> Whosoever therefore shall humble himself as this little child, the same is greatest in the kingdom of heaven. And whoso shall receive one such little child in my name receiveth me ... But whoso shall offend one of these little ones which believe in me, it were better for him that a millstone were hanged about his neck, and that he were drowned in the depth of the sea.

The royal commission raised the question of "wilful blindness", a legal term. It leads to consideration of a broader category, the moral politics of attention. Giving attention is a moral act. Withholding attention can be an immoral act. It is also a political act, because the powerful always command more attention than the powerless. Many Newcastle clergy and parishioners engaged in what I call "determined inattention", or inattention with a motive. If their gaze was fixed sympathetically on the powerful male perpetrators, who was it they were refusing to see or listen to?

Children.

For some in the church there was a complete failure of moral imagination – an inability or refusal to acknowledge the soul murder of abuse victims. Why this blindness? The answer is terrible. *Because the victims were children.*

We recognise that prejudices such as homophobia, racism and sexism do immense harm. But we haven't yet faced what psychoanalyst Elisabeth Young-Bruehl has called *childism*: a form of prejudice against children that permits every form of injustice because of a distorted and dehumanising view of the world that values adults more than children. In relation to child sexual abuse, childism results in greater value being given to the testimony of adults than to that of children. The royal commission found that it was rare for children to lie about sexual abuse, yet so often children's testimony is not believed. Children who reported abuse were thought to be lying. They had their faces slapped or their bodies beaten; they were punished for telling the truth. Sexual crimes against them were considered less significant than the need to preserve a man's reputation – because he was an adult and they were mere children. They were powerless.

Where we choose to look, whom we choose to listen to and what we choose to see are the key to understanding – and stopping – child sexual abuse. The halo effect protects powerful perpetrators, even more so than coercing, threatening or shaming the child victim. But childism, the unconscious bias and prejudice against children, is also a hugely important piece of the puzzle.

CHAPTER TWENTY-SIX
THE PEACH TREE

FOR STEVE, THE royal commission was an extraordinary vindication. Described as a "truthful and compelling witness",[1] he walked out a different man to the one who had walked in. A considerable portion of the hearing into the Newcastle Anglicans was devoted to Steve's case. Priests and laity who had loomed so large over his life now seemed puny as they were taken apart by royal commission lawyers.

There were many satisfying moments. Steve's account of the abuse he suffered was accepted. His evidence was preferred over Bishop Appleby's on the question of their 1984 meeting, at which Steve told Appleby about Parker's and Rushton's abuse. The commission made adverse findings against Bishops Appleby, Herft, Holland and Shevill, as well as against Graeme Lawrence and Keith Allen. There was fierce cross-examination of Allen and Peter Mitchell over the question of who falsified the register that was pivotal in providing an alibi in Parker's 2001 trial. There was no doubt it had been altered, but the commission did not make a final judgement as to who had made the alterations. There was another damning adverse finding of "deliberate obstruction" concerning the scurrilous behaviour of Team Church before Parker's trial, led by Mitchell, Allen and Lawrence, and their refusal to tell the police and DPP when Parker had been at Gateshead.

In another pivotal moment, Peter O'Brien, Steve's lawyer, managed to extract an apology from Mitchell for his offensive account of Parker's trial in the *Anglican Encounter*, which had deeply wounded Steve when he was at his lowest ebb. Mitchell admitted, "I would wish at the time there'd been more grace and care and compassion in what I have written there, and I apologise to your client for that."

Mitchell also said that "the withdrawal of the charges [against Parker] was absolutely a travesty … if Parker has to answer questions, then he should do so." To which O'Brien replied: "Those, sir, are hollow words, hollow words."

Bishop Farran told the commission how "contaminated" he felt by the treatment of Steve by the Anglican Church. He recalled his 2010 meeting with Steve, just after the outing of Rushton: "I just knew how damaged he'd been. I mean, he could have been, I think, quite a brilliant person, really. He probably is, still, but he could have achieved lots of things, and I just felt that he'd been so wronged."

In another moment that affected Steve deeply, the barrister John Booth, appearing for Paul Rosser, approached Steve and shook his hand, saying, "No one should go through what you have." That acknowledgement meant a lot to Steve.

As a consequence of the royal commission's trust in Steve's testimony, he was accorded a very high honour – he was one of just five survivors who spoke at the final general hearing in March 2017. Justice McClellan said that the commission had started with survivors and it was important that it end by listening to survivors.

For Steve, who had battled for forty years to be heard, it was an extraordinary moment. He went last. He spoke with authority and gravitas. It was essential, he told the commission, that all professional standards matters were completely independent of the church. Steve advised the commission that criminal sanctions, fines and withdrawal of tax benefits should be imposed on institutions if they did not comply with mandatory reporting. All allegations should go to two independent agencies (professional standards and case management) within twenty-four hours of the allegations being made, and those agencies should be required to follow up without delay. Steve suggested emergency support be given immediately to any complainant when they made an allegation. "No alleged victim should leave a situation where an allegation of child sexual abuse has been made, without direct and immediate care being offered." Steve spoke from the heart when he said:

> The responsibility for the safety of children falls solely upon adults. Parents, lawmakers, enforcement agencies, institutions and the community in general are responsible wholly to protect and nurture the minds and

bodies of all children and our future. We should never again find ourselves in this situation where generations have been devastated and lives
have been lost due to the indifference and self-serving attitudes of institutions in this country. We as a community need to send a clear message
to potential offenders and those institutions that would seek to protect
them that we will act swiftly and decisively to protect our children and
their future ... A zero-tolerance approach is the only approach that we as
a community can adopt.[2]

He thanked the commission for the opportunity to "finally have my
voice heard ... and on behalf of those who haven't survived, I also thank
you." Steve was thinking of all those who had committed suicide, like his
childhood friend Michael. The commission, the gallery, the courtroom, the
media and the nation, via live streaming, listened with attention.

*

While the royal commission was happening, Steve's legal suit against
Parker had to wait. But once it was over, Detective Little was ready. "Jeff
had it well in hand, he knew what he was doing," Steve said.

On 23 December 2016, Steve was driving home from Newcastle when
Little called him.

> Jeff rang me and said, "Where are you, mate?" I said, "I'm just driving up
> Carney Avenue", and he said, "You might want to pull over." I pulled over
> and he said, "I've got some news for you." "What's that?" Jeff said, "I'm
> in Ballarat."
> Oh.

Little usually held his cards close to his chest, but he now announced
proudly: "I've just charged Parker with the offences which were no-billed
in 2008, and I've reinstated them. I've given him another twenty, in relation to you."

Recalled Steve:

> And I felt ... you can't imagine!
> There was no question then. No one could ever turn around to me and

say that there was nothing in this. Jeff had done the most extraordinary investigation, had been all over the country and interviewed people everywhere, about Parker. Jeff's a really good guy, a really good cop ... What you need for a detective, is that doggedness and determination ... that's him in a nutshell. He lets nothing go and misses nothing.[3]

When news of Parker being charged reached the media, Little described Steve and his brother to *The Australian* as "bare-knuckled, bloody-fisted fighters".[4]

Little was confident the case would proceed to trial and that there was a good chance of a conviction. He told the media that "children's innocence was stolen by a criminal who was protected" by the church. Steve hugged Little outside the court. "Forty-two years it's taken to get to where we are today," Steve told Dan Box of *The Australian*. "If it gets to the steps of the court, we won't settle it there, we're going inside. If they haven't figured out that I'm going to fight, they haven't been listening."

Parker died of cancer just before the committal hearing in early 2017. Little had seen him a few weeks earlier and offered him the chance to confess, to achieve atonement before he died. Parker refused. Steve was devastated and told the ABC:

> I feel really cheated I guess ... you spend all that time and effort and heartache, and it just ends like this ... Parker, as he was dying, still wouldn't admit to what he did. So, I'll never forgive him. Even his funeral notice was a kick in the guts for us.[5]

In a final gesture of defiance, Parker wrote his own obituary, published in the *Ballarat Courier* on 13 January 2017.

PARKER George Alexander – Priest Passed away at Ballarat on January 11, 2017. Aged 79 yrs. Son of George William and Elsie Parker (both dec) and brother of Kelvin and Colin (dec). "You are a priest forever, in the order of Melchizedek." The Society of the Holy Cross, male members.

Melchizedek, in the Christian tradition, means "holy, blameless, unstained". The bishop of Ballarat, Garry Weatherill, rang Steve and apologised.

He was sincere in his apology. Weatherill said, "I wasn't aware of [the obituary] ... I didn't attend his funeral and I told my priests not to attend his funeral" ... Weatherill told me the obituary was prepared and submitted by Parker himself before he died. And he said, "I'm really, really sorry." I said, "Garry, you didn't do it, mate."[6]

Despite Steve's disappointment that Parker had evaded justice, he took comfort in the fact that the court record shows that the charges against Parker were never dismissed, and that Parker died before the trial. Little's painstaking investigation, the new charges against Parker, the apology and compensation from the church and Steve's vindication at the royal commission all made a huge, transformative difference to Steve's life. He felt heard, believed, recognised and respected.

On 11 November 2017, in front of friends and family, Steve married Rachael. It was a non-religious service, but Greg Thompson gave a reading.

*

One of the most disappointing aspects of the royal commission was that those found to have lied under oath or to have covered up child sexual abuse faced no legal consequences. However, after the commission, Bishop Stuart, along with Cathy Rose (the new director of professional standards, a former policewoman with a background in child protection, who took over after Michael Elliott left on stress leave) and the Professional Standards Board, took disciplinary action against Bishop Appleby, who had an adverse finding against him. Steve thought Appleby had zero insight into what he had done, unlike Bishop Herft. The central issue for Steve was that Appleby refused to apologise, or even to make a truthful, lucid admission recognising the harm he'd done.

He hasn't acknowledged anything ... If they don't acknowledge it, what are you forgiving them for? If they acknowledged it, I was the most forgiving bloke in the world in those circumstances. But if you're not prepared to put your hand up and say I stuffed up, then you cannot grant forgiveness.[7]

A Professional Standards Board hearing on 19 February 2019 recommended that Appleby be defrocked for ignoring credible allegations of child sexual abuse from 1983 to 1992. The board described Appleby as "unfit permanently" to hold church office. The board noted that the royal commission's findings against Appleby's evidence about his lack of knowledge of Stephen Hatley Gray's criminal charge, and his "incorrect evidence" about his diaries not showing any meeting with Steve, "has caused us to proceed with caution in assessing Bishop Appleby's evidence". In contrast, the commission stated that:

> Steve Smith presented as a truthful and compelling witness who gave a clear and precise account of the circumstances in which he disclosed his abuse to Assistant Bishop Appleby. No reason was suggested as to why Smith would fabricate an account that he disclosed his abuse to Assistant Bishop Appleby [who] ... told Smith that he would look into it.[8]

However, Appleby's lawyer appealed, and on 27 August 2019 a review board decided against the defrocking but imposed strict conditions. He was not to be licensed for three years, he couldn't dress as a bishop and he had to satisfy the director of professional standards that he was committed to reporting future disclosures of child sexual abuse.

Steve was furious at the reversal. He told the *Newcastle Herald*, "Bishop Appleby could have changed my life in 1984 if he had acted on my allegations about Parker ... The Royal Commission found he took no action. I'm absolutely outraged. After all the processes we've been through, we get this."

Bishop Stuart issued a statement acknowledging that the "royal commission found that Bishop Appleby failed to investigate allegations against George Parker", and confirming the restrictions would be placed on Appleby's ministry. Stuart added, "George Parker has inflicted great harm and was subject to multiple charges prior to his death. His survivors have shown great courage in speaking of their experience. They are remarkable men." He noted the "considerable graciousness" with which Steve had treated the diocese, "given all that he had experienced".[9]

*

During Lawrence's trial for raping Ben Giggins, one day Steve and I were walking back to the courthouse after lunch when Steve spotted a man cleaning people's shoes. The man was dressed scantily in thongs and shorts in the chilly Newcastle winter. Steve chatted to him, quickly finding out his name and his story. Donny was unemployed, homeless and sleeping in his car. Although Steve was a disability pensioner, he threw $50 into Donny's money box.

The next day, I noticed that Donny was wearing long trousers, socks and shiny lace-up shoes; he'd taken the money Steve gave him to an op shop and bought warm clothing. Every day at the trial, I watched Donny chat with Steve, who followed his progress with the shoe-shining business and put photos of him on Facebook. Soon Donny was well known all over Newcastle and doing a roaring trade.

Steve had recognised that Donny needed help and quietly offered it in a straightforward, practical way. He treated Donny respectfully. About the same time, I heard someone call homeless people by the disparaging moniker "deros", i.e. derelict. It was one of many occasions when I reflected that Steve would have made an extremely good priest, with more genuine care for the "least and the lost" than most of the clergy he had dealt with.

Or a good detective. In 2001, Team Church had told the DPP that the servers' guild did not exist. Of course, it did exist, and there was evidence for it in the registry book produced at Steve's trial. Steve also had proof in the form of a servers' guild medal, which altar boys wore around their necks, but in 2001 he couldn't find it. That denial that the guild existed – with the implication that Steve was a liar – had rankled him. After twenty-one years of searching, he finally found and purchased a server's medallion from a collector in the United Kingdom. It did exist! He sent me the photos of the medal, triumphant.

And he fights on. After Lawrence was jailed for the rape of Ben Giggins, Steve wrote many times to the Australian Honours and Awards Secretariat, asking that Lawrence's 2004 Order of Australia be revoked.[10] In his last letter, on 24 June 2020, Steve pointed out:

> I have now written to you at least 12 times since 2012 in relation to the holding of an OAM by Former Anglican Dean of Newcastle Graeme Russell Lawrence. Lawrence was defrocked in 2012 for engaging in group sex with a child. He was convicted in 2019 of raping a 15-year-old boy and sentenced to 8 years in prison.

Steve's lengthy campaign eventually succeeded. In late June 2020, Law-rence resigned his Medal of the Order of Australia (OAM). Once feted, he had now been stripped of every honour. Steve got the *Newcastle Herald* to do a story on it. The days of being blown off by journalists were over. Now journalists all over Australia seek him out.

One of Steve's new battles is taking on the federal government's re-dress scheme, established after the royal commission to make things easier for survivors. He approached the scheme seeking an apology from the NSW Department of Education for letting Parker repeatedly take him out of school, thus enabling all the sexual assaults. Steve didn't want money; he had compensation from the Anglican diocese. He just wanted them to admit the wrong and say sorry. Dealing with the redress scheme was a lengthy bureaucratic nightmare, during which Steve was subjected to offensive, intrusive questioning about his sexual abuse, including how much penetration there was, despite them having his detailed police state-ment on file. Even after appeals and years of wrangling, at the time of writing the redress scheme still refuses to give a simple apology on behalf of the Department of Education. Steve hasn't given up and has enlisted his lawyer, Peter O'Brien. He wants to highlight that the redress scheme is not really working. If it is hard for him, with years of experience and a good lawyer, a supportive wife and family, how impossible would it be for an isolated, depressed and penniless survivor to battle through it?

Steve keeps on battling for justice. During the previous NSW Libe-ral Coalition government, Steve wrote to ask the then attorney-general, Mark Speakman, for an apology for Judge Coolahan's conduct and com-ments at the 2001 trial of George Parker. Speakman did not reply. After a Labor government was elected in 2023, Steve tried again, this time with the new attorney-general, Michael Daly. Daly granted Steve a meeting. Steve explained what had happened to him and presented the transcript of Coolahan's comments from the beginning and end of the trial.

The response this time was different: warmer and kinder. Because of the independence of the state from the judiciary, it still fell short of an apology for Coolahan's behaviour. However, the letter Daly sent meant a great deal to Steve. He read it many times. Daly wrote, "I am truly sorry for the trauma and distress that you have experienced as a result both of the abuse that you endured and the comments of Judge Coolahan." Daly commended Steve and his brother for their "strength and courage ... to report the abuse you suffered." He also acknowledged Steve's "devastation" at the outcome of the trial. He noted that the royal commission's final report described Coolahan's trial comments criticising Steve and his brother for taking so long to come forward as "intemperate and ill-conceived". Daly noted that section 294(2) of the *Criminal Procedures Act 1986* meant that in sexual assault trials, where there is a delay in a person making a complaint, "the Judge must direct the Jury that ... Delay in complaining does not necessarily indicate that the allegation is false", and:

> There may be good reasons why a victim of sexual assault may hesitate in making, or may refrain from making, a complaint about the assault.
>
> Further, the Judge must not direct that delay in complaining is relevant to the victim's credibility unless there is sufficient evidence to justify such a direction.

Daly told Steve that as he considers the current research commissioned by the NSW government into the experiences of sexual offence complainants in the criminal justice system, he would keep Steve's experience in mind, and his bravery "will stay with me ... Thank you for your courage, perseverance, and strength."[11]

Steve is now working as a delivery driver for a supermarket chain and loves it. If the delivery is to someone vulnerable or elderly, he goes inside, unpacks the groceries and puts them away. A lot of elderly people, living on their own, are grateful for his help. Once, while unpacking the shopping for an old woman on a walking frame, he noticed light globes in the bags and a light out in the hall. He "couldn't have her trying to get up on a ladder", so he offered to help, found the ladder, climbed up and put in several light bulbs around the house. He has also finally found his vocation, working a second job in aged care. He told me how he loves sitting with residents and talking with them for a long time, listening to the rich stories of their lives. "Anne, the stories they have to tell!" He coaxes residents out of rooms and builds relationships with them, finding novel ways of connecting with dementia patients. Steve told me he wished he'd discovered this work years ago, he loves it so much. "They deserve such respect and kindness." I realised that whatever job Steve does, he gives expression to the ideals of care he learned from his parents as a child in Edgeworth parish.

When Bishop Farran observed to me what a brilliant person Steve could have been, he then corrected himself, noting that he "probably still is". That way of seeing Steve, of focusing on his lost potential and what might have been if not for Parker's abuse, is only a partial truth. It does an unintentional injustice, because Steve has become a finer human being than any job title could convey. His courage and implacable determination to fight on in the face of injustice is a beacon for other survivors. His inner strength, his ability to get up off the floor of life time and again, is remarkable. He is a leader among survivors and a tireless advocate for victims of child sexual abuse. He never gives up agitating and holding the church to account, because he believes churches are "just one bishop away from it happening again". All it would take is a weak or ambivalent bishop or a complicit professional standards regime.

In March 2023, Archbishop Hollingworth, after a secret hearing by Kooyoora, the Melbourne Anglican professional standards body, escaped defrocking over his failure to act on clear evidence of child sexual abuse while archbishop of Brisbane. Most of the survivors affected by Hollingworth's behaviour were not even notified of the hearing. The investigation took more than five years – longer than the entire royal commission took to examine thousands of cases. The decision drew widespread condemnation. The Kooyoora debacle showed that the Anglican disciplinary system is still deeply flawed in some areas. The primate, Archbishop Geoffrey Smith, salvaged the situation by calling for Hollingworth to resign. He finally did so.

Archbishop Smith asked Steve to write an article for the Anglican *Guardian*, the magazine of the Adelaide diocese. Steve wrote an eloquent piece, calling for a national audit of the Anglican disciplinary process and for a centralised, standardised and transparent national approach. Despite having spent more than fifty years fighting for justice against the church, Steve was generous and fair-minded. He wrote, "The Anglican Church is an organisation that does much good in the community but is struggling to regain the trust that is so vital to its continued ability to do that work."[12]

Smiley, that boy who sat in the peach tree listening avidly to his father, grandfather and the local priest talk about fairness and justice, who climbed down to ask perceptive questions before climbing back up again into the leafy canopy, is still there.

Steve never stopped being a fighter. "If something is wrong, it's wrong. You have just got to go on fighting. Don't ever give up."

ACKNOWLEDGEMENTS

THE ESSAY I wrote in 2017 for *The Monthly*, "Rape Among the Lamingtons", opened many doors in Newcastle. One was Steve's. He wrote to *The Monthly* after I published that essay in May 2017. He wrote, "I was incredibly impressed with the way Ms Manne wrote this article and would like to speak to her about my story." He passed on his contact details. I was greatly relieved that I had not got a survivor's story wrong. I wrote to him, eager to learn more, but could not then take further my desire to delve more deeply into this extraordinary story, because in late 2016, my husband Rob had a recurrence of throat cancer. He had to have a life-saving but also life-changing operation of a laryngectomy.

Needless to say, I postponed the writing of the essay on the Anglican hearing until the following May. Nick Feik, then editor of *The Monthly*, was very understanding, as was Chris Feik, who was my editor at Black Inc. for the book I was researching on the royal commission. After that, however, there were so many health crises, it was necessary for a time not to publish any work with a tight deadline. We spent time with each other and our daughters and son-in-law and grew vegetables, especially peas, as Rob got used to his new life post-surgery, which included chronic pain.

Throughout his slow recovery, Rob kept urging me to go back to the Newcastle Anglican story. It was his encouragement and implacable belief in its importance that was vital in helping me persist. Two years on, in early 2019, I felt he, we, were strong enough for me to commit to travelling regularly to Newcastle to do the interviews with Steve and all the others who made this book possible. I contacted Steve again. It was the beginning of many, many hours of interviews and conversations. We hit it off immediately and developed an easy rapport. He is such a remarkable person, so crystal clear on right and wrong and in his belief in justice. I felt privileged to know him, and to bear witness to his extraordinary story, and it has been an honour to tell it. I made sure Steve and his wife Rachael read the book before publication but also gave him the right to veto his part of the book if he felt uncomfortable in any way – unusual perhaps but in my view part of an essential ethic of care for victim-survivors. Thankfully, he was extremely enthusiastic about the book in its final form.

I interviewed many of the main people in 2019, but then in early 2020, Covid struck. I was locked down in Melbourne for much of the next three years. I did some more interviews by Skype, Zoom and phone, but partly because of regulations and then because of Rob's health, I was unable to return to Newcastle.

People often asked, when they knew I was stepping into the dark territory that is child sexual abuse, how do you cope? How do you keep going? My answer is that one part of a writer's vocation has to be an unflinching resolve to shine light on the dark areas of human life, but above all to bear witness to the stories of survivors. It is not without cost. Sarah Ferguson once commented, after completing her superb program *Revelation* about Catholic child sexual abusers, that "it leaves deep lines in your soul". This is undoubtedly true. As a writer or broadcaster, you have to accept that.

However, I also admit the experience was even darker than I expected, because of Covid. During the many lockdowns, there were no trips up to Newcastle to see the people I'd come to care so much about, who had inspired me by their courage, fortitude and determination to see justice done. No seeing friends, family or attending events, apart from visiting my mother, who had ever worsening dementia. Day after day, year on year, immersed in the dark territory of child sexual abuse. There were times when I struggled, and wondered if I could continue. To keep me going, Rob suggested putting the photo of Steve as a boy of nine, just before the abuse began (reproduced on page 8 of this book), on my study wall. There he still looks at me: shining, happy, bursting with the joy of life.

That worked! I also turned to examining the huge pile of thousands of pages of church documents, statements, emails, letters and transcripts as part of the royal commission. Part of my training was as an historian, and thankfully, I love creating a history from the raw primary materials of documents. That work was a relief, because it was a different task with different emotions, one that put the whiff of pursuit in my nostrils, piecing together who the predators were and who were their protectors in the laity and clergy, mapping their sinister network.

That said, writing this book was by no means all dark. Why not? I met such inspiring people. As surely as this book has within its pages a story of evil, it also has many good people trying to change the network of power that had allowed it to flourish. There was the astonishing courage of the survivors, but also the whistle-blowers, lay people and clergy, as well as police prosecuting the crimes.

Although writing is a solitary exercise, once the book is handed to the publisher, a truly collegial process takes place. Chris Feik was extremely kind, understanding and patient as Rob healed. He is a brilliant editor, highly intelligent, dedicated, perceptive, completely without ego, able to see the architecture and shape of a manuscript and see (sometimes with a rather too ruthless clarity) where cuts are needed. The first draft at almost 150,000 words was too long. So, between February and June 2023, some 40,000 words hit the cutting-room floor. It hurt, but I knew it was needed. Chris was ably assisted by Denise O'Dea, a senior editor at Black Inc. who proved a sensitive reader and tireless worker, over many months, always meticulous and careful, asking me good questions to clarify the text or justify what I had written. I deeply appreciate the fine work these editors did, and the book is the better for it. The amount of time and energy Black Inc. spent on getting the book right was admirable. Morry Schwartz, the creative genius behind all the Schwartz Media publications, makes sure the highest quality is achieved. Nick Feik, the morally acute and empathetic former editor of *The Monthly*, also deserves especial thanks for supporting my first essay, and the others I wrote on child sexual abuse, including on the trial of Graeme Lawrence. As an editor, he was always onto the issues that really mattered. Some of the research in this book, in different form, was previously published in *The Monthly* as "Rape Among the Lamingtons" (May 2017) and "The Trial of Graeme Lawrence" (September 2019), and in *Right Now* as "Catholic Clergy and Child Sexual Abuse" (November 2013).

I would like to express my gratitude to all those I interviewed: Steve of course, his lovely wife Rachael, and also Paul Gray, Phil D'Ammond, Ian Smith, Colin Elliott, Rob and Bronwyn Walls, Ben and Jane Giggins,

Lance Johnston, Rod Bower, John Cleary (who also won the Lake Macquarie Citizen of the Year award for his whistle-blowing), Reverend Colvin
Ford, Canon Paul and Noreen Robertson, Reverend Roger and June Dyer,
Reverend Tim Costello, former Newcastle Bishops Brian Farran and Greg
Thompson, the current Bishop Peter Stuart, Joanne McCarthy, Kirsty Raffan, Richard and Lyn Rudkin, as well as several sources who wish to remain
anonymous. All were extremely generous with time, provided invaluable
insights into what had gone wrong in Newcastle and pointed me in helpful
directions. Steve kept saying to me that I had to talk to Detective Jeff Little, as no one knew the case better than he did, and he was right. Jeff Little
is wary of tabloid-style journalists, but Steve was persuasive, and Jeff also
explained that the "Rape Among the Lamingtons" essay gave me credibility.
Once persuaded, he was generous with his time and forensic understanding of paedophilia and the issue of child sexual abuse, both among the
Anglicans and the Catholics, as he was the lead investigating officer on
Strike Force Lantle and Strike Force Arinya, and successfully prosecuted
Graeme Lawrence for the rape of Ben Giggins.

The royal commission is a researcher's treasure trove. It had almost
1000 documents on the Newcastle Anglicans alone. However, it was
not easy to navigate after the commission was over, as it was sent to the
National Library, but beyond the first page of exhibits none of the links
to the documents worked! I was lucky to have Pearl Longden to do her
superb transcribing of all the interviews. Her daughter, Cate O'Neill, a brilliant archivist at Melbourne University, gave me invaluable help navigating
the difficult and labyrinthine process of accessing the National Library
archive of royal commission exhibits. Without Cate's generous help, this
book could not have been written.

I was fortunate to have many discussions with two friends, Professor
Frances Salo Thompson and Dr Jan Hepburn, a UK-based psychoanalyst,
who were wonderfully supportive throughout, and were extremely insightful about child sexual abuse, its origins and consequences, and the
widespread denial of it. Jan Hepburn organised, with Neuroscience UK,
a webinar on child sexual abuse, where I first presented the new work on
powerful perpetrators in relation to Newcastle, and also a valuable in-
person day seminar in Melbourne, in August 2023. Gerry and Dee Gill
were wonderful friends and interlocutors. Gerry and I shared an interest
in denialism – his was in white denial of Indigenous history, while mine

was in the church's denial of child sexual abuse. Gerry sadly died of cancer in 2019; I feel so lucky to have known him. I have continued the warmest of friendships with Dee, who has followed the progress of the manuscript with attentive care. Professor Julie Stephens, too, was a very good friend throughout. She's an extremely intelligent, kind and empathetic listener, who shared many insights from her understanding of sexual perversity as a Lacanian psychoanalyst, as well as her inestimable common sense. Mark Aarons and Robyn Ravlich were wonderful friends throughout Rob's illness and the aftermath, and were patient, interested and encouraging listeners to my early (no doubt garbled) accounts of the Newcastle story. Likewise, Raimond Gaita and Yael Gaita are precious friends, as are Stephanie and Alex Miller, generously listening with insightful comments to my story. Ramona Koval gave early and much appreciated support for the project, as did our dear friends Tim and Merridie Costello.

My family means everything to me. On the way home from Newcastle early on, when I was still half thinking of writing about another case too, I met my younger daughter, Lucy, in a pub in Sydney. One of the most perceptive readers I know, Lucy told me she'd like to read about just one story, in real depth, to really dig down and understand it, how it happened and why. I realised immediately that she was right, and the shape of the book changed. She has followed the book's progress with care and attention, as has my elder daughter Kate. Both are making stellar contributions to the public realm, Lucy in the area of climate change, Kate as a feminist philosopher. The years of writing of the book also saw an event bringing great joy to us all: the birth of our granddaughter Sophie, who is vibrant, joyous and full of fun. Kate and Daniel are wonderful parents.

The greatest debt, however, is to my beloved husband Rob, who has endured so much over the years of writing with a quiet grace and courage, but always giving his unstinting love, encouragement and support, despite the demands of his own work and whatever health issues he faced. Rob read and edited every draft carefully, made great suggestions, but above all cared about the book and the people in it. To Rob, I give my heartfelt thanks and deepest gratitude.

NOTES

CHAPTER ONE: SMILEY

1   Author's interviews with Steve Smith, 2019 to 2023.
2   Author's interviews with Steve Smith, 2019 to 2023.

CHAPTER TWO: THE KIDNAPPING

1   Steve Smith, police statement, page 18.
2   Steve Smith, police statement, page 15.
3   Joanne McCarthy, "Paedophile ring used boys home," *The Sydney Morning Herald*, 23 September 2013.

CHAPTER THREE: THE BODY REMEMBERS

1   Bessel van der Kolk, *The Body Keeps the Score: Brain, Mind and Body in the Healing of Trauma*. Viking, 2014, p. 66.
2   Van der Kolk, *The Body Keeps the Score*, p. 68.
3   Van der Kolk, *The Body Keeps the Score*, p. 543.
4   Sam Tomlin, "Victims of Derby rapist John Melverne Bodey get compensation from WA Education Department", ABC News, 21 April 2021.

CHAPTER FOUR: SMOKING VOLCANOES EVERYWHERE

1   Ken Singer, *Evicting the Perpetrator: A Male Survivor's guide for Recovery from Childhood Sexual Abuse*. NEARI Press, 2010.
2   Max Lean, camp director, report of accident, 21 March 1976.
3   I have read a written copy of the eulogy, from which these excerpts are taken. From Steve Smith's files.

CHAPTER FIVE: BREAKDOWN

1   When cross-examined at the Royal Commission into Institutional Responses to Child Sexual Abuse, Appleby denied ever meeting Steve. When the royal commission subpoenaed his diaries, however, they showed a meeting with Steve Smith in 1984. The royal commission said Appleby's credit, as a witness, was now "at issue". Appleby then claimed he didn't remember what the meeting was about. His diary also showed he met with Dean Graeme Lawrence and others shortly after meeting Steve. Appleby denied that meeting, too, but it was in his diary.
2   Letter from Robert Smith to Bishop Alfred Holland, 25 September 1985.
3   Author's interview with Steve Smith.

4   File note, Graeme Lawrence to Bishop Herft, 29 April 1996, Royal Commission, Case Study 42, exhibit ANG.0050.002.2960_R.
5   File note, Graeme Lawrence to Bishop Herft, 12 January 1999, Royal Commission, Case Study 42, exhibit NSW.0037.001.0443_R.
6   Letter from Graeme Lawrence to Steve Smith, 22 January 1999, Royal Commission, Case Study 42, exhibit NSW.0037.001.0077_R.

CHAPTER SIX: TEAM CHURCH

1   Roger William Dyer, statement to the Royal Commission, exhibit STAT.1076.001.0001_R, and the author's interview with Dyer, 3 February 2020.
2   Letter from Bishop Herft to Father George Parker, 26 February 1996, Royal Commission, Case Study 42, exhibit ANG.0050.003.4678. The letter is regretting a lack of a farewell, which is described as Parker's decision. "I find the decision not to allow anyone to farewell you rather difficult, although I can sense the pain and anguish …" As Parker did not show at any other time a dislike of ceremony or attention, it is compatible with Roger Dyer's case about him being forced to leave by Assistant Bishop Appleby.
3   W. Brown, file note, 9 February, Royal Commission, Case Study 42, exhibit ANG.0050.003.9059_R.
4   Royal Commission, *Report of Case Study No. 42: The Responses of the Anglican Diocese of Newcastle to Instances and Allegations of Child Sexual Abuse*, Commonwealth of Australia, 2017; Theresa Kerr, file note, Royal Commission, Case Study 42, exhibit ANG.0050.003.9058_R.
5   File note by Theresa Kerr in relation to Father George Parker (CKC), 9 February 2000, Royal Commission, Case Study 42, exhibit ANG.0050.003.9058_R 09.
6   Graeme Lawrence, transcript of evidence to the Royal Commission, Case Study 42; Royal Commission, *Report of Case Study No. 42*.
7   Handwritten police note, Royal Commission, Case Study 42, exhibit NSW.0037.001.0372_R.
8   Letter from Peter Mitchell to Keith Allen, 17 February 2000, Royal Commission, Case Study 42, exhibit NSW.0037.001.0305_R.
9   Handwritten police note Royal Commission, Case Study 42, exhibit NSW.0037.001.0372_R.
10 Handwritten police note, Royal Commission, Case Study 42, exhibit NSW.0037.001.0372_R.
11 Royal Commission, Case Study 42, transcript of cross-examination of Mr Keith Allen by Mr O'Brien for Steven Smith, 9 August 2016, page C16785.
12 Faxed letter from Peter Mitchell to Mr O'Connor, solicitor for Public Prosecutions, 3 August 2001, Royal Commission, Case Study 42, exhibit NSW.0037.001.0311_R.
13 The royal commission called it "deliberately obstructive": Royal Commission, *Report of Case Study No. 42*, page 48.
14 Royal Commission, *Report of Case Study No. 42*, page 48.
15 Robert Caddies, transcript of evidence to the Royal Commission, Case Study 42; cross-examination by Naomi Sharp, 16 November 2016, page 23136, and subpoena for production issued in the criminal prosecution of Father George Parker (CKC) addressed to Graeme Lawrence, 16 July 2001, exhibit IND.0519.001.0010_R.
16 Bishop Herft, transcript of evidence, Royal Commission, Case Study 42, 30 August 2016, pages C17434 and C17448.

CHAPTER SEVEN: MISCARRIAGE OF JUSTICE

1   Author's interviews with Steve Smith.
2   John Cleary, file note of a meeting on 26 March 2015 with Keith Allen, Bishop

Thompson and John Cleary. Royal Commission, Case Study 42, exhibit ANG.0132.001.0008_R.

3 For example, Allen was the defence lawyer for Stephen Hatley Gray in 1990. Gray got a good behaviour bond for anally raping a fourteen-year-old boy.

4 Author's interview with Philip D'Ammond.

5 Coolahan came from a Catholic family. His brother, Monsignor Frank Coolahan, was a senior figure in the Catholic Education Office in the Newcastle Maitland Catholic diocese. Along with Monsignor Vince Dilley, he'd employed a teacher who warned them during an interview that in 1962 he had been convicted of sexually assaulting two young boys at a Hunter public school. They employed him anyhow. The teacher became a notorious sex offender. Parents raised the alarm about him on at least three occasions during the 1980s. Monsignor Coolahan did nothing. For a fuller account of Frank Coolahan's behaviour, see Suzanne Smith, *Altar Boys*, ABC Books, 2020.

6 Letter from Keith Allen to Paul Rosser QC, 12 June 2001. Royal Commission, Case Study 42, exhibit IND.0501.001.0034_R.

7 Transcript of trial and Coolahan's comments, Royal Commission, Case Study 42, exhibit NSW.0037.001.0455_R.

8 Ian Smith (CKL), statement to Royal Commission, Case Study 42, exhibit STAT.1084.001.0001_R, and discussion with the author in August 2019.

9 File note by Michael Elliott, 17 May 2016.

10 Noelle Freeman, statement to the Royal Commission, Case Study 42, exhibit STAT.1112.001.0001_R, page 2, point 10.

11 Paul Rosser, transcript of oral evidence to the Royal Commission, Case Study 42, day 164, cross-examination by Mr O'Connell, page C17531.

12 Sonia Roulston, statement to the Royal Commission, Case Study 42, exhibit STAT.1116.001.0002_R.

13 Rosser, transcript of evidence; author's interviews with Steve Smith; see also transcript of Peter O'Brien's cross-examination of Keith Allen, Royal Commission, Case Study 42, 8 August 2016, page 16689 ff.

14 Sonia Roulston, statement to the Royal Commission, Case Study 42, exhibit STAT.1116.001.0002_R.

15 File note by John Cleary following a meeting with Keith Allen, 11 February 2015, Royal Commission, Case Study 42, exhibit ANG.0132.001.0014.

16 Royal Commission, *Report of Case Study No. 42*, page 218.

17 Royal Commission, *Report of Case Study No. 42*, page 218.

18 Author's interviews with Steve Smith.

19 Transcript of proceedings, District Court of NSW, Criminal Jurisdiction, 13 September 2001, Royal Commission, Case Study 42, exhibit NPF.045.010.0096_R.

20 Transcript of discussion between Rosser, Coolahan and Huggett at the end of the trial, Royal Commission, Case Study 42, exhibit NPF.045.010.0096_R.

CHAPTER EIGHT: THE FIGHTER

1 Letter from Steven Smith to Bishop Roger Herft, 3 October 2001. Steve Smith's archive, and Royal Commission, Case Study 42, exhibit STAT.0221.001.0032_R.

2 Letter from Peter Mitchell to Steve Smith, Royal Commission, Case Study 42, exhibits ANG.0050.003.9148_R.

3 Letter from Keith Allen to Paul Rosser, 12 June 2001, Royal Commission, Case Study 42, exhibit IND.0501.001.0034.

4 Draft letter, "Steven Andrew Smith", sent by Robert Caddies to Peter Mitchell on 16 October 2001. Royal Commission, Case Study 42, exhibit ANG.0050.003.9215_R.

5   Peter Mitchell, "Confusion over false action", *Anglican Encounter*, October 2001,
     Royal Commission, Case Study 42, exhibit ANG.0207.001.0065.
6   Peter Mitchell, facsimile to Keith Allen, 14 September 2001, Royal Commission,
     Case Study 42, exhibit ANG.0050.003.9304_R.
7   Mitchell, "Confusion over false action".
8   Bishop Herft, transcript of oral evidence, Royal Commission, Case Study 42,
     12 August 2016, page 17258. His words were, in answer to a question from Justice
     Peter McLellan about the process of handling child sexual abuse complaints,
     "Yes, Your Honour. Looking back on it, it is an extremely inadequate and
     hopeless process."
9   Author's interviews with Steve Smith.
10   Media statement, "A statement from the Diocese of Newcastle", Royal
     Commission, Case Study 42, exhibit ANG.0207.001.0146_R.
11   Peter Mitchell to Nicholas Cowdery, 3 October 2001. Royal Commission, Case
     Study 42, exhibit NSW.0037.001.0313_R.
12   DPP memorandum, draft response to Keith Allen, "Parker memorandum
     of costs, Friday 30 November", Royal Commission, Case Study 42, exhibit
     NSW.0037.001.0264_R.
13   Nicholas Cowdery to Peter Mitchell, 29 November 2001, Royal Commission, Case
     Study 42, exhibit NSW.0037.001.0425_R.
14   Keith Allen to Bishop Herft, 18 September 2001, Royal Commission, Case Study 42,
     exhibit ANG.0050.004.2850.
15   Tim Mawson, Royal Commission, Case Study 42, exhibit, STAT.1110.001.0001_R.
16   Meeting of Newcastle Diocesan Council, 24 January 2002, Royal Commission, Case
     Study 42, exhibit ANG.0048.002.4939.
17   Author's interview with Rod Bower.
18   Letter from Bishop Herft to Reverend Peter Lord at Bateau Bay, NSW, 11 March
     2002; Rod Bower's experiences from the author's interview with Bower.
19   *Newcastle Herald*, "Church thief: jail for man who stole from trusts", 26 October
     2002.
20   Author's interviews with Steve Smith.
21   Gary Grant, psychologist's report, 20 June 2002, for Stacks Law Firm Port
     Macquarie. Steve Smith's files.
22   Author's interviews with Steve Smith.

CHAPTER NINE: LAWYERING UP ON HIS WAY TO CANTERBURY
1   Biographical details for Peter Hollingworth from https://www.gg.gov.au/
     biography-dr-hollingworth-and-mrs-hollingworth
2   AAP, "Key dates in the life of Peter Hollingworth", *The Age*, 12 May 2003.
3   Belinda Hawkins, "Secrets in the suitcase that still haunt Anglican church sexual
     abuse survivor Beth Heinrich", ABC News, 8 May 2023.
4   AAP, "Church committee says GG was warned", *The Age*, 24 February 2002.
5   Tracy Grimshaw, interview with John Howard, *The Today Show*, Channel 9,
     18 February 2022, at https://pmtranscripts.pmc.gov.au/release/transcript-12548
6   Report of the Board of Inquiry into Past Handling of Complaints of Sexual abuse
     in the Anglican Church Diocese of Brisbane, May 2003, Royal Commission, Case
     Study 34: The Response of Brisbane Grammar School and St Paul's School to
     Allegatioins of Child Sexual Abuse, exhibit Ang.0044.001.0796.
7   Media statement by the Anglican Archbishop of Brisbane, Dr Phillip Aspinall, on
     the Independent Inquiry into Past Handling of Allegations of Sexual Abuse or
     Misconduct in the Anglican Diocese of Brisbane, 1 May 2003, Royal Commission,
     Case Study 34, exhibit ASQ.210.016.0002.

8   Author's interview with Brian Farran, 2 December 2019.
9   Author's interview with Canon Paul Robertson, 23 January 2020.
10 Author's interview with Colvin Ford, 1 December 2019.
11 Author's interview with Rod Bower, 2 April 2019.
12 Bishop Herft, transcript of oral evidence to the Royal Commission, Case Study 42, 30 August 2016, page 17445.
13 Letter from Keith Allen to Bishop Herft, 28 April 2003. Royal Commission, Case Study 42, exhibit ANG.0050.003.9150.
14 Michael Elliott's confidential "yellow envelopes" report refers to a meeting held with Keith Allen on 29 January 2013, at which he told Bishop Stuart about a review committee consisting of Rosser, Mitchell, Hoare, Lawrence, Caddies, Allen, Sanders and others: "the review practice was that if the complainant in any given matter had not engaged legal representation that was actively attempting to progress the matter the standard response was to 'do nothing.'" Royal Commission, Case Study 42, exhibit ANG.0207.001.2373_R, page 2.
15 Memorandum from Bishop Herft to Tim Mawson and Bruce Hockman, 18 March 2003.
16 Letter to Bishop Herft from Steve Smith, 15 April 2003.
17 Raimond Gaita, *After Romulus*, Text Publishing, 2010, page 160.
18 Bishop Herft to Steve Smith, 1 May 2003.
19 Bishop Herft to Keith Allen, 6 May 2003, Royal Commission, Case Study 42, exhibit ANG.0050.001.2584_R.
20 Keith Allen, letter to Bishop Herft, 13 May 2003.
21 Fax from Robert Caddies to Bishop Herft, 3 June 2003, with excerpt on meaning of "without prejudice".
22 Confidential "Notes re Meeting Smith", of a meeting attended by Bishop Herft, Jean Sanders, Bruce Hockman, Graeme Lawrence, Robert Caddies, Keith Allen, 19 June 2003.
23 Author's interviews with Steve Smith.
24 Email from Steve Smith to Bishop Herft, 7 May 2003.
25 Author's interviews with Steve Smith.
26 Herft admitted that he realised Steve was telling the truth at his meeting with him during the royal commission. See transcript of oral evidence, Royal Commission, Case Study 42, cross-examination by Mr O'Connell, 29 August 2016, pages 17409–14.
27 Steve Smith's email to Bishop Herft, 15 June 2003.
28 Bishop Herft to Steve Smith, 18 June 2003.
29 Steve Smith to Bishop Herft, 10 August 2003.
30 Bishop Herft to Steve Smith, 20 August 2003.
31 Bishop Herft, confidential file note, outlining Robert Caddies' advice on correspondence being in hard copy, not email.
32 Bishop Herft to Steve Smith, 22 August 2003.
33 Steve Smith to Bishop Herft, 3 October 2003.
34 Steve Smith to Bishop Herft, 27 September 2003.
35 Letter from Bishop Herft to [CKA], 23 June 2003, Royal Commission, Case Study 42, exhibit: PS.0532.001.0031_R; letter from Herft to Caddies regarding advice concerning child protection issues and CKA and CKU, 9 September 2003, exhibit ANG.0050.003.8965_R; letter from Caddies to Herft re CKA, 3 September 2003, exhibit ANG.0050.002.2593_R; file note by Herft of meeting with CKA and Graeme Lawrence, 13 June 2003, exhibit IND.0486.001.0402_R.
36 Steve Smith to Bishop Herft, 12 October 2004.

CHAPTER TEN: A NEW REGIME

1   Bishop Brian Farran, statement to the Royal Commission, Case Study 42, exhibit
    STAT.1072.001.0005_R page 1.
2   Jean Sanders, statement to Royal Commission, Case Study 42, exhibit
    STAT.1104.001.0004_R
3   Bishop Herft's evidence to the Royal Commission, Case Study 42.
4   Jean Sanders, statement to the Royal Commission, Case Study 42, exhibit
    STAT.1104.001.0003_R.
5   Jean Sanders, statement to the Royal Commission, Case Study 42, exhibit
    STAT.1104.001.0003_R.
6   Author's interview with Bishop Farran, 2 December 2019.
7   Author's interview with Bishop Farran, 2 December 2019.
8   John Cleary, file notes, Royal Commission, Case Study 42, exhibits
    ANG.0132.001.0008_R, ANG 0132.001.0016_R, ANG.0132.001.0015_R and
    ANG.0207.001.0279_R.
9   All quotes are from the author's interview with John Cleary, 16 June 2019.
10 Letter from Steve Smith to John Cleary, 25 January 2008.
11 Email from Gwen Vale to Steve Smith from the Professional Standards
    Committee, 7 November 2007, Royal Commission, Case Study 42, exhibit
    ANG.0050.002.2476_R.
12 Paul Robertson, statement to the Royal Commission, Case Study 42, exhibits
    STAT.1166.001.0007_R.
13 Letter from Bishop Farran to Michael Hough, Bishop of Ballarat, 3 March 2008,
    Royal Commission, Case Study 42, exhibit ANG.0334.001.0122.
14 Letter from Gwen Vale to Bishop Farran, 15 February 2008.
15 Author's interviews with Steve Smith.

CHAPTER ELEVEN: AN ALLY ARRIVES

1   All quotations from the conversation between Steve Smith and Michael Elliott are
    from the author's interviews with Steve Smith.
2   "S11 Information Form No. 11", George Parker, respondent
3   Letter from Keith Allen to Bishop Herft, 28 April 2003, Royal Commission, Case
    Study 42, exhibit ANG.0050.003.9150.
4   Letter from Bishop Holland to Peter Matthews, 26 October 1988.
5   *Newcastle Post*, 12 October 1988, page 42.
6   Letter from Bishop Holland to Peter Matthews, 26 October 1988.
7   Letter from Bishop Holland to Peter Matthews, 26 October 1988.
8   *Newcastle Post*, 9 November and 15 November 1988.
9   Author's interviews with Steve Smith.
10 Letter from Keith Allen to Bishop Herft, 28 April 2003, Royal Commission, Case
    Study 42, exhibit ANG.0050.003.9150.
11 Michael Elliott, file note, "Area under discussion George Parker, 30 September
    2009", written immediately after the conversation.
12 Michael Elliott, undated file note, "Intel re Peter Mitchell"; written after 2012, as
    it refers to Bishop Farran seeing a photo of Mitchell, Herft and Hoare together at
    Beaulieu in the diocese of Winchester in the UK. This was the former parish of the
    first Bishop of Newcastle, William Tyrrell, whose bishopric ran from 31 January
    1848 until 24 March 1879.

CHAPTER TWELVE: THE OMERTA CODE AND THE FAKE CELIBATES

1   Patrick Parkinson, "Child sexual abuse and the churches: a story of moral failure?",

Current Issues in Criminal Justice, vol. 26, no. 1, 31 October 2013, http://ssrn.com/abstract=234841; Paul Robertson, Royal Commission, Case Study 42, exhibit STAT.1166.001.0001_R, and author's interview with Robertson.

2   Author's interview with Tim Costello, 21 September 2021.

3   Bishop George Browning, statement to the Royal Commission, Case Study 42, 28 July 2016, exhibit STAT.1105.001.0001. Browning did not think a paedophile ring was nurtured at Morpeth College, but "rather if a ring existed I am more inclined to the view it existed within a small group who shared the same ecclesial and theological perspective and that their passage through St John's Morpeth as students was not in itself germane to their predatory behaviour."

4   Author's interview with Rod Bower, 2 April 2019.

5   Pamela Wilson, transcript of evidence to the Royal Commission, Case Study 42, 3 August 2016, pages C16295–C16303; Valerie Hall, statement to the Royal Commission, Case Study 42, 12 October 2016, exhibit STAT.1120.001.0002; Lesley Danger, statement to the Royal Commission, Case Study 42, exhibit STAT.1120.001.0002.

6   Chrisopher Hall, statement to the Royal Commission, Case Study 42, 12 October 2016, exhibit STAT.1213.001.0003_R.

7   Pamela Wilson, statement to the Royal Commission, Case Study 42, exhibit STAT.1092.001.0006_R.

8   Bishop Holland, transcript of oral evidence to the Royal Commission, Case Study 42, 3 August 2016, page 16313.

CHAPTER THIRTEEN: WHERE HAVE ALL THE MEN GONE?

1   Reverend Hugh Bright, statement to the Royal Commission, Case Study 42, 26 August 2016, exhibit STAT.1164.001.0004_R, especially dot points 16 and 17.

2   Pre-sentencing report, Reverend David Williams (former probation and parole officer for NSW), 1971–77, 12 September 1989, Royal Commission, Case Study 42, exhibit ANG.0207.001.0618_R.

3   Roger Dyer, statement to the Royal Commission, Case Study 42, 22 July 2016, exhibit STAT.1076.001.0001_R, dot point 13.

4   Author's interview with Roger Dyer, 3 February 2020.

5   Roger Dyer, statement to the Royal Commission, Case Study 42, 22 July 2016, exhibit STAT.1076.001.0001_R, dot point 18.

6   Author's interview with Roger Dyer, 3 February 2020.

7   Roger Dyer, statement to the Royal Commission, Case Study 42, exhibit STAT.1076.001.0001, dot point 22; and author's interview with Dyer, 3 February 2020.

8   Author's interview with Roger Dyer, 3 February 2020.

9   For example, see Bishop Farran, presidential address to the third session of the forty-ninth synod, Royal Commission, Case Study 42, exhibit ANG.0050.001.0168.

10   Author's interview with Roger Dyer, 3 February 2020.

11   Email from Bishop Stuart to Dr Frost, 11 August 2009, Royal Commission, Case Study 42, exhibit IND.0496.001.0006

12   Roger Dyer, email to Dr Adam, 30 July 2009, in which he told his doctor he believed his mental-health issues were symptomatic not causative, Royal Commission, Case Study 42, exhibit IND.0496.001.0005_R

13   Michael Elliott, file note of phone conversation with Jim Brown, 13 September 2010, Royal Commission, Case Study 42, exhibit ANG.0050.001.1822_R. Jim Brown's trial was on 20 September 2010.

14   Michael Elliott, file note, 7 December 2015, about a meeting between Bishop Thompson and Reverend Lindsay McLoughlin.

15 Lindsay McLoughlin, statement to the Royal Commission, Case Study 42, exhibit 1115.001.0001_R.

16 Lindsay McLoughlin, statement to the Royal Commission, Case Study 42, exhibit 1115.001.0001_R. In his statement, McLoughlin mentioned that he thought Parker knew Rushton was abusing boys.

17 Author's interview with Paul and Noleen Robertson, 23 January 2020.

18 Dan Proudman, "Former Anglican priest Lindsay Thomas McLoughlin jailed for preying on two boys in 1980s", *Newcastle Herald*, 7 December 2016. The article also mentions: "The court heard McLoughlin had been in a 'sexually abusive and manipulative' relationship with Rushton for three years."

19 Email from Roger Dyer to Bishop Farran, 10 December 2009, Royal Commission, Case Study 42, exhibit ANG.0050.003.5076.

20 Author's interview with Roger Dyer, 3 February 2020.

21 Roger Dyer, email to Michael Elliott, 12 April 2010, Royal Commission, Case Study 42, exhibit ANG.0050.004.3008_R.

22 Email from Michael Elliott to Roger Dyer, 12 April 2010.

23 Author's interview with Paul Robertson, 23 January 2020.

24 Author's interview with Bishop Farran, 2 December 2019.

25 Joanne McCarthy, "Hunter priest's evil child sex secrets", *Newcastle Herald*, 19 October 2010.

26 Author's interview with Bishop Farran, 3 February 2020.

27 Rushton's close friend, Greg Hansen, for example (see his statement to the Royal Commission, Case Study 42, exhibit STAT.1027.001.0001_R) and John Woodward, Lawrence's lawyer.

28 Email from Roger Dyer to Michael Elliott, in 2010.

29 Bishop Brian Farran, address to synod, 23 October 2010, Royal Commission, Case Study 42, exhibit ANG.0323.001.0092.

30 Author's interview with Dyer, 3 February 2020.

31 Author's interview with Dyer, 3 February 2020; Dyer's statement to the Royal Commission, Case Study 42, exhibit STAT.1076.001.0011_R. For Chris Bird on his membership of the Society of the Holy Cross (SSC), see his statement to the Royal Commission, Case Study 42, exhibit STAT.1100.001.0004_R, pages 4–5, point 14.

32 Author's interview with Dyer and Dyer's statement to the Royal Commission, Case Study 42, exhibit STAT.1076.001.0011_R.

33 The omission in the minutes was eventually corrected by the Newcastle Diocese, after Dyer's testimony and the royal commission hearing, at the full synod on 10 December 2016. It recorded Roger Dyer's motion on the necessity of acknowledging the impact of child sexual abuse on victims at the 2010 synod. It also acknowledged the warm acclamation he received. The acting synod secretary wrote to Dyer on 12 December 2012, informing him of the correction. Roger Dyer, submission to the Royal Commission, Case Study 42, exhibit SUB.1042.003.0001.

34 Email from Bishop Farran to Roger Dyer, 26 August 2010. Roger Dyer's archive.

35 Author's interview with Dyer, 3 February 2020.

36 Email from Steve Smith to Bishop Farran, 19 October 2010.

37 Author's interview with Bishop Farran, 3 December 2019. Media statement from Bishop Brian Farran published in *The Anglican Encounter*, 1 December 2010, Royal Commission, Case Study 42, exhibit NG.0050.001.1819_R.

38 Media statement from the Anglican Bishop of Newcastle, The Right Reverend Dr. Brian Farran, 18 November 2010. Published in the *Newcastle Herald* and *Anglican Encounter*.

CHAPTER FOURTEEN: THE WOLF HIDING IN PLAIN SIGHT

1 Author's interviews with Steve Smith.
2 The committee membership for 1994 to 2008 can be found at Royal Commission, Case Study 42, exhibit ANG.0322.001.0002.
3 For laity membership of key committees, see Royal Commission, Case Study 42, exhibit ANG.0322.001.0002.
4 Robert Walls, statement to the Royal Commission, Case Study 42, 3 August 2016, exhibits STAT.1117.001.0003_R; and author's interview with Bronwyn and Robert Walls, 16 October 2019.
5 Robert Walls, statement to the Royal Commission, Case Study 42, 3 August 2016, exhibit STAT.1117.001.0003_R; and author's interview with Bronwyn and Robert Walls, 16 October 2019.
6 Letter from Bishop Herft to Mr and Mrs Wall, 13 July 1995, Royal Commission, Case Study 42, exhibits ANG.0347.001.001. It has Herft's name but is unsigned. It was accepted as from Bishop Herft by the Royal Commission.
7 See Reverend Brian Kelly's letter to Archbishop Goodhew, 18 December 1996, Royal Commission, Case Study 42, exhibit STAT.0221.001.0031_R.
8 Follow-up letter from Reverend Kelly to Archbishop Goodhew, 18 February 1997, telling Goodhew that Herft had not responded, with record of phone call to Bishop Herft, and Goodhew's handwritten comments. Royal Commission, Case Study 42, exhibit STAT.0221.001.0030_R.
9 Richard Henry "Harry" Goodhew, statement to the Royal Commission, Case Study 42, exhibit 1053.001.0001_R, pages 5–7; file note on Reverend Tony Drayton and Mr David Andrews, exhibit STAT.0221.001.0022; and letter from Kelly to Goodhew with Goodhew's handwritten comments, exhibit STAT.0221.001.0030_R.
10 Goodhew, statement to the Royal Commission, Case Study 42, exhibit 1053.001.0001_R, page 7.
11 CKH, statement to the Professional Standards Board Hearing, Royal Commission, Case Study 42, exhibit STAT.1078.001.001_R.
12 For Rev. Duncan's behaviour see CKH, statement to the Royal Commission, Case Study 42, exhibit STAT.1078.001.0001_R, pages 2 and 3.
13 CKH, statement to the Royal Commission, Case Study 42, exhibits STAT.1078.001.0001_R, page 4.
14 Legal advice provided to Michael Elliott by Garth Blake, 19 October 2010, Royal Commission, Case Study 42, exhibit NSW.0030.005.0156_R.pdf.
15 CKH, statement to the Royal Commission, Case Study 42, exhibit STAT.1078.001.0005_R.
16 Royal Commission, Case Study 42, exhibits OMB.0005.002.0057_R, OMB.0005.002.0092_R and OMB.005.002.0093.
17 Royal Commission, *Report of Case Study No. 42*, page 259.
18 CKH, statement to the Royal Commission, Case Stuy 42, exhibit STAT.1078.001.0005_R, page 23, pinpoint reference 73.
19 Statement of CKH, Royal Commission, Case Study 42, exhibit STAT.1078.001.0005_R; Professional Standards Board determination on the matter of Lawrence and sexual abuse of CKH, December 2010, Royal Commission, Case Study 42, exhibit IND.0577.001.0001_R.
20 John McNaughton, statement to the Royal Commission, Case Study 42, 24 June 2016, exhibit STAT.1030.001.0001_R.
21 CKH, statement to the Royal Commission, Case Study 42, exhibit STAT.1078.001.0005_R.

22 Author's interview with Joanne McCarthy, 14 April 2019. See also CKH's statement to the royal commission, in which he said he was approached by McCarthy but did not want to talk to the media.
23 Author's interview with John Cleary, 16 June 2019.
24 Author's interview with Bishop Farran, 2 December 2019.

CHAPTER FIFTEEN: TOO MANY NUTTY PEOPLE

1 For example, Joanne McCarthy, "Diocese's future a 'deep concern'", quoting John McNaughton and other anonymous clergy about the board hearing as a "kangaroo court", "toothless tiger" and "star chamber". *Newcastle Herald*, 17 December 2010. Royal Commission, Case Study 42, exhibit ANG.0048.001.4643_R.
2 All quotes from the author's interview with Joanne McCarthy, 14 April 2019.
3 Author's interview with Joanne McCarthy, 14 April 2019.
4 Author's interview with Bishop Farran, 2 December 2019.
5 Emailed letter from Bishop Farran to All Clergy, 23 November 2010, Royal Commission, Case Study 42, exhibits ANG.0041.001.0470_R.
6 Author's interview with Bishop Farran, 2 December 2019.
7 Author's interview with Colin Elliott, 12 March 2020.
8 Author's interview with John Cleary, 16 June 2019.
9 Author's interview with John Cleary, 16 June 2019.
10 Email from Chris McNaughton to Bishop Farran, Royal Commission, Case Study 42, exhibit ANG.0050.003.4910_R.
11 Email from Geoff Spring to Bishop Farran and John Cleary, 1 September 2010, Royal Commission, Case Study 42, exhibit ANG.0041.001.0671_R. For being "berated" by Rosser, see Geoff Spring, statement to the Royal Commission, Case Study 42, exhibit STAT.1099.001.0004_R.
12 Email from Michael Elliott to Bishop Farran, 9 September 2010. "I am concerned about the lack of formal consultation with myself with regard to the proposed amendments to date. Since it is my role to apply the ordinance in a practical sense, I would have expected that close consultation with my office was warranted." Royal Commission, Case Study 42, exhibit ANG.0041.001.0154_R.
13 Draft amendment, "An Ordinance to Amend the Professional Standards Ordinance 2005". For the Diocesan Council, see Royal Commission, Case Study 42, exhibit ANG.0041.001.1343.
14 Author's interview with Brian Farran, 2 December 2019.
15 Chris Bird, questions to the bishop and the chancellor at the synod, synod minutes, first day, pages 6 and 7. Royal Commission, Case Study 42, exhibit ANG.0006.001.0721_R.
16 Email from Paul Rosser to John Cleary, 24 August 2010, Royal Commission, Case Study 42, exhibit ANG.0041.001.0649_R.
17 Email from Paul Rosser to Bishop Farran, Peter Stuart and John Cleary, 31 August 2010, Royal Commission, Case Study 42, exhibit ANG.0050.004.3306_R.
18 Bishop Farran, transcript of evidence to the Royal Commission, Case Study 42, 17 November 2016, 23244: 8–12.
19 Email from Bishop Farran to John Cleary, Royal Commission, Case Study 42, exhibit ANG.0061.001.1478_R; Bishop Farran, transcript of evidence to the Royal Commission, Case Study 42, 17 November 2016, 23243:31, SUBM.0042.0.
20 Paul Rosser's resignation letter, hand-delivered to Bishop Farran, 26 November 2010, Royal Commission, Case Study 42, exhibit ANG.0048.001.3015_R.
21 Email from Paul Rosser to Bishop Farran, 16 December 2010, Royal Commission, Case Study 42, exhibit ANG.0050.003.7859_R.
22 Letter from Michael Elliott to Grame Lawrence, 11 August 2010, Royal

Commission, Case Study 42, exhibit OMB.005.002.0056_R.

23 That John McNaughton and Robert Caddies didn't attend long enough to evaluate the evidence is made clear in their statements to the Royal Commission, Case Study 42, exhibits STAT.1030.001.0001_R, 42-0100, and STAT.1070.001.0001_R; see also transcript of Robert Caddies' evidence to the Royal Commission, 30 August 2016, 17553:13-16.

24 See Caddies' and McNaughton's statements to the Royal Commission.

25 This separation of powers was entirely consistent with the 2005 Ordinance. See "Further Statement of Michael Elliott", Royal Commission, Case Study 42, exhibit STAT.1088.001.0001_R.

26 Author's interview with Bishop Farran, 2 December 2019. See also Royal Commission, Case Study 42, exhibit STAT.1072.001.0001.

27 Letter from Bishop Farran to Colin Elliott, Royal Commission, Case Study 42, exhibit ANG.0041001.0714_R.

28 Letter from Colin Elliott to Bishop Farran, Royal Commission, Case Study 42, exhibit ANG.0041.001.0165_R.

29 Phillip Aspinall, statement to the Royal Commission, Case Study 42, exhibit STAT.1153.001.001_R. The conference commenced on 27 February 2011. He met with the disgruntled cathedral parishioners the same day.

30 Joanne McCarthy, "Cathedral wrangle: clergyman concedes concerns in diocese", *Newcastle Herald*, 3 March 2011. Royal Commission, Case Study 42, exhibit ANG.0050.005.6597.

31 Aspinall remembers this slightly differently: that he was not trying to get Farran to resign but was simply looking for a way forward. See Aspinall's statement to the Royal Commission, Case Study 42, exhibit STAT.1153.001.001_R.

32 Author's interview with Bishop Farran, 2 December 2019.

33 Justice Sackar, Supreme Court New South Wales, Equity Division Decision Graeme LAWRENCE & Graeme STURT-V-Bishop Brian Farran Professional Standards Committee Professional Standards Board 27 April 2012, at NSW.0030.005.0005

34 Justice Sackar quoted in Royal Commission, *Report of Case Study No. 42*, pages 259 and 281, and *Sturt & Anor v Bishop Brian Farran & Ors* [2012] NSWSC 400, exhibit NSW.0030.005.0004 at 0130[396].

35 Author's interview with Bishop Farran, 2 December 2019.

36 Author's interview with Bishop Farran, 2 December 2019.

37 Author's interview with Bishop Farran, 2 December 2019.

38 There was also now provision for a panel review of the board's decision, which could also overturn it.

39 Michael Elliott, transcript of evidence to the Royal Commission, Case Study 42, 11 August 2016, 17056:9–25.

40 The conflict between Cleary and Farran and file notes of their meetings can be found in John Cleary, email to Bishop Farran regarding Professional Standards, 27 August 2012, exhibit IND.0487.001.0407_R; Cleary, file note of meeting with Bishop Farran regarding Lawrence and others, in which Farran admits being "intimidated" by Lawrence and his networks, 27 August 2012, exhibit IND.0487.001.0163_R; Farran, file note of conversation with John Cleary, 27 August 2012, exhibit ANG.0323.001.0197.

CHAPTER SIXTEEN: UNLEASH THE DOGS OF WAR

1 Letter from Michael Elliott to Dylan Kerslake, senior Optus customer relations executive, requesting a silent number for Steve, 2 July 2014.

2 Author's interview with Colin Elliott, 12 March 2020.

3 Author's interview with Colin Elliott, 12 March 2020.

4   Bishop Stuart, transcript of evidence to the Royal Commission, Case Study 42,
     18 November 2016, page 23355..

CHAPTER SEVENTEEN: I THOUGHT THEY ENJOYED IT

1   "Most child sex abuse in out-of-home care: commission", *Otago Times*, 15 August
     2016.
2   Author's interview with Philip D'Ammond; see also Philip D'Ammond, statement to
     the Royal Commission, Case Study 42, exhibit STAT.1080.001.0001_R.
3   Royal Commission, Case Study 42, exhibit STAT.1080.001.0001_R, page 3,
     pinpoint 9.
4   Except where otherwise indicated, all quotes are from the author's interview with
     Philip D'Ammond.
5   Author's interview with Philip D'Ammond.
6   Joanne McCarthy, "Revered Anglican priest named as predator of children",
     Newcastle Herald, 15 October 2015.
7   Phil D'Ammond, statement to the Royal Commission, Case Study 42, exhibit
     STAT.1080.001.0001, page 11, pinpoint 51.
8   D'Ammond, statement to the Royal Commission, page 11, pinpoint 50.
9   Author's interview with Phil D'Ammond.
10   Transcript of police interview of James Michael Brown on 15 November 1996,
     exhibit NSW.0030.011.0418_R.
11   Author's interviews with Steve Smith.
12   "Court hears 20 families fractured by child sex abuse", ABC News, 25 November
     2011.
13   "Court hears 20 families fractured by child sex abuse", ABC News, 25 November 2011.
14   Sentencing remarks outlining Brown's crimes and the reasons for increasing prison
     time, R v Brown [2012] NSWCCA 199, 31 August 2012, NSW.0087.001.0028.
15   Author's interviews with Steve Smith.
16   "Anger at church as worker is jailed over abuse", ABC News, 2 March 2012.
17   "Anger at church as worker is jailed over abuse", ABC News, 2 March 2012.
18   "Sentence doubled for paedophile church worker", ABC News, 18 September 2012.

CHAPTER EIGHTEEN: GASLIGHTING THE BISHOP

1   Most quotes in this chapter are from my interview with Bishop Greg Thompson,
     12 April 2019, except where otherwise indicated.
2   Bishop Thompson, transcript of evidence to Royal Commission, Case Study 42,
     24 November 2016, pages 23639–23640.
3   Thompson, transcript of evidence, pages 23640:39–23641:12.
4   Thompson, transcript of evidence, pages 23640:39–23641:12.
5   Author's interview with Thompson.
6   Author's interview with Thompson.
7   Author's interview with Joanne McCarthy, 14 April 2019.
8   Giselle Wakatama, "Newcastle Anglican bishop Greg Thompson apologises for
     church's handling of child abuse", ABC News, 17 June 2015.
9   John Cleary, file note, 26 March 2015, Royal Commission, Case Study 42, exhibit
     ANG.0132.001.0008_R.
10   Cleary, file note of meeting with Bishop Thompson and Keith Allen, 26 March 2015,
     Royal Commission, Case Study 42, exhibit ANG.0132.001.0008_R.
11   John Cleary, file note, Royal Commission, Case Study 42, exhibit ANG
     0132.001.0016_R.
12   Cleary, file note, exhibit ANG.0132.001.0008_R.
13   Cleary, file note, exhibit ANG.0132.001.0008_R.

14 Cleary, file note of meeting with Keith Allen, 11 February 2015, Royal Commission, Case Study 42, exhibit ANG.0132.001.0015_R.

15 Michael Elliott, confidential file note, 29 January 2013. Allen's disclosures were reported to police, Detective Sergeant Rob Waugh, Newcastle, 12 March 2013.

16 Cleary, file note, exhibit ANG.0132.001.0009_R.

17 Cleary, file note, exhibit ANG.0132.001.0014_R.

18 Cleary, file note, 11 February 2015, exhibit ANG.0132.001.0015_R.

19 Email from Bishop Thompson to Keith Allen, 13 April 2015, Royal Commission, Case Study 42, exhibit ANG.0195.001.0109_R; email from Bishop Thompson to Keith Allen, 16 April 2015, exhibit ANG.0195.001.0041_R; letter from Keith Allen, 15 April 2015, exhibit ANG.0195.001.0040_R.

20 Anne Connolly, "Newcastle Anglican bishop says child abuse cover-up like 'religious protection racket'", 7.30, ABC TV, 24 November 2016.

21 Author's interview with Bishop Thompson, 12 April 2019.

22 Author's interview with Bishop Stuart, 15 January 2019.

23 Connolly, "Newcastle Anglican bishop says child abuse cover-up like 'religious protection racket'", 7.30, ABC TV, 24 November 2016.

CHAPTER NINETEEN: THE HEART OF DARKNESS

1 "Paedophile dentist gets longer jail term", ABC News, 4 May 2010.

2 Dan Proudman, "Priest accused over teen sex abuse", The Sydney Morning Herald, 10 October 2008.

3 John Parmeter's evidence at a preliminary hearing in October 2009.

4 See the account of the Parmeter brothers and Brock in Joanne McCarthy, "The Catholic Church's dirty secrets: abuse, injustice and a damning letter", Newcastle Herald, 19 September 2014. The investigation into Brock's abuse, and the Parmeter testimony, precipitated the investigations into child sexual abuse in the Catholic Church in the Newcastle region by Strike Force Georgiana, a special unit of Lake Maquarie detectives.

5 "Full Story: How the church continued covering up for this priest", Broken Rites, updated 20 September 2020, https://www.brokenrites.org.au/drupal/node/120.

6 Stephen Ryan and Dan Proudman, "Crime files: Repeat offender paedophile eligible for parole in March", Newcastle Herald, 25 July 2014.

7 Stephen Ryan, "Pedophile dentist Ashleigh Edward Jarrold's sentence nearly doubled", 4 May 2010, Newcastle Herald, 4 May 2010; Stephen Ryan and Dan Proudman "Crime files: Repeat offender paedophile eligible for parole in March", Newcastle Herald, 25 July 2014.

8 Statement of CKG, Royal Commission, Case Study 42, exhibit STAT.1090.001.0001_R.

9 Royal Commission, Case Study 42, exhibit ANG.0367.001.0001. Reports of abuse allegedly perpetrated by Father Peter Rushton compiled by the Royal Commission staff on 21 November 2016.

10 "Sex abuse response still woeful: mother", The Sydney Morning Herald, 2 September 2002.

11 Michael Elliott, file note, 5 August 2010.

12 Author's interview with Joanne McCarthy, 14 April 2019.

CHAPTER TWENTY: THE GOOD COPPER

1 James Wood, Report of the Special Commission of Inquiry into Child Protection Services in NSW, vol. 1, page 137, pt 8.290.

2 Joanne McCarthy, oral evidence to the Special Commission of Inquiry, day 12, 25 June 2013, pages 1265–7.

3   Jason Gordon, "Fox rode on 'saddle of lies'", *Newcastle Herald*, 24 June 2013.
4   NSW Special Commission of Inquiry, 26 June 2013, transcript of Detective Chief Inspector Wayne Humphrey's cross-examination by Mr Hunt, 25 June 2013, pages 1332–1338.
5   NSW Special Commission of Inquiry, 17 May 2013, transcript of Ian Lloyd's evidence, pages 1015–1018.
6   Detective Inspector Jeffrey Little, curriculum vitae, 2018.
7   All quotes from Steve Smith in this chapter are from the author's interviews with him.

CHAPTER TWENTY-ONE: NO EXPIRY DATE FOR JUSTICE

1   Melissa Davey, "Child sexual abuse survivors praise commision's compensation proposal", *The Guardian*, 30 January 2015.
2   Author's interviews with Steve Smith.
3   Author's interview with Bishop Stuart, 15 January 2019.
4   Author's interview with Bishop Stuart, 15 January 2019.
5   Naomi Sharp, Counsel Assisting, opening address, 2 August 2016, Royal Commission, Case Study 42, exhibit TRAN.0007.001.0016_R.
6   Paul Gray, transcript of evidence to the Royal Commission, Case Study 42, 2 August 2016, page C16240; see also Gray's statement to the Royal Commission, exhibit STAT.1067.001.0001_R.
7   Gray, transcript of evidence, page C16240; see also Gray's statement to the Royal Commission, exhibit STAT.1067.001.0001_R.
8   Author's interviews with Steve Smith.

CHAPTER TWENTY-TWO: IF ONLY I'D BEEN TOLD

1   Lesley Danger, statement to the Royal Commission, Case Study 42, exhibit STAT.1120.001.0002_R; statement of Christopher Hall, exhibit STAT.1213.001.0001_R; statement of Valerie Hall, exhibit STAT.1213.001.0002_R. The statements by COE, who had been abused as a boy, and COC, his mother, were given to the commission but withheld from publication. COA, the priest, did not give evidence. Pamela Wilson gave oral evidence about attempting to write a letter to Holland when Rushton bullied her out of it by legal threats. Statement of Pamela Wilson, exhibit STAT.1092.001.0001_R.
2   Phil D'Ammond, transcript of evidence to the Royal Commission, Case Study 42, 2 August 2016, pages C16252–16265.
3   David Frost, statement to the Royal Commission, Case Study 42, exhibit STAT.1122.001.0001. Susan Aslin, statement to police about Jim Brown, 2010, Belmont police station;. Suzan Aslin, statement to the Royal Commission, Case Study 42, exhibit NSW.0030.008.0290_R. Ian Ross-McGowan, statement to the Royal Commission, Case Study 42, exhibit STAT.1106.001.0003_R.
4   Royal Commission, *Report of Case Study No. 42* (unredacted final report), page 128.
5   Richard Appleby, transcript of evidence, Royal Commission, Case Study 42, 4 August 2016, page C16511.
6   Statement of facts concerning Stephen Hatley Gray by a detective sergeant (name withheld), Toukley Police Station. Royal Commission, Case Study 42, exhibit ANG.0050.002.4900_R.
7   John Cleary, file note, 5 March 2013, Royal Commission, Case Study 42, exhibit ANG.0207.001.0279_R.
8   John Cleary, file note of meeting with Keith Allen, 11 February 2015, Royal Commission, Case Study 42, ANG.0132.001.0014_R.
9   David Williams' pre-sentencing report for presiding judge, District Court, Gosford, 3 September 1990, Royal Commission, Case Study 42, exhibit NSW.2008.001.0114.

10 John Cleary, file note, 18 February 2015, Royal Commission, Case study 42, exhibit NPF.0018.001.0024_R; and John Cleary, file note of meeting with Bishop Thompson and John Cleary, 26 March 2015, exhibit ANG. 0132.001.0009_R.

11 Cleary, file note, exhibit ANG.0132.001.0008_R.

12 Roger Herft, transcript of evidence to the Royal Commission, Case Study 42, 30 August 2016 (C164), page C17445.

13 Herft, transcript of evidence to the Royal Commission, page C17460.

14 Rev. Paul Robertson, letter to the editor, *Newcastle Herald*, 3 September 2016, and personal correspondence to Steve Smith.

CHAPTER TWENTY-THREE: THE SENIOR PROFESSIONALS OF NEWCASTLE

1   Author's interview with Joanne McCarthy, 14 April 2019.

2   Robert Caddies, transcript of evidence to the Royal Commission, Case Study 42, 30 August 2016. See also Robert Caddies, transcript of evidence, 16 November 2016.

3   Joanne McCarthy "Newcastle Anglican Bishop Greg Thompson and the 'coordinated opposition' against him", *Newcastle Herald*, 2 September 2016.

4   Joanne McCarthy, "Christchurch Cathedral's governing parish council has been sacked after evidence of 'coordinated opposition' to Bishop Greg Thompson", *Newcastle Herald*, 7 September 2016.

5   Jean Sanders, statement to the Royal Commission, Case Study 42, exhibit STAT.1104.001.0001_R.

6   Robert Caddies, transcript of evidence to the Royal Commission, Case Study 42, 16 November 2016, pages 23113-23114.

7   Robert Caddies, transcript of oral evidence to the Royal Commission, Case Study 42, page 23143.

8   Caddies, transcript of oral evidence to the Royal Commission, Case Study 42, page 23144.

9   Author's interview with Rod Bower, 2 April 2019.

10 Raymond Manuel, statement to the Royal Commission, Case Study 42, exhibit STAT.1236.001.0002.

1   Matthew Kelly, "Ben Giggins urges victims to speak up after Graeme Lawrence jailed for eight years," *Newcastle Herald*, updated 27 December 2019.

CHAPTER TWENTY-FOUR: THE TRIAL OF LAWRENCE FOR RAPE

2   Sage Swinton, "High price of justice for survivor Lyn Rudkin who sued the Anglican Church and the State of NSW", *Newcastle Herald*, 5 March 2022.

3   Margaret Sidis, president, Newcastle Anglican Church Professional Standards Board, Determination Part 1 and Determination Part 2, 18 August 2022; Ian Kirkwood, "Anglican Professional Standards Board finds Reverend Chris Bird at St Stephen's Adamstown failed to report allegations that defrocked Graeme Lawrence had sexually assaulted a parishioner in 2018", *Newcastle Herald*, 18 August 2022.

4   Richard Appleby, transcript of evidence to the Royal Commission, 5 August 2016, page 16566.

5   Ian Kirkwood, "Vindicated again: Anglican abuse survivor Stephen Smith physically assaulted by Reverend Bird at Synod in 2016", *Newcastle Herald*, 18 August 2022.

6   Professional Standards Board Determination, PSC versus Reverend Chris Bird (part 1).

CHAPTER TWENTY-FIVE: POWERFUL PERPETRATORS

1   Marcus Erooga, Keith Kaufman and Judith G. Zatkin, "Powerful perpetrators, hidden in plain sight: an international analysis of organisational child sexual abuse cases", *Journal of Sexual Aggression*, vol. 26, no. 1, 2020, pages 62–90.

2   Erooga et al., "Powerful perpetrators", page 63.
3   Erooga et al., "Powerful perpetrators", page 82. For points about the similarities
     between community offenders and powerful perpetrators, see also K. Kaufman
     and L. Patterson, "Using sex offenders' modus operandi to plan more effective
     prevention programs", in K. Kaufman (ed.), *The Prevention of Sexual Violence: A
     Practitioner's Sourcebook*, NEARI Press, 2010; K. Kaufman et al., "Factors influencing
     sexual offenders' modus operandi: an examination of victim-offender relatedness
     and age", *Child Maltreatment*, vol. 3, no. 4, 1998, pages 349–61; J. Sullivan and E.
     Quayle, 'Manipulation styles of abusers who work with children', in Marcus Erooga
     (ed.), *Creating Safer Organisations*, John Wiley, 2012; S.K. Wurtele, "Preventing the
     sexual exploitation of minors in youth-serving organizations", *Children and Youth
     Services Review*, vol. 34, no. 12, pages 2442–53.
4   Carla van Dam, *Identifying Child Molesters: Preventing Child Sexual Abuse by
     Recognising the Patterns of Offenders*, Routledge, 2011 edition, first published 2001.
5   Gavin de Becker, *Protecting the Gift*, The Dial Press, 1999, page 67, quoted in van
     Dam, *Identifying Child Molesters*, page 170.
6   van Dam, *Identifying Child Molesters*, pages 146–7.
7   BBC TV, *Exposed: The Church's Darkest Secret*, part 1, 2020.
8   Harriet Sherwood, "Friendship with Prince Charles made paedophile bishop Peter
     Ball impregnable", *The Guardian*, 14 January 2020.
9   Harriet Sherwood, "Justin Welby orders review of church's handling of sex abuse
     bishop case", *The Guardian*, 6 October 2015.

CHAPTER TWENTY-SIX: THE PEACH TREE

1   Royal Commission, *Report of Case Study No. 42*, page 159; see also see Bishop Peter
     Stuart, "Statement by the Anglican Bishop of Newcastle …[on] Bishop Richard
     Appleby", 2 December 2019, Diocese of Newcastle.
2   Royal Commission, Final Hearing, 31 March 2017 (270), PANEL 3, 6 pages C27875
     onward.
3   Author's interviews with Steve Smith.
4   Dan Box, "Brothers sue Anglican Church after priest accused of child abuse dies",
     The Australian, 3 February 2017.
5   Giselle Wakatama and David Marchese, "Priest dies weeks after child abuse charges
     reinstated", ABC Newcastle, 15 January 2017.
6   Author's interviews with Steve Smith.
7   Author's interviews with Steve Smith.
8   Royal Commission, *Report of Case Study No. 42*, page 159.
9   Joanne McCarthy, "Bishop Richard Appleby was denied procedural fairness in a
     Newcastle Anglican board decision, a review has found", *Newcastle Herald*, 28 August
     2019. See also George Conger, "Australian bishop's sentence of defrocking for abuse
     coverup overtuned on appeal", *Anglican.Ink*, 21 September 2019.
10   Joanne McCarthy, "Steve Smith has tried for seven years to have Anglican child
     sex offender Graeme Lawrence lose his Order of Australia", *Newcastle Herald*,
     23 August 2019.
11   Letter from Hon. Michael Daly, Attorney-General of NSW, to Steve Smith,
     15 November 2023.
12   Steve Smith, "The Anglican Church disciplinary delays rip open survivors' old
     wounds", *Guardian: A Publication of the Anglican Diocese of Adelaide*, 17 March 2023.

INDEX

YMCA 23, 36, 41, 45–6, 50
Yondaio youth camp 2, 4, 232–3
Young-Bruehl, Elisabeth 281–282
    see also childism

Printed in the USA
CPSIA information can be obtained
at www.ICGtesting.com
CBHW031133090524
8303CB00010B/231